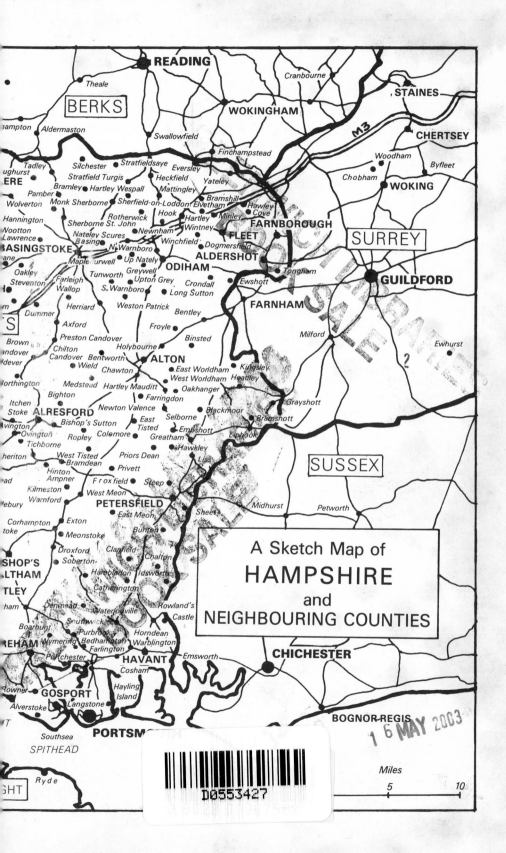

A Sketch Map of
HAMPSHIRE
and
NEIGHBOURING COUNTIES

READING

BERKS

Theale
Aldermaston
Swallowfield
Tadley
Silchester
Stratfieldsaye
Eversley
Stratfield Turgis
Heckfield
Bramley
Hartley Wespall
Mattingley
Monk Sherborne
Sherfield-on-Loddon
Hook
Rotherwick
Sherborne St. John
Newnham
Nateley Scures
Winchfield
Basing
N. Warnboro
Up Nately
Maple urwell
Oakley
Farleigh
Tunworth
Greywell
Steventon
Wallop
Upton Grey
S. Warnboro
Herriard
Weston Patrick
Dummer
Axford
Froyle
Preston Candover
Holybourne
Brown
Chilton
Candover
Bentworth
andover
Wield
ALTON
dever
Chawton
orthington
Medstead
Hartley Mauditt
Bighton
Farringdon
Itchen
ALRESFORD
Newton Valence
Stoke
Bishop's Sutton
East
vington
Ropley
Tisted
Ovington
Colemore
Greatham
Tichborne
West Tisted
Priors Dean
heriton
Bramdean
Privett
Hinton
Ampner
Froxfield
Steep
Kilmeston
West Meon
ebury
Warnford
PETERSFIELD
Corhampton
Exton
East Meon
toke
Meonstoke
Buriton
Droxford
Clanfield
SHOP'S
Soberton
Chalton
LTHAM
Hambledon
Idsworth
TLEY
Catherington
ham
Denmead
Rowland's
Boarhunt
Waterlooville
Castle
Southwick
Horndean
Wymering
Purbrook
Warblington
REHAM
Bedhampton
Farlington
Portchester
HAVANT
Emsworth
Cosham
GOSPORT
Hayling
Alverstoke
Langstone
Island
T
PORTSM
Southsea
SPITHEAD
GHT
Ryde

WOKINGHAM
Cranbourne
STAINES
Finchampstead
M3
CHERTSEY
Woodham
Byfleet
Chobham
WOKING
Bramshill
Elvetham
Hawley
Minley
Cove
FARNBOROUGH
SURREY
FLEET
Dogmersfield
ALDERSHOT
Tongham
Ewshott
GUILDFORD
Crondall
Long Sutton
Bentley
FARNHAM
Milford
Ewhurst
Binsted
2
East Worldham
Kingsley
West Worldham
Headley
Oakhanger
Grayshott
Blackmoor
Bramshott
Selborne
Empshott
Liphook
Hawkley
Liss
SUSSEX
Sheet
Midhurst
Petworth

CHICHESTER

BOGNOR REGIS
1 6 MAY 2003

Miles
5   10

D0553427

HAMPSHIRE HARVEST

To
HILDA,
my wife
the dear companion who shares so many
of my Hampshire memories, and has
helped me to record them

HAMPSHIRE HARVEST

A Traveller's Notebook

Robert W.F. Potter

PHILLIMORE

First published 1977 by
PHILLIMORE & CO. LTD.
Shopwyke Hall, Chichester, Sussex, England

CORRECTED REPRINT 1984

© Robert W. F. Potter, 1977, 1984

ISBN 0 85033 241 9

Printed and bound in Great Britain by
BILLINGS BOOK PLAN
Worcester, England

Contents

List of Illustrations

Plates

Line Drawings by the Author

Maps

Acknowledgments

The publication of this book was my father's long-cherished ambition, for it was his desire to put the village of Mapledurwell 'on the map'. He passed away in February 1974, only three months before the book was accepted for publication, and as was his wish, was 'laid to rest' at the church of Mapledurwell. His gravestone is fittingly inscribed: 'With the spirits of just men made perfect'. Not only would he have been delighted to know that his book was to be published but also that it was to be illustrated with his own sketches, most of which he drew whilst in his late teens.

Many people have helped me enormously in preparing the book for press, and to all of them, my mother and I tender our deepest thanks. Dr. T. C. Thomas, Professor E. G. White and Mr. H. H. Burchnall of the University of Liverpool were instrumental in the award of a generous donation from the University's Rankin Fund. By aiding in problems of identification, by giving me the benefit of specialised knowledge, and by providing help of various kinds, many people rendered invaluable assistance, in particular, my colleagues, Mrs. Catherine Ball, Mr. Bill Paton, Mrs. Dorothy Chamberlain and Mr. Bryan Turnbull; Professor John Hay, Mr. John O'Kane and Mr. Mark Holland of the University of Liverpool; Mr. Robin Geldard; Mr. Elgan Davies; Mr. Bernard Crossland and his staff; and Mr. Fred Young and his daughters, Mrs. Freda Woods and Mrs. Elsie Furlong of Mapledurwell.

The lovely photographs in this book date from near the turn of the century to the present day, and for the more recent ones, special thanks are due to Mr. Dennis Wolohan; Mrs. Ena Wells, Mr. Peter Rosser and Mr. Andy Williams, contributors to *Hampshire*, the county magazine; Mr. Arthur Attwood of the *Basingstoke Gazette*; Mr. S. L. Hunter-Cox of Ocean Pictures Ltd., Southampton; and a valued colleague, Mr. Roy Chamberlain. My mother and I also wish to put on record our appreciation of the generous hospitality shown to us on many occasions by the people of Mapledurwell, which has enabled us, in the warmest way, to keep in touch with the life of the village.

University College,   HUGH L. POTTER
Cardiff

Foreword

AT NO TIME have I lived more fully than in those weeks and months spent in Hampshire during each year of my life. It was my good fortune and happy lot to go there as often as four times in a single year, and to see it at all seasons. Not even two world wars were to break the sequence of annual visits which has continued until now. I inherited my mother's affection for Mapledurwell—most beautiful of names!—and am certain that there was a prenatal disposition in my nature to return as often as possible to the home of my maternal forebears. It has always been a compulsive attraction from which I could not escape. My love of the county is so well known to my friends that, when I was a patient for some weeks in a Liverpool hospital some years ago, one of them sent me the following consolatory poem:

> Dear Bob, When on your bed you lie,
>   With naught to look at but the sky,
> O let your thoughts with pleasure fly
>   To Hampshire.
>
> Where, with your pad upon your knee,
>   You sketched the cottage and the tree
> To make a happy memory
>   Of Hampshire.
>
> May present troubles fade away,
>   Like dew upon a summer's day,
> And all your world be bright and gay,
>   Like Hampshire.

Retirement has given me greater leisure, and what happier use could I make of it than to record my recollections.

My early journeyings took place before I had read any books about that part of the country, so I started off by making my own discoveries. As time went 'on, I came to know the writings of Telford Varley, D. H. Moutray Read, Sir George Dewar, W. H. Hudson, and Edward Thomas, and these were kindred spirits.

During childhood, my summer holidays lasted seven or eight weeks, but in the year of the railway strike (1911) ran to 12 weeks. I roamed far and wide by the time I was 14; thought little of walking up to 30 miles in a day, and once did forty-two. The acquisition of a bicycle enabled me to treble the distance I formerly covered, and put most of Hampshire within the bounds of a return journey on the same day. This means of transport served me well for over 40 years: I could go anywhere off the beaten track where buses, coaches and trains never ran, and I was not subject to the tyranny of a time table. The hills saw to it that walking was not neglected! Eventually the motor-car—the line of least resistance—enabled me to travel leisurely and comfortably, and to spend more time in distant beauty spots or far-flung towns and villages.

This book describes Hampshire in general, and north Hampshire in particular. The latter is not a tourist country, as is south Hampshire; many of its villages go unmentioned in the county guides and are virtually undiscovered country. It also paints a picture of a village which remained unchanged for a longer period than most, and notes the changes in the agricultural scene over a lifetime.

The M3 motorway slices through a lengthy sector of north Hampshire, especially that part of it which I know better than any place on earth. The resultant disruption of the countryside has affected the lower part of Mapledurwell through which ran the Basingstoke Canal, whose course the motorway follows for a short distance. This forms part of the stretch of motorway between Lightwater in Surrey and Popham in Hampshire, and includes Black Dam, Basingstoke, which was opened in the first half of 1971. The old country road between the Cob Tree and the Hatch, also

Green Lane, have been mutilated, and those quiet lanes in the Lyde valley at Andwell—whose beauty and charm were praised so highly by Sir George Dewar—have been disfigured, and fly-overs have had to be built over the Andwell and Nately Scures roads to span the motorway.

This then is a harvest of recollections and a tribute to Hampshire: it also serves as a valedictory to those other northern parts of the county which are still to be despoiled and to become only a memory.

My thanks are due to many people for their kindly interest and co-operation. To my wife, and to my son, Hugh, for all their help; to all my friends, especially those in and around Mapledurwell; to several Hampshire clergymen; I am particularly grateful to Mr. Adrian Bell for allowing me to quote four lovely lines from a poem which he wrote when a youth of 17; to *Punch*, for kind permission to reprint Mrs. C. Fox Smith's poem, *Stoke Charity*; and to Professor John Davis, Professor of Child Health and Paediatrics at the University of Manchester, and Professor John Hay, Professor of Child Health, at the University of Liverpool, for their appreciation and encouragement.

Irby, Wirral,
Cheshire.   *October 1973*

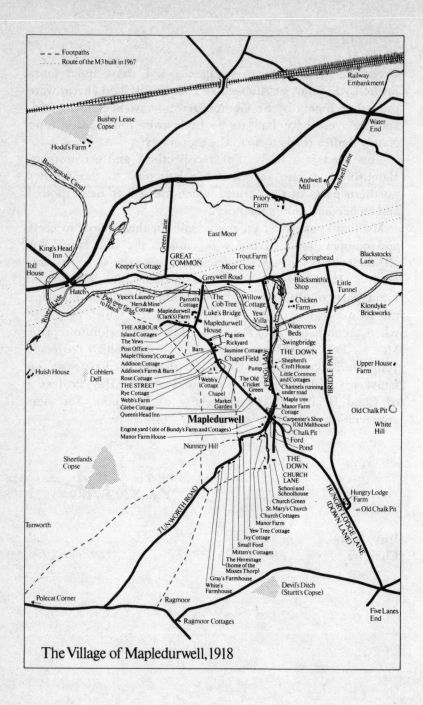

Footpaths
Route of the M3 built in 1967

Railway
Embankment

Bushey Lease
Copse

Hodd's Farm

Water
End

Basingstoke Canal

Andwell
Mill

Andwell Lane

Priory
Farm

King's Head
Inn

East Moor

Toll
House

GREAT
COMMON

Trout Farm

Springhead

Blackstocks
Lane

Keeper's Cottage

Moor Close

Hatch

River Lyde

Greywell Road

Blacksmith's
Shop

Little
Tunnel

Vince's Laundry
'Hers & Mine'
Cottage
Path over fields
to Hatch

Parrott's
Cottage

The
Cob Tree

Willow
Cottage

Chicken
Farm

Klondyke
Brickworks

Mapledurwell
(Clark's) Farm

Luke's Bridge

Yew
Villa

THE ARBOUR
Island Cottages
The Yews
Post Office
Maple ('Home') Cottage
Addison Cottage
Addison's Farm & Barn
Rose Cottage
THE STREET
Rye Cottage
Webb's Farm
Glebe Cottage
Queen's Head Inn

Mapledurwell
House

Pig-sties

Watercress
Beds

Rickyard

Swingbridge

Barn

Jasmine Cottage

THE DOWN

Chapel Field

Shepherd's
Croft House

Pump

Little Common
and Cottages

Webb's
Cottage

The Old
Cricket
Green

Channels running
under road

Chapel

Maple tree

Market
Garden

Manor Farm
Cottage

FROG LANE

BRIDLE PATH

Upper House
Farm

Old Chalk Pit

White
Hill

Huish House

Cobblers
Dell

Mapledurwell

Carpenter's Shop
(Old Malthouse)

Engine yard (site of Bundy's Farm and Cottages)

Chalk Pit

Manor Farm House

Ford

Pond

Nunnery Hill

THE
DOWN

Sheetlands
Copse

CHURCH
LANE

School and
Schoolhouse

Hungry Lodge
Farm

TUNWORTH ROAD

Church Green

Old Chalk Pit

St. Mary's Church

Church Cottages

HUNGRY LODGE LANE
(DOWN LANE)

Tunworth

Manor Farm

Yew Tree Cottage

Ivy Cottage

Small Ford

Mitten's Cottages

The Hermitage
(home of the
Misses Thorp)

Gray's Farmhouse

White's
Farmhouse

Polecat Corner

Ragmoor

Devil's Ditch
(Sturtt's Copse)

Five Lanes
End

Ragmoor Cottages

The Village of Mapledurwell, 1918

1
Mapledurwell

So I'll remember thee,
  Thy quiet ways,
Thy well-loved names
  Thy vanished yesterdays.

Adrian Bell

MAPLEDURWELL (the maple by the well) is three miles
south-east of Basingstoke. Though maple trees and maple
hedges are common in north Hampshire, nowhere are they
more prolific than here. No wonder they have given their
name to the village. When I was a child and travelled south
by train, I imagined that the wheels as they sped over the
track rhythmically spelt out the four syllables of the name
of my destination.

My introduction to Hampshire was when I was taken as
a baby to Mapledurwell to be exhibited to my mother's
family and baptised in the little church there. A significance
may attach to this, for quite early in life I became interested
in its churches.

My grandfather was an only child who resolved that if
he married, there would be no lonely child in his home. In
the course of 25 years of married life he had 10 children—
one daughter (my mother) and nine sons—all of whom
reached maturity. The eldest, Edgar, was the 19-year-old
godfather of John, the youngest. All are now dead, their
average life-span 72 years.

My grandmother died at the age of 50, and it devolved on
my mother, who had known little leisure in helping to bring
up eight younger brothers, to take over the domestic

responsibilities, to make many of their clothes (including dozens of shirts), and to keep her father's accounts. My grandfather, a tall, patriarchal figure and much respected, was a market gardener, seedsman, farmer and land-measurer, who lived for all but seven of his 78 years in his native village. He owned several cottages which he rented to villagers, and was churchwarden at Mapledurwell for a quarter of a century; after his death in 1917, his twin sons, Bill and Joe, successively held that office for a further 27 years. My mother stayed there long enough to see her youngest brother starting to make his way in the world, and when she married my father, a south Hampshireman, went to live in Liverpool. So strong was her love for her old home, however, that she returned annually during the next 42 years to spend lengthy spells—they could never be called holidays—in looking after her father and the brothers who lived with him, and keeping things going until she returned the following summer. This continuous association made it a second home for my sister and me, a sheet anchor in the deep countryside which gave us a peculiar and lasting sense of belonging to the place.

In order to provide an outlet for the activities of his large and growing family, my grandfather decided in 1894 to rent Addison's Farm, Mapledurwell, eventually farming 60 acres of land there, in addition to his horticultural and other activities. He had green fingers, and a kindly, understanding way with animals. He worked 12 hours a day, and at 75 was cheerfully measuring land with chains, in company with an elderly-looking white-haired man who, feeling the pace and the heat of the day, lamented that he was 50 years of age! Grandfather was lithe, spare, alert and always on the go until two months before his death. His second son, Bill, took over the newly-acquired farm, married and lived there; later he was assisted by two of his brothers, Joe and Harry. In 1921 they bought the farm, but finally sold it in 1937. By then, agriculture had changed out of all

1. Addison's Farmhouse, Mapledurwell, 1918.

recognition since the days when a self-binder, drawn by horses, harvested the corn. A gradual mechanisation had been going on all the time, and the shocking of sheaves and autumnal threshing ceased as farming moved into the new era of combine-harvesting. The old method was picturesque and romantic, and a more communal effort, but the new way was labour-saving, the corn being reaped and threshed at one and the same time. Harvesting which formerly spread over several weeks was done in a matter of days. Farmers were less at the mercy of the weather, but one disadvantage was the poorer quality and shorter length of straw used for thatching cottages and barns. Of farming skills I greatly admired the craftsmanship which the neat thatching of ricks involved. Threshing required a steady supply of coal and water, and frequent journeys with horse-drawn tubs to local streams and the ford at Andwell had to be made. Country milling has disappeared during the last half-century, and everywhere machines have replaced horses.

I liked not only the countryside, but the people, their dialect and turn of phrase. Expressions like 'I'll see you again when the sun shines on both sides of the hedges' from uncle Joe to our little son when the time came to return home, and the child's exclamation on setting foot in Mapledurwell at the beginning of a holiday, 'We're in Hampshire, let's pick flowers', live in the memory. Each of the hundred holidays I spent there entailed a 200-mile journey each way, and the railway ticket from Woodside (Birkenhead) to Basingstoke was a passport to happiness far more valuable to me than any other piece of paper, and infinitely more than the return half!

I cycled to Hampshire from Liverpool three years running in the 1920s, and during the last decade have often gone by car. Growing up with a farming background, I was familiar with the life of the countryside and liked to join in harvesting activities, particularly fruit-picking. Much of the hard manual side of agricultural work has gone, and so

have the low wages which in pre-1914 days were 14s. a week.
I remember a man, his wife and nine children trying to
subsist on that sum, with a house, garden and £5 harvest-
money as the only perquisites! His farmhouse bore the
name of Hungry Lodge long before he ever went to live
there!

The population of Mapledurwell has for many years
hovered round the 200 mark. The farms and cottages are
scattered, but in the last 15 years there has been more new
building than during the whole of the previous century.

Most of the local landmarks are listed in a resident's verse,
Our Village, which I thank Miss Annie Henness for permitting
me to quote:

> In winter's cold or summer's heat,
>   Our village is most wondrous sweet.
> Its cottage gardens full of flowers
>   Wherein are passed some shining hours.
> Its new tiled and old thatched cottage homes,
>   Are by the lanes wherein one roams.
> The church and farms lie round about
>   And the ford where children play and shout.
>
> Its farm with soldier on the wall
>   Is a landmark now well-known to all.
> The school and chapel are now closed
>   And never used as in days of old.
> At Hatch, King Henry's head is seen.
>   At centre of village is the 'Queen'.
> The cob tree at the crossways seen,
>   Its autumn gold, and spring's first green.
> And now I leave you, one and all
>   To think upon our village small.

The Cob Tree stands on the triangular patch at the junction
of lanes leading to Mapledurwell, Up Nately and the Hatch
(or Mapledurwell Hatch of coaching days). The Great
Common from this point to Hatch was part of the common
lands enclosed sometime between 1760 and 1850.

Opposite the thatched post office there were, until 1927,
two very tall, gaunt silver spruces, visible for miles around,

2. 'Home (Maple) Cottage' and the Post Office, Mapledurwell, 1917.

3. The Post Office, Mapledurwell, 1917.

their trunks bare for most of their height and crowned by a flourish of sparse branches which made them look like flue brushes. One of them was surely the highest tree in north Hampshire: a lofty Lombardy poplar close by only accentuated its fantastic height. At this point an unimpeded view across the Arbour, past Island Cottages, stretched away to the canal and Old Basing, and beyond to my uncle John's house high up at Norn Hill on the Reading road, Basingstoke, over three miles away, which was clearly discernible before houses in Hatch Lane sprang up like mushrooms and blotted out the fine vista. A path over the fields to the Hatch, with sweeping views on all sides and a glimpse of Huish House, was a short cut for pedestrians. Cobblers Dell to the left of the path contains tumuli. A century and a half ago or more, a boy who was supported by the parish cut a stick from a hedge of this wooded dell, and for this offence was transported to Van Diemen's Land (Tasmania). He subsequently carved out a successful career for himself there.

The Soldier on the Wall, painted on a stable at right angles to the road from the post office to the Cob Tree, belongs to Mapledurwell Farm. It probably dates from Crimean War days. The artist knew not only how to paint the smart colourful uniform of the time, but also which pigments to use to preserve it for years against all weathers. It cannot have been easy to paint such a figure so well on small Tudor bricks with thin layers of mortar in between. The last member of the Clark family who farmed here died in 1914, his forebears having been farmers in Mapledurwell for many years, and the Grenadier Guard was first painted by an uncle of his, who repainted it at intervals. The soldier is somewhat larger than life, standing two to three feet above ground level, with scarlet tunic, dark blue trousers with a stripe in them, white belt and bandoleer, resplendent with medals, and a large black bearskin and white flash, which makes him look very tall. At one time

4. The Soldier on the Wall, Mapledurwell, 1918.

he had sergeant's stripes, and his rifle was held, strange
to relate, in his left hand at an angle of 45 degrees. Changes
were made when he needed a fresh coat of paint before the
First World War, and for some reason his stripes mysteriously
disappeared, never to be replaced! His rifle and bayonet were
repainted in a horizontal position at the ready, and transferred to the right hand. An essay I wrote in 1916 before
joining up, records 'I still remember seeing on the wall the
rubbed red brick which showed the original slant of the
rifle', and I have photographs of it in both positions. I
wonder if he was reduced to the ranks for having held his
rifle in the wrong hand!

A young member of the Clark family was furious when
he heard that one of our captured officers had been forced
to surrender his sword to the Boer General, Piet Cronje.
On being asked what he would have done in the circumstances, he replied, taking up a warlike stance: 'I'd have
said, "Here is my sword, and this is the way you use 'un!"'

A landmark which lent quaintness to part of the village
opposite the ford was the old malthouse, pulled down in
1965. Part of its frontage prior to 1914 was occupied by
the carpenter's shop, its large folding doors wide open
during his long working day. The sheds were used for
stabling and storage, but the malthouse in the rear had not
fulfilled its original purpose for over a century. The
remainder of the frontage, formerly covered in, was a curving
flint wall pierced unobtrusively by small circular openings
used as peep-holes, pointing in various directions up and
down the lanes converging on the ford, enabling a person
inside to warn his companions of the approach of excisemen
whose duty it was to see that no illicit brewing took place.
One day two men working at the forge there, who had
borrowed our heavy anvil (which weighed close on two
hundredweight), were arguing about getting a cart to
transport it back to our cottage: when they had gone
for lunch, my uncle Ted, who had little time for *talking*

5. The *King's Head* inn, the Hatch, Mapledurwell, 1918.

about work, shouldered it and carried it home single-
handed—600 yards, uphill most of the way!

There are two attractive inns, over a mile apart. The
Queen's Head is serenely set at the foot of the village street
near the ford: one can sit outside the inn and enjoy the
peace and beauty of the countryside. The *King's Head,*
at Hatch, is the most distant outpost of the village: it is
a well-preserved example of a posting house, whose façade
has always been kept freshly painted, usually cream or
white. Lying back a few yards from the busy A30 highway,
its sunny appearance is shown off to the best possible
advantage. The interior retains its old-world characteristics
too, and is as pleasing as that of any Hampshire coaching
inn I know. Mallows and columbines at one time adorned
its front, enhancing the light colouring.

The Lyde, little more than a brook here, flows under the
Mapledurwell road, through the garden behind the inn, and
prattles on under the Green Lane to Andwell Priory farm.
In the streams of the Green Lane were crayfish (locally
called 'crawfish'), and children used to paddle in search of
'Tom Chugs' (millers'-thumbs or bullheads). The country
round about was moorland—the haunts of peewits, moorhens, dabchicks and coots—and woodland, but since the
Second World War most of the trees on East Moor and
copses near the Moor Close have been cut down, so that
one could see from Mapledurwell the movement of traffic
along the A30 between the Hatch and Waterend.

'Jasmine Cottage' was the home of my forebears—the Prince
family—who are mentioned in Mapledurwell church registers
for 200 years. My great-grandfather was born there in the
year of Trafalgar. It had an acre of garden, and within its
confines was a smaller cottage and a well, 60 feet deep,
which served both houses. 'Jasmine Cottage' was thatched,
the walls covered with ivy, cool in summer, warm in winter.
Its windows were small and many-paned, and its beams
were of ships' timbers. Grandfather loved the winding oak

6. 'Jasmine Cottage', Mapledurwell, looking towards Addison's Farmhouse, 1918.

staircase and used to say it was 'a bit of old England'. One
large bedroom, with a five-foot door under a crossbeam,
had a skeleton frame of oak beams reaching to the roof,
and it behoved one to remember this, otherwise one could
get a nasty shock. The open fireplace in the kitchen once
had an inglenook, and if one peered up the stepped chimney,
the open sky was visible. There were old-fashioned guns on
ledges over the mantelpiece, and a wooden bacon rack
suspended by hooks from the ceiling. Countrymen in past
centuries must have been of shorter stature than they are
today, for the low-ceilinged rooms were certainly not built
for six-footers like grandfather and myself. He liked his
garden, which included an orchard of fruit trees (apples,
plums, pears and damsons) and fruit bushes (gooseberries,
raspberries ·and red, white and black currants). One year
he grew strawberries! There were all manner of vegetables,
including runner and broad beans, to both of which all of
us were very partial, but I never cared for the horse-radish
which grew in profusion near the box hedge. There were
a couple of bay trees whose leaves were sometimes used
for flavouring rice puddings, and a kerria or two, a small,
fluffy yellow flower with beautifully-shaped leaves.
Grandfather took pride in his zinnias, asters, stocks,
marigolds, sweet williams, and peonies. He also grew under
glass frames cucumbers, tomatoes, and vegetable marrows—
and got a surprise when my mother made marrow and
ginger jam—and young cabbage plants which sold in their
hundreds. Vines shut out the sunlight as their tendrils spread
inside the roof of the long greenhouse, and at the back and
front of the ivy-covered cottage were ancient staddles
without their mushroom tops. In the cottage were catalogues
of well-known southern seed firms, many of them containing
brightly-coloured illustrations of flowers. Pictures in black
and white of vegetables with unusual names—kohl rabi,
endive, salsify—appealed to me in early childhood, and I
specially liked the varieties of mangold, mangel-wurzel,

7. 'Jasmine Cottage' kitchen, 1914

8. Water-tubs, staddle stones, and pigsties in the yard at
'Jasmine Cottage', 1917.

and turnip because they were successfully grown in large sizes in our fields. In the pantry were handsome wooden measures—half-gallon, gallon, and bushel—steel bound.

Addison's Farm, 60 yards away, was named after the captain of the Hackwood Park Cricket Club, Mr. Joseph Addison, who lived there, and was probably responsible for the building of the Congregational Chapel on the ground at the foot of his garden in 1864: this chapel fell into disuse and after the Second World War was converted into a bungalow. Lieutenant-Colonel John May's *Cricket in North Hants,* recorded that Mr. Addison died suddenly while out with the Garth Hounds in 1888, at the age of seventy-eight. The mid-18th-century whitewashed timbered farmhouse abutted sideways on to the village street, the date of the building—WO1786—being marked on the mellowed red bricks of the roadside wall. Its downstairs rooms, six in number, were small, except the kitchen: indoors a tall heavy pump stood over a boarded well. There was any amount of cupboard space on both floors, two staircases (apart from the stone stairway to the dairy cellar), and a dark pantry off a narrow passageway near the front door. In the farmyard was a barn, thatched with Norfolk reeds, which was large enough to accommodate 30 soldiers of the Leinster Regiment in the winter of 1914/15, before they proceeded to the Dardanelles. The central portion was floorboarded and partitioned off, one side being used for storing provender and farm machinery; the other, covered with straw and empty sacks, for storing fruit and vegetables. There was ample space for chaff-cutters, carts and traps and sack-carts, which were a child's delight. During our family's tenure of Addison's Farm (1894–1937), they usually had four or five horses, twice as many cattle and even more pigs, which, incidentally, were all black. Few of ours were heavy cart-horses: some were carriage-horses. Violet, a black mare, was 42 when she died. Her daughter, Diamond, was high-spirited, and once ran away with the self-binder when

9. The chapel and 'Rye Cottage', Mapledurwell, 1927.

she heard the clatter of the knives behind her. She lived
till her 30s, and was always touchy and difficult to handle
unless you knew her well. What upset these highly-strung
dual-purpose mares more than anything else was the hissing
of a steam-roller or the whistle of an engine on the way to
town. They would prick up their ears and shy, so that the
machines invariably had to stop, while the frightened
animals, their backs as straight as willows, would strain to
get away from the noise.

The rickyard looked down our fields to the banks of the
Basingstoke Canal on which barges and small craft plied
before the turn of the century. The view took in Luke's
bridge, Hodd's Farm and the copse at Old Basing, the railway embankment near Waterend, and beyond, surrounded
by high trees, Newnham church and the water tower of
Tylney Hall, Rotherwick. The clank of metal as trains sped
along the lines to and from London was pleasant, familiar
music to us a mile and a half away. Chalets had sprung up

on the slopes of Scures Hill, and Butterwood, between Nately Scures and Hook Common, formed a well-wooded background for the tall chimney of Klondyke brickworks. The view also included a farm on the down at Up Nately, with cottages on the Little Common nestling in the valley below: here, using buckets, we filled the horse-drawn 'tubs' from the cress-bed stream. The local cottagers used a pump on an embankment in mid-stream, and boys tickled trout where channels ran under the road. When water was but a trickle, the tubs clanked on to Andwell ford, which seldom ran dry. A bridle path ran along the horizon all the way from the Little Tunnel to Hungry Lodge Farm, to meet the road from Mapledurwell to Five Lanes End. The evening air was often so still that I could recognise the voices of villagers leaning on the swing-bridge rails as they talked to each other nearly half a mile away. On the upper portion of the Chapel Field, lucerne, clover or sainfoin were grown, the lower portion devoted to corn, mangolds, or potatoes in rotation. In this and other fields were cultivated oats, barley and wheat (sometimes the bearded variety which frustrated the depredations of birds when the corn was ripening). Rarely did I ever see rye, never here.

Another farmhouse—Webb's Farmhouse—close to the chapel had a most attractive façade, pale yellow and red hollyhocks in the front garden harmonising perfectly with the colour-washed walls and weathered tiles. Opposite was a thatched cottage with a fragrant rose garden behind high hedges. A field off a cart track looked towards Sheetlands and beyond to Tunworth, and the village street ran down to the ford past a market garden, the old cricket green, 'Glebe Cottage' (said to be the old parsonage) and the *Queen's Head* inn, which always looks gay and inviting. Between here and the ford were Bundy's Farm and adjacent cottages destroyed by fire in 1881, sparks from which started fires which ravaged buildings further afield: no less than four farmsteads, with machinery, implements and livestock, suffered from the effects, or were destroyed. For 50 years the site of Bundy's Farm served as an engine yard, and here were congregated several large ploughing engines and smaller threshing engines, ploughing tackle, winnowing machines, elevators, and sleeping vans which resembled shepherds' huts. A progressive farmer in the village had added steam ploughing and threshing to his other agricultural pursuits. For three decades his engines puffed and rumbled as they made their ponderous way along the country roads, incidentally causing our old farmhouse to tremble, until I thought my bedroom, which faced on to the road, might collapse! The outer wall had already been strengthened by an S-shaped iron staple. For two decades these machines spent their last days in honourable retirement in the engine yard, eventually rusting away. They were taken out of service when all heavy vehicles with iron-ridged wheels using the new tarmac roads had to change over to non-metallic tyres.

The young 'boss', son of the farmer who owned the ploughing tackle, would be heard early each morning dashing through the village on his way to the distant downland country wherever the engines happened to be, to make sure that all was going according to plan. Each steam plough—six furrows in the ground and six in mid-air—drew acres of land into its huge maw, and devoured square miles as the weeks wore on. An engine at one side of the field was connected with another on the far side by a huge coil of wire cable, which drew the multi-ploughs or a large scarifier backwards and forwards across its entire width. As each traverse was completed, the machines would move cautiously forward a yard or so, one taking its turn pulling, while the other did the winding. Agricultural wages were low in those days, but acreage money (two or three pence an acre) and overtime brought the enginemen's wages in the busy months to nearly double those of the ordinary farm labourers, whose working hours were from 6 a.m. to 5.30 p.m. This meant working all the daylight hours from dawn to dusk, however. It needed good management, careful calculation, and being constantly on the spot, for the contractor to estimate the acreage of ploughing which could be undertaken and new commitments to be entered into with other farmers seeking his services. Each set of ploughing tackle had its own team of men, who went as far afield as Chilbolton, Micheldever and Cranborne, near Wonston. The threshing tackle seldom ventured as far, perhaps because competitors operated from Mattingley and Popham. The ploughing tackle men came home only at weekends on their bicycles or motor-bikes, and were back at work first thing on Monday mornings. These engines consumed 12 to 15 hundredweights of coal a day, and in order to reach their destinations had to avoid the old brick bridges and travel a long way round by roads which permitted them to replenish their water supplies from wayside streams every seven or eight miles.

I recall happy, sunny summer days when the ploughing engines were at work in large, lonely fields between Popham and Woodmancote. The man perched on the iron seat of the scarifier had to sit firm, and if a headstrong youngster hung on tight in a standing position it was still perilous, for at the beginning of each traverse the teeth plunged nearly a foot into the earth and shook him up. If he were to lose his foothold in transit, he could be dragged under, and nothing could then stop the moving coil of steel rope or the progress of the cultivator in time to save him.

The open-air meals which my young friend, Jack White, the cook, provided were always enjoyed. Sometimes he caught a rabbit for the pot. There used to be a flint church at Popham, built between 1875 and 1878, but little did we dream in 1915 that a land-mine would fall near it in a second world war, and be the cause of its demolition in 1946; neither did I think that he would soon see service with the Hampshire Regiment in India, Sudan, Egypt, and Palestine before the war came to an end, and return home safely,

only to be accidentally killed on Wellock's Hill, outside
Basingstoke, on his way to the country with the ploughing
tackle. For several years a chalk cross on the embankment
marked the spot.

Life could be tragic in the country in the old days. An
elevator or heavy machine could collapse and crush a
labourer, leaving him maimed or permanently paralysed,
and literally looking out on life from a cottage door for
the rest of his days.

Frog Lane ran past the Little Common cottages and
over the canal swing-bridge to the Greywell–Hatch road.
Thousands of small frogs moved along it at times: I once
saw the lane covered with them. Years later, I saw a
'Jack Hern' (heron) standing statuesque and ankle-deep in
a marshy meadow off the lane, and in the same field came
across a bee orchis and a fly orchis; there were the commoner
orchises in other boggy places, where the cotton-grass also
flowered. There was a trout farm here whose stream joined
the Lyde, and also a large cress-bed between Springhead
and Andwell which provided a further supply of water to
the little river near the Priory Farm. A pair of bittern,
uncommon nocturnal marsh birds, were seen in Mapledurwell
in 1962—the first for over 60 years. They are the size of
herons, but more hunched in appearance and with plumage
of more protective colouring, but less leggy, as they stand
motionless in the water when fishing.

Down Lane, a pleasant climb from the ford, past the chalk
dell to Hungry Lodge and Five Lanes End, is rewarding for
its view of the village, particularly of the church green which
nestles like a bowl in the valley. The sides of the lane are gay
with many varieties of wild flowers, St. John's wort, poppies,
toadflax, scabious and knapweed. Further up the hill, wild
Canterbury bells, mallows four feet high, sloes and wild
rose bushes flourish, with lowly vetches and yellow trefoil
carpeting the verges. The face of the chalk pit at the foot of
Down Lane is in parts obliterated by plant life now that

10. The Ford, Mapledurwell, 1918.

chalk is no longer cut out of it. Maple and hawthorn trees line the sides of the overgrown entrance, and in late August, juniper hedges are in berry. White campions, woody night-shade (bittersweet) and wild thyme grow on the downland overlooking the dell. Earlier in the year the swards are covered with bird's-foot trefoil, ladies' slippers, and blue-eyed germander speedwell.

The Tunworth road runs from the ford past the manor farm, Nunnery Hill, Gray's farmhouse and old Farmer White's farmhouse. A garden grew up the bank opposite Gray's farmhouse years ago. The lawns and gardens behind the farmhouse were also carefully tended by the farmer's three daughters: their short cut to the church through the garden and over stiles by a path skirting the fields and sheltered by tall trees, was much treasured.

Church Green, on which stood the school and school-house, the church and Church Cottages, has changed greatly since 1911, when a tall flagstaff was erected to celebrate George V's coronation: this disappeared long before the school closed in 1938, after 75 years' service. Nearly a century ago, the village children, when they reached a certain age, had to leave and walk to Old Basing school to complete their education, but in my young days this was no longer the case. At busy times of the year during the last century, children were permitted to stay away from school and help with farmwork, and scholars who reached the fourth standard by the time they were 12 could leave school if their parents so desired. The Green is now overgrown in places, but has the beauty of comfrey, campions, mildfoil, cranesbill, agrimony, purple blind nettles and oxeye daisies.

Church Lane, like the village street, was once lined with tall elms, but nearly all have been uprooted by high winds during winter storms over the years. Very few of the old majestic walnut trees of my youth, under which cattle sought respite from plaguing flies, are still standing. In the summer of 1956, Church Cottages, which had been empty for a year

or two, were destroyed. Church Green was a perfect setting
for a pastoral picture, and many a painting was made of it,
notably one by Wilfrid Ball, reproduced in the Rev. Telford
Varley's large book on Hampshire, published in 1909, and in
a smaller revised edition issued in 1926, the year of the
author's death. Painters often exercise artistic licence by
putting human figures into a picture to lend life and veri-
similitude to the scene. I remember showing a painting of
the Green—the accompanying colour plate is a copy of it—
which the artist had embellished with a woman in a sun-
bonnet and a few ducks, to 'old Albert' who lived at Church
Cottages for well over 50 years. His comments were to the
point: 'That ain't my old woman' and 'We never 'ad no
ducks!' The gaunt, charred chimneys stood for some years,
but in the early 1960s a bungalow was built on the site.

I recently talked with an elder brother of my boyhood
friend, casually mentioning that I had retired after 44 years'
service at the University of Liverpool. His eyes twinkled as
he said: 'Tell you where you haven't been. Mapledurwell
school!' To which I replied: 'Oh yes I have. Back in 1905,
when I was six, I was there for two months with Jack'.
That summer I had yearned for the company of the other
children who were attending school, and though few
preferred school to holidays, I must have done so, for when
I returned North, the school mistress presented me with two
'Never absent, never late' cards issued by the Hampshire
Education Committee, with county views on the reverse
sides, covering my two months' attendance. School was
leisurely and sunny there compared with that in Liverpool.
The school adjoined Church Green, and the paths, hedgerows, meadows and fields on the Down were an ideal place
for nature-study rambles which extended to Devil's Ditch
(Sturtt's Copse) on the way to Ragmoor, and to Hungry Lodge
Farm (then in Up Nately parish). Thus I was initiated by
pleasant ways into a love for botany and country life.

Mapledurwell church, a 14th-century building of flint,
forms the background of the Green; no longer hidden by

11.   Mapledurwell school and schoolhouse, 1917.

elms, it can be seen from all directions. The slightly-elevated
churchyard is surrounded by a long wall, and the church is
approached by a rising, winding path. The large weather-
boarded bellcote is tile-roofed and surmounted by a
weathercock. Three bells, one of which is pre-Reformation,
gently chime over the fields; the wooden tower would
not stand their being rung. Never did they sound so smooth
and melodious as when 'old Albert' chimed them, for over
half a century prior to his death in 1954. He used both
arms and hitched one foot through a rope looped near the
ground, never losing his balance. He led the singing, and
was a faithful custodian of the church, as, indeed, are his two
daughters who succeeded him. A few years before his death,
we heard the church bells in mid-week—a rare event—and on
inquiry the old man confessed that he was celebrating his
birthday! We thought it most appropriate and well deserved.

The surname of Albert Kinge's predecessor as parish
clerk was Ifould, the oldest family name hereabouts for

12. The church, Mapledurwell, 1918.

close on three centuries at that time, with that of Gary (or Geary) a close second, and that of Prince well in the running.

There is a good 15th-century rood-screen and a brass (1525) to the memory of John Canner (a local farmer and town bailiff) and his family on the chancel floor. The name crops up again and again during the 15th, 16th and 17th centuries in Baigent and Millard's *History of Basingstoke*. I remember the old tall box-pews with doors, which were replaced by low open pews. A former rector once said that he thought the view of the Down from the sanctuary of Mapledurwell church was unrivalled: as harvest-time drew near, the cornfields over towards Hungry Lodge Farm, Five Lanes End, and Sturtt's Copse, must have seemed a benediction. It certainly formed a marvellous pastoral background, and the broad aspect of the sunny Down covered with gently swaying ears of golden corn is one I shall always associate with our little church. It was not always so, however, for relatives have told me that in the latter part of the 19th century there was resentment among the parishioners when the rector caused the large stained glass east window to be moved to Newnham church, in which village his rectory was situated. Evidently his view was that 'tuppence-coloured' was preferable to 'penny-plain', but when I see the dark interior of Newnham church, I am happy to realise that what had seemed to be theirs was ours in reality. We not only enjoy an incomparable view of the Down, but daylight and sunshine flood through the plain diamond glass panes of the east window. The only stained glass left is a tiny window at the back of the organ-blower's seat in the chancel.

In the summer of 1929 I sketched the interior from near the organ, looking towards the open west door. A swallow had built her nest inside the church, and she was teaching her young to fly from the rafters and cross-beams. The quiet rustle of their wings and an occasional chirrup were

13. The interior of Mapledurwell church, 1916.

the only sounds to be heard. By the time I had finished my drawing the young swallows had become competent short-distance fliers, almost ready to dart through the doorway out into the open air.

One summer, Father Reginald H. Tribe, Director of the Society of the Sacred Mission at Kelham, who was also a medical practitioner, took services at Mapledurwell. A week or so later we met again when he preached in Liverpool cathedral: I mentioned the contrast between the two places, and he told me that on one occasion he had celebrated the Eucharist at Old Basing church at eight one morning, and at 6.30 that evening had preached at Newcastle-on-Tyne. It hardly seemed possible then, considering Sunday railway restrictions, but was nevertheless true. During the inter-war years he sometimes acted as locum for the vicar of Old Basing, and his figure, clad in a flowing cloak and cassock, cycling round our villages, was a familiar one. It was a tragedy he was killed by a V-bomb near Bristol in 1945.

Few people visit country churches in the week-time, so I often indulged my hobby of playing the flute there. Mapledurwell church is in a corner of the Green, which is a cul-de-sac at one end of the village. This made for privacy, and I could practice unhindered to my heart's content. The mood engendered was summed up for me in essence by the opening line of *The Deserted Village*—'Sweet Auburn, loveliest village of the plain', by Oliver Goldsmith, himself a flautist sufficiently accomplished to earn his living abroad as an itinerant player.

Church services can sometimes be very personal and homely. When the organ was out of action one Sunday, the rector asked if someone would choose a hymn and start up the singing. Everyone seemed to have been suddenly struck dumb, but feeling ashamed at the lack of response and, despite a certain self-consciousness, I suggested a favourite hymn and began to sing. Fortunately the pitch was just right, and everyone joined in. On another occasion my son and I were asked to join in the bell-ringing: he also acted as server, and I took the collection, using the old wooden collecting-shoe—quite a family affair!

There were sad days too, when one by one my grandfather's large family were laid to rest in the churchyard, until, in 1961, there was no-one left of the older generation.

There remained one special wish of mine still to gratify—apart from a desire to repose there myself eventually—and that was realised in 1964. I had known Mapledurwell during each month of the year over six decades, yet I had never been able to attend a harvest thanksgiving here, due to the fact that, for over 40 years, my busiest time at the University was just before and after the opening of each new session early in October, when students had to be interviewed and enrolled. I had long before made up my mind that if I ever reached retiring age, I would attend a harvest festival service here, and, at last, it came to pass. Flowers, fruit, and corn filled every corner of the church: I counted 48 apples in a row on the top of the rood-screen, and—perhaps with special significance!—there was 'old man's beard' (traveller's joy) in the lancet window of grandfather's pew in which I always sat. This visit to Mapledurwell was my shortest—six hours—but it was well worth while, and a red-letter day in my life.

Just as in old vases unearthed after excavation there sometimes lingers the scent of jasmine or other fragrant perfume they once contained, so are old churches hallowed by the worship and prayers of generations of the faithful.

Sixty or 70 years ago, little girls used to chant 'The first of May is Garland Day, please to see my fine garlands', as they went the rounds of the village in the early morning of May Day, calling at farmhouses and cottages to exhibit posies of cowslips they had gathered and made into large balls of shining yellow blooms, tied to sticks, in the hope of receiving pennies and small silver. It is many years, however, since this colourful country custom was observed here.

We children liked to roam the downland after the harrow, drag or scarifier had traversed the fields and thrown up flints, for we knew we might come across shepherds' crowns—fossilised sea-urchins—which cropped up occasionally: they are also found on Salisbury Plain. Geologists conjecture that parts of southern England were under water millions of years ago; that these fossils were originally fragile shells on the chalk bed of the sea; and that they were eventually covered with mud and rocks, remaining buried until the sea subsided or molten rocks were thrown up by volcanic eruption, to form solid accretions. A volume of essays, *Shepherds' Crowns,* was published in 1923 by Pamela Grey, the second wife of Earl Grey, one-time Foreign Secretary. Children and farm labourers took these shepherds' crowns home as souvenirs and sometimes used them as window-stops or paper-weights. They were one to three inches high. Some, conical in shape with a slightly pointed tip and an elliptical base, had a triangular appearance; others with bulbous sides and rounded tops were hemispherical. Most had stripes, some narrow, some wide, running from apex to base, and some had rows of dots on each stripe, suggesting a crustacean origin aeons ago. There was a preponderance of flint, and also some chalk in their content. They were often ornamental: even the commonplace ones had regularity of shape. The most perfect were sometimes multi-coloured with distinctive stripes, beautifully marked. In these days of mechanisation and greater speed of movement, they are less likely to be seen by the farm worker on his tractor as he crosses the fields.

Occasionally we came across what country people called 'thunderbolts'—probably meteorites, or maybe iron pyrites which, when broken, reveal crystals radiating from the centre. They occurred in the lower part of the chalk, were roundish in shape, rusty, and pitted on the surface, varying in size from one to two inches in diameter.

The first adder or viper I ever saw was one preserved in a bottle at Finchampstead in Berkshire, just over the Hampshire border. I was six years old at the time, and we made the long journey there and back by trap one Sunday: we went by way of Newnham Green, Mattingley, Hazeley Heath and Bramshill. I knew that adders were common in the New Forest, and that 'Brusher' Mills caught them for zoos.

One hot day when cycling near the Moor Close, Mapledurwell, I saw what looked like a short coil of thin halter rope lying on the grass sward. Being curious, I dismounted and turned back. The short 'piece of rope' uncoiled, and I beheld a rearing head with the gun-metal sheen of whipcord, a flickering aspect, and a tiny tongue, and it was then, seeing its markings, that I realised it was an adder. As it was neither cornered or menaced, it did not attack me, and soon slunk away into the undergrowth. It was one of the most fascinating sights I had ever witnessed. It was near here that my sister saw another snake and her young at play in East Moor. When the mother perceived danger, by sight or more likely by footfall, she emitted a warning sound which brought her small brood scurrying to her and they disappeared into her mouth. My sister was unaware that other persons had reported having seen this phenomenon, and that their statements had been discredited because no field naturalist had actually seen it. I think it was W. H. Hudson who said that snakes do not swallow their young when danger threatens, and others have maintained that it is a myth, and that such ophidia are not adapted anatomically to permit of the young taking refuge in the mouth or throat. Nevertheless, my sister, who was a keen observer and not fanciful by nature, saw it take place in a clearing, thus precluding the possibility of an optical illusion.

Country people used to put sloughed snake-skins found along the canal bank and lanes, inside their hats as a remedy for headache.

14. In the Moor, Mapledurwell, 1927.

Grass snakes are far more prevalent in our part of
Hampshire. We once had a dog at the farm who was a
'dabster' at catching them and bringing them home, which
reminds me that years ago, there was an even more deadly
enemy of snakes—a mongoose—at Mapledurwell House.
I remember seeing a large grass snake slithering into the
church just as my mother, sister and I had arrived early for
the afternoon service. We sought the help of 'old Albert',
the verger, who quickly procured a broom and brushed the
unwelcome visitor from behind the church door out on to
the path where it mounted the bank and slid sinuously away
through the grass between the graves, and that was the last
we saw of it. I also recollect sitting quietly in a shady grassy
paddock of Mapledurwell House close to some medlar and
quince trees, and a Wellingtonia which I often climbed when
young. I was enjoying the utter peacefulness of my surroundings, for those were the days when cars were seldom heard
on country roads. The book I was reading was absorbing,

but I suddenly realised that I was not alone: there was a stealthy movement in the grass, and then the greenish coil of a snake slid slowly out of sight.

I have seen what country children called 'water snakes' (grass snakes) twisting and turning in the canal as they disported themselves in the shadow of the Little Tunnel; and near Penny Bridge, Up Nately, my fiancée and I saw a grass snake four feet long. Years later, we were having lunch in 'Jasmine Cottage', the back window wide open, when suddenly we heard a sharp frantic squeak. I rushed out to ascertain the cause, and saw a terrified frog: facing it was a long grass snake which seemed to mesmerise it. I drove the snake off down the garden, turning the frog in the opposite direction out of danger's way. Years later, I went into the orchard one evening to view the moonlit downs and was puzzled by the sound of heavy breathing from behind a box hedge near the cottage: later I wandered round the garden hoping to hear the unusual snoring sound again, and sure enough, 20 yards away, it recurred. By the light of my torch, I discovered that it emanated from two hedgehogs, nose to nose, in the preliminaries of love-making!

I call to mind a fox with a russet coat and a paler bushy brush skirting a hedge between two of our fields, rooting about in blissful ignorance of being watched from a distance. I also remember seeing a weasel with four young ones, her high-pitched squeal warning them to keep close behind, as she sought to elude my advance. On another occasion, sitting on a bank by a cornfield, I saw a stoat emerge from behind tall stalks of bearded wheat. I kept quite still, and it seemed unaware of my presence, or else regarded me as part of the landscape, and eventually went on its way unperturbed.

My uncle Hugh was fond of cats, several of which would follow him around. One day a favourite black kitten fell down the well—which was 60 feet deep—so he lashed two long ladders together and went down to rescue it. It had

managed to scramble on to a ledge near the bottom of
the well, and was so frightened that he could not hold it
and climb the ladders at the same time, so to make sure
it did not get away, he put it inside his shirt. It scratched
him, but he brought it up to the top safely. I thought he
deserved a medal for his courage and humanity. He once
had a ginger cat which brought home a dead weasel for
his inspection!

I have of course seen owls, woodpeckers, jays, bullfinches,
wrens, and most of the common English birds round about
the village, but have not heard the corncrake for years. In
late summer the telegraph wires were blackened by flocks
of swallows preparing to migrate, but woe betide the swift
if it fell to the ground, as its tiny feet and long wings made
it almost impossible for the bird to become airborne again.
House martins and swallows built their mud nests in the
eaves of farmhouses, cottages and outbuildings, sometimes
returning summer after summer.

Bats flitting to and fro in country lanes as the shadows of
evening fell, were familiar companions. Occasionally we
discovered yellow-bellied lizards behind the mass of blue
flowering periwinkle which grew close to the walls of
'Jasmine Cottage'. Newts or efts were called 'evvets' by the
country folk, just as ants were invariably known as
'emmets'.

Most British butterflies frequented the gardens, lanes
and downs, and even the Camberwell Beauty has been
seen in the neighbouring village of Old Basing. The Purple
Emperor and White Admiral are not unknown to Hampshire, but I never saw Swallowtails there. Meadow-browns,
chalk-blues, orange-tips, fritillaries, brimstones, and the
greater and lesser tortoiseshells were plentiful. The most
gorgeous were the Red Admirals, Peacocks and Painted ladies,
but the spraying of crops in recent years has played havoc
with butterflies in general, and I miss their graceful shapes
and brilliant colours. They were much attracted by the

purple buddleia which I first saw at Hook Cross; this shrub has been known for generations as the 'butterfly bush' Giant dragonflies flashed and glittered as they darted over the canal. In contrast, there were big-bodied Basingstoke spiders, with legs two to three inches long, which occasionally crept forth from cottage rafters and bedroom ceilings at night.

Hampshire is richly endowed with wild flowers, and in the springtime the countryside is a riot of marsh marigolds, cowslips, oxlips, celandines, primroses, violets, wood anemones and wild hyacinths—roughly in that order. Most beautiful is the blossom of apple, cherry, plum and pear trees, also Japanese cherry, lilac, almond and forsythia. Many of the summer flowers are mentioned in this book: it would take a very long list to include them all, but I must not forget such favourites as bachelors' buttons, cotton grass, rest harrow, figwort, chicory (a lovely shade of blue), cornflower, and an ever-diminishing number of varieties of orchis. The yellow musk (mimulus), which we called 'monkey flower', grew on the banks of streams, but is far less common than it used to be. The dainty forget-me-not gladdens the eye, when bracken and the leaves of deciduous trees are turning from green to gold, copper or fiery red.

I may have given the impression that I saw Hampshire only at its best, but in December 1927 we travelled south for Christmas. Next day—Christmas Eve—snow fell silently and continuously, enveloping the countryside like a heavy blanket. We had no idea we were to be marooned till New Year's Day. Snow was three feet deep everywhere, and six feet or more in the drifts. A path was shovelled out so that people could walk single file down the village street. It would be hard to imagine a more traditional Christmas scene, unless we had ridden on horseback to church! My mother at the cottage, and my aunt at the farmhouse—60 yards away— only saw each other when we arrived and when we left nine days later, by which time cars and lorries on the London

road were just beginning to be dug out. Conditions were
much worst at Winklebury, outside Basingstoke, for there
the drifts were 16 feet deep, and food had to be dropped
by 'plane to the beleaguered inhabitants.

Three sisters of independent means, daughters of the
leading farmer who died in 1912, were wholeheartedly
devoted to the welfare of the village in which they spent
their lengthy lives, and the country folk who dwelt there.

The eldest, Miss Florence Thorp, was the church organist
for over half a century, and also at Old Basing for a number
of years. Like her sisters, she was an enthusiastic amateur
gardener. I associate Hampshire in my earliest days with one
of Mendelssohn's *Songs without Words*, 'Consolation', no. 9
in E, op. 30, no. 3, which she often played as the opening
voluntary at church services. To me it is her theme song.
I have only to hear the opening bars of this simple tune,
and a picture of her gentle personality is conjured up in
my mind. She succeeded her brother as churchwarden.

The second sister, Miss Mabel Thorp, nursed all and
sundry in the village whenever there was sickness, having
served in Queen Alexandra's Auxiliary Nursing Service in
Egypt during the First World War. She was deputy organist
when Mapledurwell church services clashed with those at
Old Basing, and ran the Sunday School, taught the children
there, and organised their gathering of small bunches of
primroses which graced each grave—unmarked as well as
marked—in the churchyard at Eastertide—a custom which
is also observed at Weston Patrick. This reminds one of a
similar Easter practice, linking the living with the departed,
at Clyro churchyard in 1870, which is recorded in such
unforgettable phraseology by the Rev. Francis Kilvert in
his *Diary*.

The youngest of the three, Miss Nora Thorp, assisted in
the work of the garden, farmhouse, and church. She arranged
the flowers in church for the Sunday services, and revealed
an exquisite sense of symmetry and beauty. I specially liked

to see the heavenly blue morning-glory blooms from her farmhouse wall which were often placed before the small figure of the Virgin and Child in the nave. She was a member of the Hampshire Field Club, and had a flair for research, collaborating with the Rev. J. H. E. Whittaker in a short history of Mapledurwell and Andwell, dating back to the Domesday Survey. She also served as a churchwarden.

I knew them well for 60 years. They invariably extended a warm welcome to us when we arrived for our holidays, and there was always an invitation to view their fragrant, well-tended garden and greenhouses after a Sunday evening service, and to sit down in their cool old-world farmhouse drawing-room and talk about family news, the village they and we loved, and the world outside. All three were interested in the discoveries I made on many excursions all over the county. They also took pleasure in preserving Victoria and Orleans plums from our orchard. The personalities of these three ladies endeared them to everyone, and all relied on their varied and kindly ministrations, particularly in times of trouble. They were often to be seen cycling through the village on errands of help and service, and long will they be remembered. But of all their work, including the dedicated service they rendered so willingly and unstintedly to the villagers over many years, they placed first and foremost the welfare of the little church they served so long and faithfully.

It is sad to record that no sooner had the two elder sisters died—in 1960 and 1961—than the youngest was afflicted with continuous ill-health, and had to leave her beloved farmhouse to enter a nursing home near Winchester for the last four years of her life, where she passed away in 1965.

We shall not see their like again, and we sadly miss their physical presence. When I read books about Schubert and the Fröhlich sisters, who are referred to as 'the four Graces', I think of these three happy sisters.

We all have our treasured souvenirs. I have two which
concern these three old friends. I had returned from a visit
in 1946 to Gilbert's bookshop at Winchester, and was full
of a new 'find'—a mint copy of W. E. Colchester's *Hampshire
Church Bells*. Knowing their interest in the subject, I
showed them the book, which contained pedigree data
on the pre-Reformation and post-Reformation bells in
the 300 or 400 churches in the towns or country parishes.
With one accord they proposed they give the book to me,
and this they did, autographing it. The second concerns an
oil painting which had hung inside their farmhouse ever
since I could remember. It was painted about 100 years
ago by one of the Garlands of Winchester, a friend of their
father's, and was of the cottage ('Addison's Cottage') which
occupied a corner of our 'Jasmine Cottage' property. It
portrayed the entrance from the road through a latched
gate, deep thatch covering the passage past the woodhouse
to the cottage door; the narrow Tudor bricks, and the great
flat-topped stone outside the gate, which had been worn
smooth by the feet of generations. Over the fence hung
an aged green cloak which belonged to a shepherd: against
the post supporting the woodhouse rested a crook somewhat
resembling those made by the old Sussex blacksmith from
Pyecombe. It is many a long day since a shepherd lived in
our village. By the stone rested a small ringed keg and a
straw lunch-basket—a 'flag basket' made of reeds—such as
farm labourers always carried, from a corner of which a
bottle protruded. A little maid stood knitting near the open
cottage door, which gave a glimpse into the dark interior.
I had long wished to make a copy in Indian ink of this
painting, as I thought this medium would admirably suit
such an old timbered cottage; and asked if I might borrow
the picture for a day or two. Two of the sisters went and
took it from where it hung, and then, greatly to my surprise,
they presented it to me, saying that they had all wanted to
do this as the cottage had belonged to my grandfather. The

old picture is in front of me as I write, and my sense of gratitude is as warm now as it was then. Their father had more in common with me than I knew at that time, for he, too, played the flute. My boyhood friend who had recently entered his employ, asked if I might join in the harvesting activities at Sheetlands in 1911, and he agreed. Those four days were most memorable. Refreshments were sent up to the fields each afternoon from the farmhouse. I always accompanied my grandfather to church, and the following Sunday, the farmer (who was his fellow churchwarden) gave me 5s. as my wages, suggesting to grandfather that an appropriate place for it would be the collection box! How they chuckled over my discomfiture. The idea was unthinkable!

I always enjoyed fruit picking at Mapledurwell, and helped gather in the plum harvest not only from our farm and cottage gardens, but also from the large market garden which we rented for many years. One summer there was such a glut that the huge crop had to be sold to a Whitchurch jam factory for a ha'penny a pound! We did the picking and they did the collecting. As time went on, when the uncles became too old for plum picking and the farm and market garden were given up, I made a point of fixing my holidays to synchronise with the harvesting for the pleasure I got out of gathering the fruit from the cottage garden, which was more like an orchard. I sold and delivered it, too, and in the course of my activities made a number of friends. They looked forward to my annual visits, and would bring out home-made wines, and invite me to partake of their hospitality. If the crop failed to supply enough for all in some years, there would, of course, be disappointment, but they understood. They relied on me as much as I did on them! One summer I called on an old lady in Old Basing who was 'fair taken back' to see me: it transpired that she had seen an obituary paragraph in the *Hants & Berks Gazette,* but did not realise that it referred not to me, but of my father, who had died in Liverpool and been buried at Mapledurwell.

Our specialities were Victorias, Orleans and Prince of Wales. There were others—Mussels, Golden Drops and damsons—but picking damsons was a slow job. Victorias with the bloom heavy on them were a picture, so every precaution was taken not to handle or move them more than was absolutely necessary. Most people preferred the juicy Victorias, but the older generation of villagers who 'knew a thing or two' would first inquire if there were any Orleans plums—a rounder, bluish-black fruit highly prized for its excellent taste, firm texture and preserving qualities. Fifty or more years ago, fruit was sold in the country by the gallon rather than by the pound. Grandfather charged 3s. a gallon (six pounds), and the price remained the same throughout my time. One person thought I was foolish not to sell Victoria plums at market prices—upwards of a shilling a pound at the time—but I pointed out that if I did, I would sell only an odd pound or two here and there, whereas now I could easily dispose of a dozen pounds or more at a time. After all is said and done, it was a holiday pastime as far as I was concerned, and I did not want to make a labour of it! I was happy if the crop provided my uncle with a useful little addition to his income.

When he (the last of the Mapledurwell uncles) died in 1955, the parish magazine poignantly recorded: 'Hugh Prince was laid to rest near the church on his eightieth birthday, and with his passing, there is unhappily no further member of the Prince family in this village'.

2
Old Basing

OLD BASING, an ancient village and the forerunner of Basingstoke, is well-known on account of its association with the Civil War of 1642 to 1645, when for over two years the Cavaliers were besieged in Basing House. It is said to have been the last of the great houses to hold out against Cromwell, earning the title of 'Loyalty House'. After its fall, he destroyed what remained of the buildings. Occasionally cannon-balls used in the siege are found in the locality; we had a piece of one which served as a door-stop in our cottage.

A pleasant approach to the village was by the country road from Basingstoke which curved sharply as it reached a large triangle of tall sedges bounded on the other two sides by the low bridge over the Loddon and the high railway embankment between the arched viaduct and Swing-Swang bridge. That was the road we always took when we drove out from Basingstoke to Mapledurwell from the Reading (South Western Railway) side of the station, which was as countrified as the Station Hill side was towny and modern. It looked as old as a Western film setting of a railway station, for the horse was tethered at the railings which were under cover in true cowboy style! Going by way of Bunnian Place, past the thatched 'Old House at Home' and through Goddard's Lane—a thing of the past since 1966—we avoided the traffic and reached the Old Basing road which was quiet compared with the busy London turnpike (now the A30). A large tithe barn supported by king-posts flanks the lane which runs from the

Loddon bridge and under the viaduct to Barton's Mill. The
Grange Farm is walled in all the way from the bridge and
round the corner into the village street: the farmhouse
is beautifully kept, and its external appearance is essentially
the same as it was before the siege of Basing House. Indeed
the layout of the old village was strikingly similar to what
it is today. A noticeable feature was the mellowed rustic red
brick, which is still the prevailing material of the older buildings, such as the Garrison Gateway, the church, the old
cottages in the Street, and the walls and dovecote of Basing
House. These red bricks were also used in the construction
of the humpback bridges which lent beauty to the old
Basingstoke Canal on its gently curving way through Old
Basing. Bricks and tiles have been made in the village since
Roman days, and in more recent times Daneshill brickyard
earned an excellent reputation. Wherever you go in Hampshire the pale red brick of old houses, cottages, farms and
watermills is the characteristic colour of its ancient villages
and towns, which were enchantingly portrayed in Wilfrid
Ball's water-colours.

A hundred yards from the entrance to Grange Farm is
the Garrison Gateway, opposite which is Loyalty Cottage
with its large and beautifully-shaped bow-windows. A few
yards away, stagecoaches pulled up outside the *Crown*
inn. By old cottages, mud-houses and Basing Wharf canal
bridge, Crown Lane leads past Parker's (or Park-house)
farmhouse, with its charming turret-staircase, to Hatch Lane.
Oliver's Dell close by was a rifle-range long before it became
a refuse dump.

Hatch Lane, which runs from here to the *King's Head*
at Hatch, is now a suburban road lined with modern
dwellings, but it used to have fields on either side which
belonged to Farmers Wigg and Barton, of Byfleet and Grange
Farms respectively, who were often to be seen (in the first
decade of this century) on horseback severely inspecting
the work going on there: they and the Mansbridges farmed

in Old Basing for many years. The lane in those days was not yet macadamised, and slow-moving carts and wagons, even cycles, threw up a cloud of dust behind them. In a field nearby, in Milkingpen Lane, a patch of maize with large aspidistra-shaped leaves and with cobs greening to yellow, made a striking show one summer.

By far the most wonderful sight I ever witnessed in these parts was that of an aged shepherd (clad in a soiled smock and carrying a crook) talking in a quiet high-pitched voice to the foremost of his flock, who seemed to be listening and putting implicit trust in him. He was walking slowly along dusty Hatch Lane towards Old Basing—a tired, bent figure of small stature, leading his flock, with his dog busy in the rear and at the sides, rounding up stragglers. It was then that I realised that those who urged on the sheep from behind were drovers and not shepherds, and brought home in a very real way the truth of the biblical references to sheep following the shepherd and knowing his voice, and what is more, known individually by their master. That sight was a glimpse into another age, and I find it hard to believe that I am still living in the same century.

Shepherding and sheep figured less and less locally as time passed, but for another three decades or more there were skilful water diviners and dewpond makers—the Smith brothers of Old Basing—who also constructed artesian wells and artificial lakes—whose family have been associated with this ancient craft for generations.

The large parish extends from Hackwood to Huish, Hatch and Waterend, and from there across to Hodd's Farm, Pyotts Hill and Cufaude (pronounced Cuffle, and probably deriving from Cowfold), almost to Sherborne St. John and Basingstoke. An interesting little book entitled *Olden Days and Nowadays in Old Basing*, was compiled by Miss Mary Hoare with the help of friends from the local branch of the Women's Institute, and published in 1932. It was reprinted

in 1965 (the golden jubilee of the foundation of the W.I.)
by Mrs. Hilda Batchelor.

The chalk pit by Wellock's Hill, a mile from Basingstoke,
has been opened up almost as far as Redbridge, and its
deposits supply agricultural needs for miles around. Tradition
has it that Dickens Lane, not far away, is where Ethelred,
brother of Alfred the Great, was defeated by the Danes,
and Lickpit (Lych-pit) Farm commemorates their victory.
Gruesome names persist from the Civil War in Dead Men's
Lane, near Redbridge, and in Slaughter Close, not far from
Basing House ruins.

Among the families who had lived in Old Basing for many
years are the Halls, who were blacksmiths as well as parish
clerks and bellringers for a century or two. I look back on
happy times in their smithy when our horses required the
farrier's services, and can still hear the bright metallic ring
of the hammer on the anvil and the sizzle of the hooves
as the shoes were nailed on. Another familiar country sound
outside the smithy was that of the bubbling spring at the
bottom of the garden. Kindly, bespectacled Richard Hall
always gladly lent me the key to the belfry, which was
reached from a large pillar near the north vestry at the
back of the organ. The fine old church has a wide nave and
an aisle on either side, so it is very spacious. The chancel
and transepts are 11th-century, and there are 12th-century
remains in the nave, and north and south arches of the
battlemented red brick central tower. The Roundheads
stabled their horses in the church during their long seige
of Basing House, and bullet marks are visible on the walls.
That they missed despoiling the little statue of the Virgin
outside in an ivy-covered niche facing the Street, seems
providential. The peal of bells was reduced to the present
two: some say that several were melted down, whilst others
aver that four eventually found their way to Sherfield-on-
Loddon. The church, which contains tombs of the Paulet
family (Marquesses of Winchester and Dukes of Bolton),

was restored in 1664, and the Bolton chapel, in which hang iron helmets, gauntlets and heraldic decorations, in 1925. There was a church band here years ago, for that popular pair of woodwind instruments, the clarionet and bassoon, are mentioned in old records of expenditure.

The clipped yews at Peacock Corner, near the fine half-timbered *Bolton Arms* inn, are a delightful survival from the past. Down the hill is Lower Mill and another low bridge over the Loddon, and on the far side, Pyotts Hill, one of whose thatched cottages was transported brick by brick and beam by beam to the United States some years ago. There are 16th-century cottages near the railway arch in the Street, but large modern housing estates are rapidly changing the appearance of the village.

The pastoral setting of the Old Basing, Mapledurwell and Up Nately flower show, held annually for the best part of a century, occasionally in the fields of Basing House, but more often in the recreation ground between the *Bolton Arms* and the Loddon, was to my mind as attractive as the exhibition of flowers, fruit, vegetables and country crafts. The shaded background of high trees on a fine summer's day is a memory I cherish.

3
Basingstoke

BASINGSTOKE is a borough and market town 46 miles
from London, and from here Waterloo can be reached by
rail in five minutes under the hour. The market was established before the Domesday Survey, and has always been one
of the main attractions of the town, particularly to country
folk from the outlying villages. The open stalls in front of
the town hall on market days have flourished longer than
anyone can remember. The once thriving cattle market
closed in 1966. There was also the Lesser Market off Wote
and Church streets, between the town hall and the old
Corn Exchange (now the Haymarket theatre), where,
nearly 60 years ago, the evening show consisted of reels of
the big film alternating with vaudeville acts! In the shopping precinct near the fine modern bus station, there is a
new open-air market to serve the growing needs of the
satellite town, whose population in 20 years' time will be
well over seven times as large as it was in 1914. With the
extensive demolition which has taken place, it looks as
though most of the old narrow and congested streets will
soon be a thing of the past. Basingstoke is no longer the
country town of former years. Most of the older types of
houses, including those of the Queen Anne period, will
have disappeared long before the new town is completed.
The modernised town has already lost much of the individuality which was its charm: the kindly spirit which
pervaded the villages had its focal point in the old town.

A well-preserved ancient inn, the *White Hart,* on the
London road, is a picturesque survival from stagecoach days

and the old Basingstoke we knew, and it is good to know that the half-timbered *Feathers* hotel near the top of Wote Street has been spared. The old *Rose and Crown* inn in Potter's Lane—where my uncle Bill put up his horse and cart—was pulled down in 1966, and so was the *Barge* inn, built in the 1780s when the canal was being constructed, where we left our cycles when we were likely to be home late. The canal wharf terminus vanished in 1936. The slate-grey cap on the malthouse of May's brewery in Brook Street was dismantled in 1963, and three years later, other parts of the building were razed to the ground when demolition took place on a colossal scale. The list of streets, inns and old buildings scheduled for destruction from 1966 onwards made sad reading, indeed heartache, for the older generation.

When tree-lined Eastrop Lane was known as Dark Lane, Eastrop church with its three-decker roof looked out over a mile of more of wide cornfields towards Old Basing. The almshouses, founded by Sir James Deane in 1607, are still standing, and give grace to London Street.

Walter de Merton, the founder of Merton College, Oxford, was born in Basingstoke, and died in 1277. He became Chancellor of England in 1261, and a Bishop of Rochester 13 years later.

Basingstoke has literary associations with Gilbert White, the Rev. Thomas Warton (to whom there is a memorial in the parish church), and the Rev. Charles Butler (1560-1647), author of a much-sought-after treatise on bees, *The Feminine Monarchie,* first published in 1609; and, in my time—though only as birds of passage—with two Irish poets who were both in camp on Basingstoke Common in 1914-15. Lance-corporal Ledwidge, who was killed in France in 1917, was in the same battalion—the 5th Inniskilling Fusiliers—as Lord Dunsany, then a captain, who not only discovered the younger poet and fostered his talents, but provided introduction in 1914, 1915, 1916, and 1917 to *Songs of the Fields, Songs of Peace* and *Last Songs,* all four being reproduced in *The Complete Poems of Francis Ledwidge*, published in 1919. Dunsany even wènt so far as to say that if Ledwidge had lived he would have surpassed even Burns, and might have become the greatest of Ireland's peasant singers.

The old Assembly Rooms at the rear of Barclay's Bank premises opposite the town hall were the scene of the early 19th-century monthly balls attended by gentry from the neighbourhood—the Portals of Laverstoke, the Lefroys of Ashe, the Terrys of Dummer, and others, including Jane Austen during her early life at Steventon rectory.

Malting, brewing and tanning have long been among the main industries of the town. Basingstoke was engaged for many years in the manufacture of clothing, particularly the Burberry raincoat. Foundries and engineering works, notably Thornycroft's, employed a sizeable percentage of the local populace, but in recent years, pharmaceutical laboratories and precision instrument factories have been built outside the town. Agricultural and gardening implements formerly manufactured on Station Hill are now being made in great variety and numbers on higher ground beyond the station.

Golding's (the War Memorial) Park is a valuable asset to the amenities of the town. The 16th-century parish church of St. Michael, with its whitish-grey battlemented tower and fine war memorial chapel, stands serene and handsome amid the destruction it survives. Thomas Hardy's reference to the church as 'gaunt and unattractive' is even more manifestly untrue than his pseudonym of 'Stoke Barehills' for Basingstoke. I am glad that the trees close to the church have been spared. A loss to the town was the Methodist church—renovated in 1951, but demolished in 1966—whose graceful exterior harmonised so well with that of the parish church opposite. The memorial garden for the blind, in Church Square, where enemy bombs fell in 1940, is beautifully kept, and is also memorable for the manifold scents of flowers and aromatic shrubs.

Basingstoke was an important junction in both the stage-coach and rail eras. Express trains still continue to thunder through the station on the straightest of tracks to London. Station Hill overlooked the town, but the town hall, for so long a landmark from the railway, is no longer so since the 1887 golden jubilee clock-tower was taken down in 1961: its four bells were melted down to make one large bell weighing five hundredweight for the new church of St. Paul, Tadley, seven miles away. The 13th-century Holy Ghost chapel ruins in the old cemetery or Liten, look out forlornly over the railway station. The Grammar School (otherwise the Holy Ghost School) and Chapel were maintained by the Guild or Brotherhood of the Holy Ghost, of Basingstoke.

In 1966, it was reported that among the tombstones to be removed from the old cemetery were those of John Lyford (1746-1829), surgeon and 'man-midwife', who was the family doctor of Jane Austen's parents at Steventon rectory; and his son, Dr. Charles Lyford (1778-1859) who gave to the town of Basingstoke the medallion bearing its coat of arms (St. Michael and the Dragon) which hangs on the mayor's chain of office. The grave of Mrs. Blunden, who was twice buried alive in 1674, is also among those in the cemetery.

The gentle river Loddon receives honourable mention in the works of three poets, Michael Drayton (in *Poly-Olbion,* 1613-22), Alexander Pope (in *Windsor Forest,* 1712), and Thomas Warton the younger (1728-90) in his ninth *Sonnet.* The river has two sources near the junction of Flaxfield with Sarum Hill and Worting Road, and both ran close to Brook Street, uniting in St. Michael's vicarage garden to become the Loddon. From there it ran under the town to Eastrop. The Loddon is a slowly-flowing river whose course is mainly through flat meadow country via Eastrop to Old

Basing, Hartley Wespall, Sherfield, Bramley and Stratfield-saye. It then crosses into Berkshire, and at Swallowfield is joined by two Hampshire tributaries, the Blackwater (so-called because of its peaty bed) and the Whitewater (probably because of its chalky foundations), and flows on through Arborfield until it empties itself into the Thames at Shiplake. The Loddon at Basingstoke was diverted from its course in 1967, and during this operation a thousand gallons of water a minute—or roughly one and a half million gallons a day—were pumped from the bed of the Basing road at its junction with the Reading road. Hampshire's unique flower—'the Loddon lily'—still grows on the river bank below the Lower Mill at Old Basing: Loddon pondweed is described in volume six of A. R. Horwood's *British Wild Flowers in their Natural Haunts*.

From my boyhood onwards I purchased a wide range of picture postcards of Hampshire from shopkeepers and photographers, among whom I remember best the kindly personality of Terry Hunt, dressed in sports attire, and a tall familiar figure in Basingstoke between the wars. His views of the town and the surrounding villages were popular because of their excellence and extensive variety: I must have bought hundreds in my time. I once approached him about several which had long been unobtainable, and recall the trouble he took in searching through his negatives and providing me with copies I specially wanted.

The old days of the unsweetened lardy cake, caraway seed cake, faggots and draught ginger ale have gone. I miss the respected shopkeepers of the older generation, especially the long-established craftsmen whose work was always reliable; also the bakers whose home-made bread and cakes were so appetising; and a white-haired pharmacist of the old school, whose dispensary was in Winchester Street.

I count myself fortunate that I had a long innings to enjoy the old town as it was.

4
The Basingstoke Canal

ACCORDING to Baigent and Millard's *History of Basing-stoke,* the London and Basingstoke Canal, promoted in 1778 by Act of Parliament, was opened in 1789, though the 'great tunnel' excavated under Greywell Hill was not completed until 1793. It was 1,200 yards long and built of brick, and its bore was smaller than that of the bridges, as there was no towpath through the tunnel.

Apart from the original proposition for a direct route from Basingstoke to Woodham, it was mooted in 1777 that an extension might also run from Up Nately to Nately Scures, Newnham, Rotherwick, Hartley Wespall, Turgis, Heckfield, and Yateley, but this plan was defeated, owing in part to certain objections by Lord Tylney, the mounting costs of the pioneer project, and the very considerable expense which the excavation of Greywell tunnel would entail.

The canal from Basingstoke timber wharf to Woodham, near Byfleet in Surrey, was 38 miles long, and timber, flour, etc., from Basingstoke, and hand-made bricks from Old Basing and Up Nately, were transported via Greywell and Odiham to Woodham—where it joined the river Wey—from whence they were conveyed to London. Coal, iron, sugar, and other goods were the main cargoes in the reverse direction. At Greywell wharf (eastern end of the tunnel) the tow-horse had to be unhitched and led over the Greywell wooded estate to the western end. When the railways were opened at Basingstoke between 1839 and 1848, the Canal Company was faced with severe competition, and it was wound up in 1869. My mother told me that when she was a young child, she was taken through Greywell tunnel in a boat, and that the tunnel caved in in 1872, just after Mr. Burrows, a bargee from Mapledurwell, had passed through in his boat, but the damage was repaired. Bargees had to lie on their backs and 'foot' or 'leg' their way (i.e., push their feet sideways) along the wall of the tunnel, or use poles against it, and sometimes even against the ceiling to propel the barges through. The waterway, however, continued to be used, though to an ever-decreasing extent between Basingstoke and Greywell, for the next 20 or 30 years. It was sometimes referred to as 'the barge river'. Men and children used to bathe and swim in it at Old Basing and Mapledurwell well after the turn of the century. One of the barges bore the name 'Mapledurwell', a coloured plate of which appears on the dust-wrapper and as the frontispiece to P. A. L. Vine's *London's Lost Route to Basingstoke* (the story of the Basingstoke Canal), published in 1968.

After 1905, when the canal bed was cleaned out rather too vigorously, the water between Up Nately and Basingstoke seeped away in places and became shallow. The bed and sides needed repuddling with clay, but this was never done, so that for close on 70 years the water under Brick Kiln bridge on the Nately Scures road near Up Nately crossroads has been dammed with boards so as to maintain a consistent depth between that point and the western end of Greywell tunnel. Therefore, for nearly a decade before the First World War the days of the canal with its slow-moving freight from Basingstoke to Greywell were numbered. On the red brick humpback bridges were notices prohibiting heavy traction engines from using them, so ploughing machines sometimes had to make wide detours to reach their destinations. Threshing engines, being lighter, went over, though at their peril, their weight and vibration sometimes causing the bridges to shake ominously.

When I was a lad I accompanied another boy along the winding towpath all the way from Mapledurwell to Basingstoke on his quest for half a gallon of barm (yeast) from May's brewery! That boy, later Sergeant Alfred Eccott, was killed in France in 1916 at the age of 21 whilst rescuing a wounded comrade in No Man's Land, and is commemorated on the Roll of Honour on the prayer desk in his village church of Mapledurwell. The path was overgrown in places and the snake-like journey took twice as long as by road, but to me it was a novelty and an adventure. There are two swing-bridges in fields near Hatch and Huish Park, and two red brick bridges within 100 yards of the *King's Head* inn at Hatch, on the A30 to Basingstoke and on the Hatch Lane road to Old Basing. When we reached Old Basing there were several humpback bridges. Cuckoo bridge, now demolished, was near Mansbridge's (now Brown's) farmhouse and Riley's stile, which were between the low railway bridge and Old Basing school built round about 1868. Another canal bridge still stands in Church Lane, near the vicarage and Byfleet Farm. (I have a water-colour of Old Basing church showing the mellowed walls of this bridge in the foreground, the rays of the sun shining slantwise across them and displaying the lovely tints of the rounded bricks on which villagers leant as they gazed down on the towpath and waters of the canal.) A third—Basing Wharf bridge— now filled in, was in Crown Lane near some old wattle-and-daub cottages known as the Mud-houses; and a fourth— Basing House bridge—leads from the Garrison Gateway to Basing House ruins, which consists of walls, ramparts, subterranean passages, and a small museum. From the fifth (Redbridge), there is a fine view of the canal which forms a moat outside the perimeter of Basing House grounds. Not only is there incorporated within its walls an old thatched columbarium set at a most attractive angle and containing a revolving ladder for easy access to 500 nesting places, but at a distance another shapely dovecote-like

building. Tall trees with splendid foliage and an ivy-covered
thatched cottage make a picturesque background to the
Broadwater.

Between here and Basingstoke, the canal pursued a course
more or less parallel with the river Loddon close by, for the
last mile or so of its journey, both drawing on springs to the
east of the town. There was sufficient depth and expanse
of water at Basingstoke wharf for a few large barges to be
moored there permanently later on. Eventually much of
the bed of the canal between Up Nately and Old Basing
dried up and became overgrown. The water at the western
(Up Nately) end of Greywell tunnel had a steely clearness
compared with the discolouration elsewhere. From the bank
opposite the end of the towpath, it was possible to peer
through and see a small circle where the light of day shone
at the Greywell wharf (eastern) end, even though there was
a bend in the tunnel. Springs in the woods and on the land
of the Greywell Hill estate over the tunnel have always
provided some water for the canal: at the time (1932)
of the collapse of the tunnel not far from its western end,
it was conjectured that it was due to the action of springs
from the chalky land above it, and as the damage was never
repaired, the canal was thereafter practically impassable.
Basingstoke wharf finally closed down in 1936, and it
eventually became the site of the new bus station.

I well remember that in 1913, the circumstances of the
time made an indelible impression on me as the problems
of the company affected our land on both sides of the
canal, and other largely dried-up sections between Mapledurwell and Old Basing. It was rumoured that the company
might lose certain rights, including possibly the reversion
of the ownership of the canal bed, banks and towpaths to
the owners or occupiers of adjoining land if the canal
property fell into disuse for a period exceeding five years
from 1910, when the last barge had tied up at Basingstoke
wharf. It was considered imperative that an attempt be

made in the autumn of 1913 to reaffirm the company's rights, and it was decided that a boat make the journey from Up Nately to Basingstoke. This involved two members of the Harmsworth family (including the bargemaster), his small crew, a tow-horse and volunteers to cope with the labour involved in difficult situations—the six-mile stretch eventually presented problems which took several weeks to overcome. No canal traffic took place during the First World War, but there was active traffic between London and the Aldershot wharf. From 1919 onwards it slowly diminished and eventually disappeared. The Harmsworth family were professionally associated with the canal company for the best part of 108 years (1840 to December 1947, when one of the active members from the days of 1913 died). The family then sold their interests in the company.

In the canal's course from Basingstoke to Woodham there were about seventy bridges, most of which were built of the old hand-made bricks, though several were wooden swing-bridges. Some of the canal land between Mapledurwell and Basingstoke was sold to farmers and other local persons. Eastrop Lane bridge near Basingstoke wharf terminus was demolished in 1927 to permit of a wider road being built connecting the London road (A30) with that from the old market town of Old Basing. The canal had been navigable for 22 years for only 31 of its original 38 miles' course from the old Greywell wharf to its confluence with the river Wey—roughly half in Hampshire and half in Surrey. Leaving Greywell, it runs via North Warnborough, King John's Castle, Odiham, Winchfield, Pilcot bridge, Grubb's Farm bridge, Dogmersfield park, Crondall bridge, Crookham (Chequers and Malt House bridges), Fleet (Reading road and Pondtail bridges) to Aldershot, Ash Vale, and North Camp, where it leaves Hampshire. It then journeys on through Surrey via Great Bottom flash, Mytchett Lake, Frimley Green, Deepcut, Pirbright, Brookwood, and Goldsworth to the *Wheatsheaf* bridge at Woking, Maybury Hill, Sheerwater and West

Byfleet to Woodham. All of the 29 locks occur in the
Surrey reaches, six within a mile of the junction of the canal
with the Wey. The so-called 'flashes' which occur in the
course of the canal are lakes which served for barge-turning.
In Hampshire there were wharves not only at Basingstoke,
but also at Old Basing, Mapledurwell (Frog Lane), Up Nately
brickworks, Greywell (eastern end of the tunnel), Odiham,
Winchfield, Crookham, Fleet, Aldershot, and Ash. I never
visited those in Surrey.

Fishing has been permitted over certain portions of the
waterway, and nature lovers interested in the fauna and
flora along its banks enjoyed the privilege of rambling there.
Pleasure boats and canoes have been used at Winchfield and
other places, and occasionally there have been barge outings
up and down the canal. The once busy Klondyke brickyard
at Up Nately has not been worked for many years, and its
tall square chimney has long since disappeared. The chalk
and sand pits adjacent to the Little Tunnel were the nesting
places of sand martins and kingfishers, whose flashing blue
as they fished the canal was as strikingly beautiful as the
brilliant green of the 'yaffle' (woodpecker) in flight. Not
far away, near Frog Lane swing-bridge, I once saw a large
'jack' swallow another pike almost instantaneously. There
were a few trout in the canal, but they were far more
plentiful in the nearby trout farm and natural waterways
in the vicinity, especially in rivers and streams. One had
only to dig down a foot or two almost anywhere to find that
the subsoil was chalk. When the water in the canal dried
up there were hosts of empty shells apart from those of
snails embedded in the chalky, flinty banks. It has been
conjectured that these were accretions of sea deposits from
the distant past. In 1916, Luke's bridge at Mapledurwell
had moss-covered bricks and ivy-clad sides: crowning the
steep approach from the Cob Tree was a yew, with osier
willows on the opposite bank of the canal. When one looked
over the sides of the bridge, one saw only a wilderness of

reeds, rushes, arrowheads, bulrushes, meadow-sweet and aquatic flowers, and at times in the summer months one could walk over the canal bed without getting one's feet wet.

All of the old brick bridges over the canal at Up Nately, which include Brick Kiln bridge, Slade's bridge, and a tiny bridge at Klondyke brick kilns, one at Nately Eastrop (locally called 'Strip'), also the Little Tunnel (only 28 yards long) at Mapledurwell, are still standing (1973), but Penny bridge on the road from Up Nately to Hatch was pulled down in the early 1930s. Between here and the two brick bridges over the Basingstoke (A30) and Old Basing roads near Hatch, which were levelled during the middle 1920s, there were several bridges in Mapledurwell—two small wooden foot-bridges not far from Hatch and Huish House, a larger wooden swing-bridge half-way along Frog Lane, and the fine old Luke's bridge, both of which vanished about 1923. Our farmland stretched downhill to these two bridges, and on both sides of the canal for nearly half a mile of its length. In 1949—in which year a renovation appeal was made—the canal was sold to a group of enthusiasts (the New Basingstoke Canal Co., Ltd.), whose object was to save it from extinction by keeping it navigable and open as a waterway. House-boats were moored on it, and old canal-boats converted for the purpose. Great credit is due to Mrs. Joan Marshall, its former general manager, for the way in which the amenities and beauty of the canal could still be enjoyed by the public, despite all the difficulties and expense which its upkeep inevitably entailed. She promoted interest in its maintenance by her hard work, and by persuading people to take a share in its preservation. In addition to the permanent staff, a large number of honorary bailiffs patrolled its banks and towpaths to this end. This applied to the portion of the canal east of Greywell, the haunt of anglers, ramblers and lovers of wild life. There were the ever-present problems of ridding the canal of weeds which caused less trouble when barges plied to and fro, and of dredging the waterway, which is 10 to 12 yards wide during most of its course. It supplied water to farms and nurseries and also for fire-watching exercises.

In August 1965 I decided to explore the course of the canal between Odiham and Greywell, and to revisit King John's Castle, which is close to North Warnborough. I made the journey on foot from the High Street, Odiham, to the humpback bridge near the *New* inn, where Odiham Common begins. The prospect of following the old waterway to Greywell tunnel, where the towpath comes to an abrupt halt, was a fascinating one, as I had not been that way since I was young. The district was rich in wild flowers, like most of the Hampshire countryside. Flowering sedge, arrow-head and large laurel-shaped leaves grew in the canal, and tall blue vetches on the bank. Willow stumps stood at the water's edge, and traveller's joy, lesser bindweed, and the dried seed-pods of hogweed were everywhere, while the scented willow-herb graced the opposite bank. The towpath was fringed with forget-me-nots, and the red berries of the hawthorn trees which lined much of the way to North Warnborough and Greywell were in great abundance. Reed maces stood high in the water, and moorhens rushed with flapping wings and noisy anxious concern across the surface. Large burdocks with purple and brown burrs, plantains, and heaps of dried-up rushes lined the path which now broadened out, flowering grasses growing to a height of seven feet on the bank.

Near King John's Castle there was a field of cow parsley, and meadow-sweet blossomed fragrantly. The castle keep, octagonal in shape, with gaping holes in its walls, was an empty shell. There were fir trees nearby, and rose bushes and ivy growing on the flint walls which were matted with creepers—this was all that remained of the castle in which King John stayed before and after sealing Magna Carta at Runnymede. David Bruce, King of Scotland, was incarcerated here for 11 years, until ransomed by the Scottish nation during the reign of Edward I. Queen Elizabeth I occasionally visited the castle. James I disposed of his royal interests there in 1618, and less than a century and a half later it was in ruins, but it is protected as a monument of national importance.

Between North Warnborough and Greywell there were two oblong patches of water at right angles to the canal, on either side of it. The water here was broader and deeper than that in the canal only five yards away: these form part of the Whitewater and inter-connect beneath the canal. The towpath widened to three yards in places, and young elms formed the hedges. Oaks bent over so low that their leaves almost touched the water, and the hornbeam's foliage rustled gently. Woody nightshade was abundant. Here, also, were masses of ragwort flowers, both the small-centred and large-centred varieties, and mallard were flushed as I walked quietly along the slippery path. I could now see Greywell waterworks through the trees on the far side of the canal which, for some reason, narrowed and was bricked for a short distance, though there surely cannot have been a lock here. Approaching the dark entrance to Greywell tunnel, I saw an old notice on a board above the arch stating that it was constructed in George III's reign. This is the wharf end, and it is reached from a road between Greywell and Hook Common through gates on the opposite side from the *Fox and Goose* inn.

I walked through the village, by a lane to Greywell Hill House and through the woods, which rise to a considerable height, Greywell Hill estate being a landmark in the vicinity. One or two of the springs along the footpath are large enough to be used for swimming pools; their prevalence and the tremendous pressure of the land-mass above the tunnel contributed to its subsidence in 1932. The Up Nately (or rather the eastern) entrance to the tunnel was so overgrown as to be well-nigh invisible. Two young escorts who knew the woods, accompanied me as far as Nately Eastrop and the Up Nately–Greywell road where we parted company, the boys going to Greywell village and I to Mapledurwell.

It is fitting to conclude with a tribute to Mark Hicks, who was the oldest canal worker in this country, having worked on barges on southern inland waterways since 1885, and as a water-bailiff on the Basingstoke Canal from 1914 until shortly before his death in July 1966 at the age of ninety-two. In accordance with his expressed wish, his body was conveyed along the canal he had loved and served so long, on a barge hauled by friends, from his canal-bank home at Crookham to Malt House bridge, and was then laid to rest in Crookham churchyard.

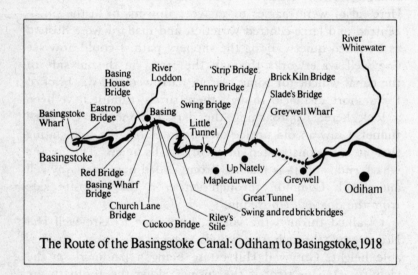

The Route of the Basingstoke Canal: Odiham to Basingstoke, 1918

5
Hook, Mattingley and Rotherwick

ONCE OR TWICE during each long summer holiday before the First World War, we walked or went by trap to Hook Cross, midway between Hook and Rotherwick, the home for 50 years of my mother's eldest brother Edgar. His wife, our aunt Thyrza, was a Cornishwoman whose maiden name was Liddicoat. Before her marriage she had spent six years in South Africa and four in France, and recalled a contingent of Uhlans' dipping their lances to her as she stood at the window of her house in Dieppe in 1871. She loved her life in the Hampshire countryside, and once said when nearly 90: 'When I look over the fields towards Mattingley, I wonder how anyone could ever wish to die'. She lived till she was 95 (1943), and throughout her long life, relatives and friends listened to her with respect and affection, and quoted many a sage remark of hers. Firm as a rock in her adherence to what she regarded as right—and how right she always was!—and generous, hospitable and sympathetic, she enjoyed hearing news of the large family at Mapledurwell and of mother's life in Liverpool. We always looked forward to our visits to Hook Cross, which was a second home in the south to us children.

Our journey was a countrified one through the lanes of peaceful Andwell by the tall mill-house, the gentle Lyde almost lapping over on to the low-lying road; to Waterend, this side of the elevated railway track; then past the tiny Norman church and manor farmhouse at Nately Scures; and Crown Lane (at the foot of Scures Hill) which meandered until it passed under the railway arch near the brickworks. At the top of shaded Newnham Hill is the village green intersected by lanes leading to the church and manor farm, and another going to Lyde Mill. A wooded road to Rotherwick bordered Tylney Hall park: the new model farm was a showpiece of Sir Lionel Phillips's time and the acme of comfort and cleanliness for cows and cowmen. Instead of taking the winding uphill road to Rotherwick village, we went along a narrow lane—Runten's Lane—over stiles and through a little wood which came out at the foot of a hill on the road to Hook. A footpath opposite led to a small lake in the woods. Near the entrance to this path I once spotted a nest of a long-tailed tit—the 'Mumruffin' of mid-Wales—whose feathers were ruffled when she sought entry through the low hedge to her bottle-shaped home. At the top of the hill was 'The Oaks', my uncle's house.

Hook Cross was a mile and a quarter from Hook and a mile from Rotherwick, whose village stores in those days was near the vicarage. The village is virtually one long street flanked by the church, school, parish hall, two inns, and a string of sizeable old-fashioned houses and cottages. tall trees lending an air of dignity to it. Where the street tapered off in the direction of Mattingley, dense woods, including an avenue of Waterloo oaks, formed the boundary of the village. A child's purchases at Rotherwick stores were almost entirely confined to stationery and sweets, so if we wanted to make more varied ones, we had to walk to Hook post office. Books, transfer pictures, and large sheets of cards of religious reformers could be obtained there in those days, and also postcard views of the district, including one of Mapledurwell Street, not obtainable elsewhere.

It was at Hook Cross as a child that one of my first creative activities developed—the sketching of Hampshire churches. The parochial magazine had on its cover pictures of the exteriors of Rotherwick, Mattingley, and Hartley Wespall churches, and these aroused in me a great interest

in Hampshire churches in general. I was fascinated by their
shapes—no two exactly alike—their spires, towers, turrets,
gable-end belfries, and, above all, bell-cotes with their
infinite variety of shapes. I began to sketch them, and soon
became proficient in reproducing unmistakably their dis-
tinguishing features. This inevitably led to rambles in search
of more, further and further afield, until many delightful
country churches, old and new, were not only committed
to paper but imprinted on my memory. If I could buy
picture postcards or photographs of them I did so, but if
these were non-existent, I made my own sketches and
snapshots. This hobby of collecting pictures of Hampshire
churches has persisted for many years, even down to today.

My three cousins at Hook Cross, though older than my
sister and me, were enjoyable companions, interested in the
country and in everything and everyone around them.
They acquitted themselves well at school, and two of them
taught. A much-respected headmaster at Rotherwick school
once told me what a tower of strength my eldest cousin
Agnes had been to him there. There were two harmoniums
at 'The Oaks' in the living room and 'Sunday room', and
all three cousins (particularly Hilda) played on them. An
amateur could make progress quickly on a harmonium, the
tone of which resembled that of a church organ, the
gradations of tone and colour being obtained by judicious
use of the various stops rather than by lightness or heaviness
of touch. The reedy quality also had its special appeal, and
by the use of hands and feet, one could warm up effectively
to satisfying crescendos.

Uncle Edgar occasionally drove us to Mattingley, Dipley
Mill, West Green, Hazeley Heath, and Hartley Row, and
once to Wild Moor, on the way to Sherfield. He was
seldom without a packet of sweets in his pockets, and saw
to it that we never went short. He loved his ponies and they
him. How we enjoyed these outings particularly when the
pony, hearing the pattering sound of uncle's feet on the

floor boards of the cart, started to gallop; but when we turned in the direction of Hook Cross, there was never any need for such persuasion, for it raced back home in next to no time. All my uncles were blessed with a boyish sense of fun, which they retained until their dying day.

Uncle Harry walked over from Mapledurwell most Sundays —five miles each way—and at busy times stayed on to help with the hay-making. His prowess as a mower had to be seen to be believed, for he was an artist with a scythe, and tireless even in the heat of midsummer, making short work of the meadows.

Uncle Edgar had a large garden, and having been trained at Kew, knew how to select and arrange a bouquet of flowers and southernwood (Lad's Love) for my mother. He it was who designated the place Hook Cross and had the post-box put up: previously it had been a bone of contention with the authorities, he having to go to Rotherwick, Hook or Mattingley to post letters. His meadow near the signpost had an unusual feature—three wells with water not far from the surface—so we had to beware when scampering over it. We played cricket in the timber yard under the oaks, and my cousin Jim, later a schoolmaster at Hook, Odiham and Merton, joined in. He was a fine player, the star of the Rotherwick team, and was promised the next vacancy in the county team, but he joined up on the second day of the war, and died of enteric fever in 1916 at Fyzabad in India, where he acted as deputy organist at the garrison church: before the war he practised on the church organ at Rotherwick. Uncle Edgar died in 1945 soon after V.E. Day, at the age of eighty-three.

Twenty years later I revisited 'The Oaks', which was soon to be sold. This time I approached it from Hook, where there is little which is old, except the two *White Harts* on the A30—one, the so-called *Old White Hart,* a modernised building opposite the foundry; the other, the *White Hart,* which faces the Reading road turning, retaining much of its ancient look externally, whose picture is associated with coaching days and coaching ways in W. Outram Tristram's book of that title, illustrated with Herbert Railton's fine-point sketches. A gaily-decorated wagon containing tubs of garden flowers stood outside. Hook church close by may be modern—it was built in 1938—but its interior is beautiful and full of peace. It is easily recognisable from the entire design and particularly the draped reredos as the work of the architect of Guildford cathedral, Sir Edward Maufe.

The home of the originator of the 'Burberry' raincoat was on the Reading road. In the hedges flourish persicaria, ragwort and goatsbeard, and the scent of the honeysuckle is as fragrant as that of the sweetbriar near Andwell Mill. Bright red and shining green virginia creepers on a house with a brick-kiln 'bottle-top' chimney call to mind those on Hurstbourne Priors church-tower. Those two typically Hampshire wayside flowers, the pink striped lesser bindweed and the white great bindweed, grow in close proximity on the verge and in the hedges, and making for variety of colour are blue and yellow vetches and the brilliant red berries of the wild arum lily.

Hook Cross signpost is at the top of the hill, where the roads from Rotherwick and Mattingley meet. A tall Lombardy poplar which sways and rustles as it battles with the wind, brings back nostalgic memories of boyhood holidays spent nearby at 'The Oaks', which is up for sale. I open the well-remembered gate. The garden, once so beautiful, is unkempt, but the fig trees trained up the walls, continue to bear their purple fruit. The scent of the buddleias, roses and tiger lilies persists, and the long-familiar phlox, Russian vine, foxgloves, and Michaelmas daisies are still there. Jasmine grows near the side door of the long house, and snowberries in the hedge by the road. The ornamental pool, once gay with goldfish and flowering reeds, is overgrown. Uncle Edgar would not have tolerated this wilderness, for he kept his garden tidy at all times. How he loved wandering round his aromatic garden with pocket knife and raffia handy to assemble a bunch of choice blooms! The pilgrimage was well worth making, bringing back memories of other days spent in good company and happy surroundings.

I decided to walk on to Mattingley. A charming old house with a tiled roof and a most beautiful timbered out-house stands near the entrance to a country lane leading to Dipley Mill. Off the Reading road is a lane to Mattingley Green, on which stands 14th-century thatched 'Crocus Cottage', beautifully restored and cared for, and the 15th-century church built largely on wooden beams, pillars and bricks laid herring-bone fashion. One of its two medieval bells is 12th-century, which, with one at Bramshaw and two at Chilworth, are probably the oldest church bells in Hampshire. An old clarionet is preserved near the font in a case with an inscription which reads: 'To live in hearts we leave is not to die', a variant of a more familiar line. A booklet published in 1965, *The History of a Hampshire Parish, Heckfield and Mattingley,* based on researches of the late Mr. W. J. James, was chained to a wooden pillar at the back of the church for the information of visitors.

Retracing my way to Mattingley post office, I left the Reading road by a quiet lane which runs past Cowfold Farm to Rotherwick. It was late August, but dog violets were still in bloom under a hedge. Further on was an avenue of oaks, commemorating the victory of Waterloo, where the raucous caws of rooks and the sharp piercing cries of jays could be heard above the more musical expletives of smaller birds in the thick overgrown copses. On the border of the parish are the Whitewater and Lyde rivers. Outside the village is Lyde Green, a tiny quiet hamlet, the terminus of a most countrified route for buses which ran on two days a week from Basingstoke through Old Basing, Nately Scures, Newnham and Rotherwick.

There are two old inns in Rotherwick's village street—the *Falcon,* and the *Coach and Horses* to which hydrangeas add a splash of colour. Masses of what look like acacia flowers grew halfway up a tall tree and seemed foreign to it. The rosy red brick tower of Rotherwick church, whose chancel dates from 1250, was 'in splints', even redder modern bricks being used in its renovation. One of its bells was cast in 1420. Rotherwick church was the most satisfying acoustically of the country churches in which I played my flute, because the building, with its wide high nave and transept, is larger than most, and there is little matting on the stone floors to muffle the sound, thus lending itself admirably to a purer and more reverberating tone. It was gratifying to me to read that other enthusiastic woodwind players had derived pleasure here, for under a glass case on the wall above the vestry door at the back of the church, a notice stated that 'these instruments, three clarionets and a bassoon, used by musicians in the gallery above to accompany the singing previous to 1870, were presented to the church by Lt. Col. Harris St. John'. Those were times when there were more amateur players in country villages than there are now, and it was a sad day for them when the fashion changed, and organs and harmoniums took their place. There are mural tablets in memory of the Tylney family. Tylney Hall, now a school, is in the nearby park.

An unusual surname, but familiar in this parish, is that of Caesar: there were Octavius and Julius Caesar who kept the stores near the church, and the post office, which was for a time at the far end of the village street.

6
Andwell, Nately Scures and Newnham

ANDWELL, which is described officially as an 'extra-parochial district', is a delightful hamlet through which runs the river Lyde, the confluence of a number of rivulets.

In 1924, Sir George Dewar wrote his little book, *The Pageant of English Landscape,* in which he paid a charming tribute to the peaceful country lanes round about Andwell Priory farm and mill, Nately Scures, and the idyllic Lyde, but I first fell in love with them 20 years before. Andwell adjoins Mapledurwell, from which place there is a network of byways to other quiet villages—Up Nately, Greywell, Upton Grey, and Tunworth—which have remained unspoilt. I hope, as I write this in 1967, that the projected M3 motorway from the Surrey border to Popham, which will cut a deep swathe through this hitherto undisturbed country-side, will not utterly destroy its beauty.

Silverweed lines the verges at the Priory Farm end of the Andwell lane, and on one side of the narrow road to Springhead and Mapledurwell is a large watercress bed. Hawkbit, bracken and brambles, maple and ash grow profusely along the lanes, with colourful clumps of comfrey; and the hedges from Springhead to Up Nately are brightened by scabious, lesser cranesbill, milfoil, mugwort, persicaria and knapweed flowers so small and close to the ground that they almost mislead one into thinking they are bachelors' buttons. In late August there are unripe hazel nuts and a few purplish-black sloes, and tall hogweed in the meadow above the bank, turning from yellowish-green to a dry brown, stands out against the sky. Over all spread the sheltering luxuriant oaks so characteristic of these parts.

At the time of the Norman Conquest, a greater Mapledurwell—which included what is now Up Nately, Newnham and Andwell—came into the possession of the de Port family. In 1130 Adam de Port of Mapledurwell founded Andwell Priory, a dependency of the Benedictine abbey of Tiron in Normandy. Even in those far-off days there was a mill at Andwell.

All that remains of the monastic buildings is associated with the Priory farmhouse, much of the ancient part of which was demolished nearly a century ago. In 1912 a wall of the old chapel with its 13th-century window collapsed. In the summer of 1966, Mr. Stacy of the Priory Farm showed me the stone coffin in the garden behind the farmhouse and the plot, 16 yards long, which was the site of the chapel, with the end walls still standing. He also showed me the porch and doorway, a receptacle in the middle of the portico, and a sealed-up doorway at the far end of it. The Priory Farm is situated on flat moorland soil, and tracks lead to the London road and to the ford. Between Andwell Mill and the gravelly slope to this ford near the Priory Farm bridge, the stream sometimes overflowed its banks. The Andwell cottagers drew their water from a dip-hole by immersing their buckets from a miniature wooden platform alongside the lane.

Over 60 years ago, Andwell Mill was nearing the end of its long period of usefulness to the local community. How well I remember the wagons conveying the golden grain there to be ground, and what a pleasant sight it was to see the horses and wains standing under the high platform projecting like a penthouse from the tall brick building. The steel waterwheel on the river side of the mill was immense, much larger than most mill-wheels. Eventually the mill became derelict, but was still picturesque in its ruinous condition.

Shortly before the Second World War the machinery and millstones were removed, and the mill was later converted into a beautiful country house. The millstream was only slightly diverted at that time, and the expanse of water near the millrace made it into a miniature lake in front of the lawn. Tall willows and poplars flank the country road and the place where the wheel once turned, lending a delicate grace to the scene. A gentle lingering fragrance of sweetbriar in the hedge by the mill-house garden permeates the air.

A few yards away are cherries and snowberries, but thick undergrowth almost blots out the Lyde where it returns to its roadside course. Trout flash in its shaded waters, and on its banks reeds, meadow-sweet, ragwort, forget-me-nots, tall purple loosestrife and scented willow-herb flower in profusion. Rosebay, milk thistles, and white blind nettles grow on the other side of the lane, and by the end of August hips, haws and woody nightshade berries are reddening. Teasels are plentiful, and puce-coloured leaves of the great bindweed trail out into the quietly flowing stream.

A major diversion in the river Lyde had to be made later (1969-70) for the M3. This involved the closure of the Springhead Lane at a point near Andwell ford and the Priory farmhouse, and the construction of a fly-over in the vicinity.

Motorists rushing along the A30 or travellers by train between Basingstoke and London may catch a fleeting glimpse of the 12th-century flint church of Nately Scures, a hundred yards from the main road, four miles from Basingstoke and 42 from Hyde Park Corner, according to an old local milestone. The late Rev. J. H. E. Whittaker, who was priest-in-charge there, described it as 'probably the most perfect example of a single cell Normal aisleless apsidal church in this country'. The chancel apse is beautiful, 16 feet in diameter, the nave 30 feet long, all built in one piece. This led people to think it was the smallest church in England, but Lullington in Sussex, 16 feet square (really the chancel of a larger building) seats 24 people, less by half than Scures.

St. Lawrence in the Isle of Wight probably holds even fewer, and Upleatham in Yorkshire only twelve. Stockwood in Dorset, 29 feet by 12½ feet; Lewcombe and Oborne, in Dorset; Brentor in Devon; Fifield Bavant and Knook in Wiltshire; Culbone in Somerset; Over Denton in Cumberland; Wastdale in the Lake District; and Upper Eldon and Ewhurst in Hampshire, are all smaller than Scures, though some are no longer used.

It has also been stated that Nately Scures is the smallest parish church in Hampshire, but that at Upper Eldon, near Romsey, is smaller, 32 feet by 16 feet 8 inches, rectangular, with a bell in its roof: priests have ministered there since 1346. When I photographed it in 1922, there was seating for 20 people. Services used to be held a few times each year, but now there are only four parishioners and the church is empty, so this likeliest contender has fallen out of the race. Ewhurst church, near Wolverton, has a nave 25 feet by 26 feet, chancel 13 feet by 12 feet, north transept and vestry nine feet square, and south transept nine feet by six feet, but there have been rumours that it is to be pulled down, so it also may have to be eliminated. If St. Lawrence's church is ruled out because it is in the Isle of Wight (though this is technically part of Hampshire), Nately Scures may soon be the smallest parish church in regular use in the county.

Nately Scures is a cosy little church, whose walls, altar, pulpit and reading desk, all chalk-whitened, reflect a measure of light. In photographs the window above the altar appears as a shining holy of holies in the dim interior.

A mermaid capital may be seen on a pillar of the Norman doorway. The local legend is that a young sailor made the acquaintance of a mermaid far away at sea. After flirting with her, he forsook her and returned to England, soon afterwards falling in love with a girl from Nately Scures. The wedding day came, but as the bridal party approached the church door, there, sitting outside it, was the mermaid.

She seized the sailor and carried him off (hence the little figure on the mermaid's back in the carving), plunged with him into the nearby stream at Waterend, and thence swam down the Lyde and the Loddon into the Thames and so out to sea. The capital was carved as a warning to all faithless youths. This story was retold in the George V Jubilee issue of *Punch* (1 May 1935), but with a happy ending. In it the mermaid and the girl, discovering the sailor's fickleness, both decide to have nothing more to do with him and depart, leaving him forlorn.

Parts of the small gallery at the back of the church were built in 1591 and others in 1786, and the organ and choir stalls are at the top of the narrow wooden steps. I remember the pleasure my father derived from being a chorister here in his later years; he who, 65 years before, had been head choirboy in Wymering church. Two bells, dated 1651, are visible in the gable, and we could hear their drowsy tinkle, like cowbells, over the meadows nearly two miles away at Mapledurwell. The manor farmhouse, very close to the church, is old, spacious and beautiful.

The railway runs close to Newnham Hill, at the top of which stands the 12th-century flint church among high trees. Its chancel and narrow south tower doorway are Norman, but the interior is darkened by too much stained glass everywhere.

The former rectory was once the home of Admiral Sir Archibald Douglas. My grandfather occasionally drove over to prune his fruit trees, and one day in 1911 at coronation time, when walking round his garden, the admiral introduced him to Admiral Togo, the hero of the Russo-Japanese war of 1904. The old man was greatly pleased at having shaken hands with the Japanese admiral, and talked of it for long afterwards.

Newnham village is on a plateau, the older houses and farms clustering round the goose green. There are several timbered houses, first and foremost among them, 'Tithe

Barn', much enlarged since I first knew it as a thatched cottage and village shop. Today it is a gracious house, with a lovely and peaceful garden: I have often enjoyed visiting this delightful place, and lingering over coffee in conversation with its charming owner, Mrs. Doris Parsons. Another attractive house with a lily-pond in front, on the edge of the hilly boundary of the parish, has an extensive view of distant woodlands and downs. The manor farm and church, a stone's throw away, complete the rural scene. A bridge over the railway leads to Hook Common and the *Dorchester Arms* inn.

Each year I visited the secondhand bookshops in Winchester, Salisbury, Andover, Oxford, and Reading. The nearest and one of the best was that of William Smith & Son of Reading: the music section alone was always well worth a visit. My last most treasured major acquisition there was the original three-volume set of Kilvert's *Diary*.

I would start out for Newnham, and bypassing Rotherwick village make for Mattingley, Hound Green and Heckfield Common (where one now and again caught a glimpse of a squirrel climbing up and down the trunks of trees and frolicking among the branches) to Riseley, just over the Berkshire border, and then on to Swallowfield Mill —now pulled down—Spencerwood, Three Mile Cross by *The Mitford* at the foot of the hill, and Whitney, past *The World turned Upside Down* (whose sign shows a rabbit taking a shot at a fleeing poacher), to Reading. London Street still retains its old-world appearance by reason of its width and hilly sweep. I feel sure that when W. H. Hudson stayed at Silchester or even Hurstbourne Tarrant whilst writing *Hampshire Days* and *Afoot in England,* he, too, must have cycled over to William Smith's bookshop to browse and rummage through its several floors and labyrinthine passages, just as he did at Gilbert's old bookshop in the Square at Winchester. You were always free to roam at leisure unhindered, and if you came away without making a purchase, which was seldom, no-one minded. You knew you were always welcome.

I often lingered on till the shop closed before cycling home up the hilly road towards Basingstoke and Odiham. Many a drenching have I had, but none dampened my ardour. Today those purchases from Smith's bring back happy memories of days when, as often as not, I was so engrossed in hunting down literary treasures that lunch was forgotten and I reached home well-nigh famished.

7
Walking and Cycling

THE FIRST TIME I walked to town and back—three miles each way—was on a shopping expedition with my mother when I was six or seven years old. Shops stayed open late in those far-off days, and it was pitch dark when we started on the return journey from Basingstoke to Mapledurwell. Practically the only vehicles on the road were bakers' carts and grocers' vans.

My uncles used to recall the exploits of Charlie Spier, clerk of St. Michael's parish church, Basingstoke, for over 47 years, who had a well-deserved reputation for his long-distance walking. London, Portsmouth, and Oxford, were roughly equidistant, as were Salisbury and Southampton. In his prime he would cover the 35 miles from Basingstoke to Salisbury on foot in less time than the stagecoach took, complete his transactions, and return even quicker than he went, reaching home late the same evening. He died in 1865.

My uncle John thought nothing of walking the 14 miles from Farnham to Mapledurwell late on Saturday night and returning in time to open shop first thing on Monday morning, but that was long before the First World War, when there were no buses or cars. Country folk had to walk or cycle to town. Sometimes a local farmer or some other well-disposed person driving there took compassion on them and would give them a lift, but he could be reported if there were more than three up on the seat. A few might obtain seats in the carriers' vans which plied between certain villages and the local town, but these only operated on specified days, usually market days. Luckily, we had our own horses, traps and market cart, and my sister and I often accompanied grandfather to Basingstoke, Old Basing and Newnham for the sake of the ride. We usually had a glass of ginger wine at *The Grapes,* draught ginger ale at the *Crown,* or a lardy cake at the *Hatch.*

I learned to ride a bicycle in 1912, and my father bought me my first machine a year later. Previously, if I wished to explore neighbouring villages, I had to go on foot; and when I was 10 years old, 10 miles was my limit. This increased a year later to 15 or more miles a day, and thus I was able to range as far afield as South Warnborough, Long Sutton, Hartley Row, and Heckfield. An overwhelming urge drove me to widen my radius of territory and to cover 20 to 30 miles on a number of occasions during 1912, when I walked to Alton, Froyle, Bentley, Wield, Silchester, Kingsclere, and other places during the summer. If I had no views of certain places, I included those villages in my itinerary, for the desire to provide my own pictures had become paramount.

One fine morning that year, armed with sandwiches, cake and a little pocket money, I set off soon after seven o'clock for Whitchurch, passing Basingstoke town hall at eight o'clock. A steady three miles or so an hour, and Oakley, Ashe, Overton, and Laverstoke were soon behind me. The road from Deane to Whitchurch had been hilly in places, but as I was making good time and had all day in front of me, I decided to break new ground, so directed by steps to Tufton and Longparish (a most beautiful village, and very aptly named), whose church (dark within) was set among chestnuts, close to lush meadows and the gently flowing Test, with islets midstream. Outside, near the lychgate, were the remains of the village stocks. The turreted tower is a pleasing sight in springtime, the background of a farmyard scene where an old tiled barn on staddle stones and several thatched cottages and sheds nestled in amongst sheltering trees. Equally picturesque in summertime is the view of the church from the opposite direction, when dairy cattle plod leisurely homeward across a plank bridge over the river.

The village street, a long and pleasing succession of cottages, farmhouses and country residences, leads to Forton, with a glory of golden thatch sloping from the cottage roofs almost down to the ground. This hamlet lies off the lane to Longparish station up above the Andover–Basingstoke road. There I bore left, skirting Bransbury Common, and caught a glimpse in the distance of the rugged tower of Barton Stacey's 12th-century church, but wisely decided not to diverge so far out of my way as the afternoon was now well advanced. Although not perceptibly tired, I resolved at Bullington Cross to make for home after pencilling in rough outline the shape of the ivy-clad Norman church with the avenue of pollarded limes leading up to it, but to include the Sutton Scotney locality in my return journey, as there were two churches there I had never seen, Wonston and Hunton, which I hurriedly sketched because I thought it might be many a long day before I was that way again. Wonston church externally is as modern as that of Dogmersfield, which it closely resembles, but its chancel arch dates from 1200. I already had pictures of the ancient and beautiful little church of Stoke Charity, so did not linger, though it was only a field or two away from Hunton church, and would have been a gentle balm to my spirit.

In my zeal, however, I had underestimated the distance involved. At Sutton Scotney I came face to face with a signpost which read 'Basingstoke 13¾'—shall I ever forget it?—and as Mapledurwell was a good three miles the other side of Basingstoke, the prospect of walking another 17 miles before reaching home was a startling reality which had to be faced. It was now six o'clock, and I put my sketching pad away, and set my course rigidly in the direction of Popham Beacon. The rare beauty of the chalk downs as I walked alongside cornfields and through open country took my mind off oncoming weariness. I called at a wayside cottage between Popham and North Waltham, and asked for a drink of water, but owing to the severe drought during that exceptionally hot summer, the family had none. However, they very kindly gave me a cup of tea from the pot which they were enjoying, and this helped me on my way. (I had a similar experience at Farleigh Wallop nine years later in the rainless summer of 1921.) A comforting thought was that every mile was one nearer home, but my legs were becoming dead tired, and I knew that if I succumbed to the temptation to sit down by the roadside and rest awhile, I should fall asleep through sheer exhaustion. I had to take a firm grip of myself and make my feet keep going at a set, rhythmic speed, with no let up, and hoped against hope that I might get a lift from a passing van, but none was forthcoming in the darkness which by then had fallen. There was nothing for it but to trudge on and on, and when I passed Basingstoke town hall and glanced up at the clock, I realised that it was just 15 hours since last I had set eyes on it.

Although very weary, I was at last on home ground, and I called on my resources to climb Wellock's Hill on the way to the Hatch, where I took the footpath over the fields, reaching Mapledurwell 10 minutes before midnight. One of my uncles was still out scouring the lanes for me: the others had given up the search much earlier. When I popped my head round the door, my grandfather exclaimed, 'Well, thank God, you're back safe', and that was the feeling of all the family. There were no reproaches for the anxiety I had caused, and I was more than glad to be home again. During the round journey I had covered 42 miles in less than 17 hours.

A year later, when I got a bicycle, I gave up long-distance walking. In 1924 and 1925 I cycled 162 miles in a day on my heavy roadster from the suburbs of Liverpool to Banbury, taking the train from there to Reading, and cycling the remainder of the journey to Mapledurwell. Sixteen hours on the way.

The Aldershot buses to Basingstoke in 1916 were the first I remember in those parts, but eight years later, buses and charabancs had come into general use, which enabled me to make long journeys cheaply without any effort. Cycle rides were confined to places inaccessible by other means of transport. Eighty or 90 miles in a day continued to be enjoyed at holiday times for many years, and I could cycle the 39 miles each way to Salisbury in daylight, and still spend eight or more hours in that lovely city.

The time came when I was able to go almost anywhere in a car, but in 1965, when neither car, bus, nor coach was available to me to visit villages in deep country which I had not seen for years, the wheels of life turned full circle, and I resumed walking. I found that I could still quietly roam the downs and bridle paths, and as I went along I noted down details of trees, flowers, birds, and other wild life observed at close quarters, just as I had done many years ago, and that really was renewing my youth.

8
Winchester

BOOKS OF VIEWS of Winchester and district formed part
of the small library in our farmhouse, so the shapes of
most of the buildings in and around the ancient Saxon
capital of England were familiar to me before I actually
saw them. On my earliest visit I went by train from
Basingstoke.

The only intermediate station on the 18-mile run to
Winchester was 10 miles from Basingstoke, at Micheldever
(pronounced Mitchel-devver), a name which still retains
the strange suggestion of wildness it had always had for
me, and which holds as strong a fascination as did the
dazzling stretches of white chalk cliffs which came into view
like shining seraphim in the heat of glorious summer days,
as the train finally emerged from tunnels in the deep
cuttings under Popham Beacon. The embankments seemed
to darken as they narrowed near Micheldever station, which
in the railway's early days was known as Andover Road. The
chalk had been excavated in 1847 to form the foundations
of docks which were being constructed at Southampton.
Whether one went by rail, or made the journey by road
from Basingstoke over Popham Beacon, from which the huge
cutting could be viewed from a height, the scene was always
striking and memorable. By the time the Second World War
had started, the cliffs were camouflaged in the interests of
national security, and their gleaming whiteness departed
for good. When I passed through by train in 1966, I found
the cutting unimpressive, a depressing grey, with weeds
growing out of the chalk: the old view had been obstructed

not only by sheds, but by railway carriages and trucks on the lines in the sidings.

Micheldever church, a mile or so from both the station and the distant village, has a curious octagonal nave (1806) and memorials by Flaxman to the Baring family who lived at Stratton House. The massive 16th-century tower can be seen for miles. There are whitewashed, thatched cottages flush with the road in Micheldever village which, like Longstock and Eversley, was noted for mats and baskets plaited from dried sedge. Whether viewed from Popham Beacon or from the shaded stretches of the Basingstoke–Winchester road, what always struck me were the miles of rolling cornfields in late summer, with few hedges; and an avenue of beech trees from Micheldever station to the Stockbridge road, and heavy foliage in the churchyard, to relieve the bare landscape. The fields round our home village could not compare with these as to size and remoteness. Popham Beacon to Popham village, Woodmancote, Micheldever, Stoke Charity, and Stratton Park, was no country for the horse-plough; consequently teams of men from Mapledurwell with their large engines and multiple ploughing tackle spent weeks in these wide open spaces.

The Bullington stream rises near Micheldever, and after flowing through Stoke Charity, Hunton, Sutton Scotney, and Bullington, joins the river Test near Wherwell.

Winchester station lies in a backwater among trees, a haven on the edge of the city at a distance from the cathedral and the High Street, as is the case with other cities such as Oxford and Salisbury. Near the station approach is a crossroads, with Jewry Street leading to the High Street. Jewry Street had a greater appeal for me as a boy, for there were curio or junk shops with stalls where old books could also be bought.

One of my favourite haunts has always been Gilbert's rambling old bookshop in the Square. It is reached from the High Street through a passageway from the Butter

Cross and past St. Lawrence's church (part of William the Conqueror's palace), rebuilt in 1449, and nowadays an oasis of peace. Gilbert's premises consist of two old houses in which 80 per cent of the large stock of books is second-hand, so that its contents are both ancient and modern. Here one can roam virtually undisturbed in the ground floor backrooms or the dimly-lit first floor rooms, reached by an ancient wooden stair with a rope serving as a balustrade. Books crowd the shelves from floor to ceiling, and centre tables are piled high with volumes having a vague sort of association of subjects. No wonder W. H. Hudson and other booklovers, many from rural parsonages and country houses browsed to their hearts' content on the treasure they unearthed there. Just round the corner of the Square is the *Eclipse* inn, formerly St. Lawrence's 16th-century rectory.

The tiny church of St. Swithun over the Kingsgate is reached by a staircase from the street. Wolvesey castle (to the south-east of the cathedral) was King Alfred's palace before Henry of Blois, grandson of William the Conqueror, rebuilt it in 1138: the keep was destroyed by Oliver Cromwell's troops, and is now in ruins.

Sometimes I visited the West Gate, the City Mill, the Itchen, Cheesehill, the College, and other old buildings, including St. Cross church, and the fine Beaufort Tower and quadrangle of its hospice, not forgetting to ask at the porter's lodge for the wayfarer's dole—founded in 1136— of bread and ale: one of the drinking horns bore the name in silver of King Edward VII. Anthony Trollope's book, *The Warden,* has its roots in ancient St. Cross.

The cycle ride home along the Basingstoke road was hilly and sometimes monotonous, and one passed through only two villages, King's Worthy and Popham, but I felt happy and satisfied with my literary acquisitions. I recall a winter evening in 1940, enemy aircraft overhead, when I rode through dark avenues of trees on the edge of Stratton Park and the approach to Kempshott Hill, with volumes of German *Lieder* and a topographical book or two in my saddlebag: thus are libraries built up, each book with a pedigree or story attached to it. I remember visits to Winchester on consecutive days when I was thirteen. In those days pocket money was limited, even at holiday times, and I espied in a stationer's shop in the High Street a large quarto illustrated book on Hampshire and the Isle of Wight, published by W. Mate & Sons, at one shilling. I had nine pence in my pocket. Receiving an assurance that it would be kept for me, I rode home in the heat of the sun, and returned next morning for the coveted volume, making the 42-mile round journey for a second time. Gilbert's shop, however, with William Smith's at Reading and Beach's at Salisbury, comprised the trinity of bookshops which I haunted in those days as much as I do now: they are lodestones which have drawn me for over half a century. No holiday has been complete unless all three have been visited at least once.

Everyone made pilgrimages to the cathedral, for was it not the longest in England? An avenue of limes in the peaceful Close leads to the west doors. The heavy massive building and square central tower stood firmly planted on the ground, or so we thought until it was reported that the foundations were far from secure and likely to collapse. The grim truth revealed that the huge sprawling edifice was built on rotting beech trunks resting on layers of peat above a mass of silt, and that parts of the structure were showing visible signs of subsidence. The beech trunks had been provided by the indefatigable Bishop de Lucy from forests for which, equally with its oaks, the county was famous. It was a horrifying thought in those days (1906) that Winchester cathedral, which had hitherto stood for everything that was permanent, should have been built on insecure foundations: yet it had survived for 800 years. It was wonderfully heartening, however—indeed providential—that

by his expert skill, courage, dedication and infinite patience,
a Liverpool diver, William Walker, should have worked six
hours a day, six days a week, in muddy water and in
claustrophobic conditions, in darkness and danger during
those six vital years, 1906 to 1912, placing in position
interminable bags of cement in deep and lengthy channels
which had first to be excavated so as to ensure new secure
foundations for the cracking and crumbling edifice. By the
incredible labour of his own two hands, the cathedral was
extensively and successfully under-pinned and thus saved.
When King George V and Queen Mary attended the thanksgiving service—most appropriately on St. Swithun's Day,
1912—William Walker was presented to them and thanked
for his unique services. Unfortunately, he died during the
1918 influenza epidemic which claimed more victims than
the whole of the dead of all the nations at war. A bronze
statuette, nearly two feet high, by Sir Charles Wheeler,
P.R.A., was dedicated to his memory on 21 March 1964:
it shows the fine face and outstretched hands of Walker in
his diving outfit, minus his headgear, at the rear of the high
altar. It is a coincidence that the names of Bishop Walkelyn,
who built the cathedral, and William Walker, who preserved
it, are so similar.

Many informative works have been written about the
cathedral city, but few are as interesting, concise and well
illustrated as Brian Vesey FitzGerald's monograph on
Winchester. The marvellous breath-taking beauty of the
cathedral's soaring vaulted nave and of the reredos (the
exquisitely carved screen behind the high altar), which I
like better than any I have ever seen, can never be forgotten.
There are tombs and chantries of famous ecclesiastics from
the Middle Ages. The cathedral used to be described to us
by 'Adams of Winchester', the senior verger at that time:
H. V. Morton paid a tribute to him in *In Search of England*.
On V. J. Day in August 1945, Mr. A. J. Adams, who was
soon to retire from his post, invited children (including my

little son), whom he was showing round the cathedral, to accompany him up the worn, winding steps on to the roof of the tower, where they watched him unfurl the Union Jack to celebrate the termination of hostilities in Asia, three months after those in Europe had ceased.

Mortuary chests said to contain the bones of several kings, including Cynegils and his son Cenwalh, Egbert, Ethelwulf (father of King Alfred the Great), and Canute, rest on the roofs of chantries at the rear of the choir stalls, and the tomb of William II—whose sudden death in the New Forest appears not to have raised the repercussions one would have expected—lies in the centre of the Choir.

While we think of William of Wykeham and other famous bishops and cardinals of the past, let us also remember one of the greatest prelates of our own time, a towering figure physically, intellectually, and spiritually—Bishop Cyril Garbett, later Archbishop of York, who, during his episcopal reign at Winchester, made pilgrimages on foot, wearing a purple cassock, his 500-year-old crook in hand, to each of the many parishes in his diocese, holding services daily in country churches and by the wayside. I remember seeing a film in a Birkenhead cinema, when he and his chaplain walked through Mapledurwell in 1935. My mother, father, uncles, and a number of villagers were in the picture, and at the conclusion of the roadside service which was held opposite our farmhouse, my father stepped down towards the camera: I almost met him midway!

While one is looking up at the memorial window to Jane Austen in the north aisle of the cathedral, one may unwittingly be treading on her gravestone. There is also a memorial window to Izaak Walton (1593–1683), author of *The Compleat Angler*, who is buried hereabouts. He is portrayed reading under a tree close to the winding Itchen, with his rod and creel by his side, and with St. Catherine's Hill in the background: underneath are the words, 'Study to be quiet'. Two other 20th-century windows—the work of Hugh

Easton—one of George VI and his Queen, and the other of George V—are strikingly beautiful.

The bones of St. Swithun, a patron saint of the cathedral and tutor of King Alfred the Great, lie buried outside in the precinct, but, alas! those of his illustrious pupil were lost through a piece of incredible carelessness when the ruins of Hyde Abbey, where they rested, were pulled down in the 18th century.

Winchester College, whose famous motto is 'Manners makyth man', is the home of the 17th-century picture of 'The Trusty Servant', which bears the following inscription:

> The Trusty Servant's portrait would you see
> This emblematic figure well survey.
> The worker's snout not nice in diet shows:
> The padlock shut no secrets he'll disclose
> Patient the ass his master's rage will bear,
> Swiftness in errand the stag's feet declare.
> Loaded his left hand apt to labour saith,
> The vest his neatness, open hand his faith.
> Girt with his sword, his shield upon his arm,
> Himself and master he'll protect from harm.

The College Cloister commemorates the 500 Wykehamists who paid the supreme sacrifice in the First World War. Many famous men were Winchester College boys, and none more to be honoured than the late Field Marshal Earl Wavell, whose collection of his favourite poems, *Other Men's Flowers,* is affectionately remembered. A valued porter whose face Queen Mary recalled after 18 years on revisiting the College, often acted as guide. There were other guides we remember—the elder resident brethren who served St. Cross Hospital and church so faithfully and described their treasures with such enthusiasm and interest.

Peter Symond's School, founded in 1607, is associated in my mind with its headmaster (1896–1926), the Rev. Telford Varley, whose book, *Hampshire,* largely historical, by no means neglects the countryside, and is admirably illustrated with reproductions of 75 water-colours by Wilfrid Ball, recapturing the beauty of the county when its roads were sandy and dusty, and time was spacious and unhurried.

St. Catherine's Hill, crowned with a clump of trees and a maze, is the pleasing downland background to water-meadows by the placid river Itchen, which has weeping willows and meadow-sweet on its banks, and rushes and the swaying leaves of aquatic plants in midstream.

St. Giles's Hill, formerly the scene of St. Giles's fair, looks down on Winchester at much closer range, with the Guildhall in the mid-distance and the cathedral to its left. Sir William Hamo Thornycroft's fine statue of Alfred the Great, erected in 1901 (the millenary of his death) occupies the centre of Broadway. It is most impressive, standing sentinel against the sky, the left hand steadying the shield by his side, and the right hand held high grasping his sword, which is in the shape of a cross.

The prevailing atmosphere about Winchester is its time-lessness: that which is modern seems unimportant compared with all that is ancient in the city. Mellowed half-timbered spacious houses amid the seclusion of luxuriant gardens and shrubs, bestow an air of grace and charm on such places as Cheyney Court and the Deanery, and if they happen to be in proximity to streams and water-meadows, as at St. Cross, their beauty is even greater. The Itchen runs below the old City Mill, under Eastgate bridge near Cheesehill or Chesil rectory (1450)—now a café—and on past the weirs to pursue a less restricted course out into the open country. Small tributaries skirt the edges of the public gardens between the Guildhall and the Eastgate bridge. St. Peter-Cheesehill church (now used by a dramatic association) has a bell-cote as ancient and shapely as any in Hampshire. God Begot House—originally a place of sanctuary, rebuilt in 1558—is now a hotel and jeweller's shop in the High Street: in a passageway running alongside it, and also in the Royal Oak Alley further down the street, are old taverns and penthouse buildings which may be even older. The *Hampshire Chronicle's* premises in the High Street, have two beautiful bow-windows: they all date from 1772 and are still going strong! The oldest house in Winchester was the former *Blue Boar* tavern, but, unfortunately, it became extremely dilapidated (1967). In the same street—St. John's Street—is the oldest church in Winchester, St. John the Baptist's, dating from 1193. The impressive West Gate at the top of the High Street has an interesting museum, and from the roof there is a panoramic view of the city. Close by is the Great Hall of the Castle, on the wall of which hangs the so-called Round Table of King Arthur: it is not as ancient as all that, but may be 700 or 800 years old.

Apart from St. Cross, there are several parishes on the outskirts of the city. Weeke (or Wyke) is not far from Winchester railway station: the church has a brass (1498) of St. Christopher and the Christ-child, and a very ancient paten dating from 1200. Nearby, off the Basingstoke road, is another 12th-century church, that of Hyde, close to the remains of Hyde abbey. Winnal lies at the foot of St. Giles's Hill, but its church, rebuilt in 1858, presents little of interest architecturally. A local inn bears the novel name of *First In and Last Out*!

The tiny downland church of Chilcomb with its small weather-boarded bell-cote, has changed little since it was built over eight centuries ago on the side of a hill outside the city. A document drawn up in 1287 conjures up the ancient scene perfectly:

> THE CHURCH SHALL RECEIVE ON ACCOUNT OF TITLE ONE LAMB, ONE CHEESE and one small ACRE OF LAND CALLED SHEPAKER.

Whenever I think of Chilcomb, its neighbour also springs to mind—Compton, in a valley whose little church of flint and rubble, almost as old (1151), has some Saxon work, a Norman font and doorway, wall paintings and a stoup. The little wooden belfries, side porches and the small narrow slits of windows in the naves and chancels of Chilcomb and Compton churches used to make me regard them as twins, but the similarity is less now because Compton has recently been enlarged.

Two other pleasant but isolated downland villages which appealed strongly to me because of their hilly, windswept open country and ancient associations were Morestead and Owslebury (pronounced Usselbury). Morestead is traversed by a Roman road, and lies in a sheltering hollow under Morestead Down: its small Norman church, restored in 1873, has an interesting roof and tie-beams, and an open gable-end bell turret. Hazeley Down, like Bramley, was a German prisoner-of-war camp in 1918. Owslebury is large compared with Morestead, and is a hill-top village whose 14th-century church, restored in 1890, has a picturesque embattled tower, a peal of six bells, a 1552 chalice, and that rare musical instrument, the serpent.

9
Farnborough

THE HEADMISTRESS of Up Nately school used to stay at our farmhouse in the years before the First World War, from Monday to Friday during term-time. She went direct from school to Hook station on Friday afternoons to spend her weekends at Farnborough, and in the summer of 1913, invited me to stay a few days at her home.

I remember attending Sunday morning service at a large modern church with a high steeple—St. George's, in the Stanhope lines of Aldershot camp—where my hostess's nephew was organist.

One day, as I was passing the gates of the mausoleum grounds of Farnborough Hill, and pondering whether I should venture inside to view the chapel containing the tombs of Napoleon III (who died in 1873 at Chislehurst in Kent), and his son, the Prince Imperial (who had been killed in the Zulu War of 1879), I saw a tall figure in black, the ex-Empress Eugénie, taking a walk in the grounds, accompanied by a priest on either side, one very short in stature. She towered above her companions, and the little group seemed wrapt in thought, except for a few words of conversation. The Empress was 87 at the time, and was to live on for another seven years. Her remains lie in the crypt of the chapel which she erected to the memory of her husband and much-loved and mourned son. Three kings, including George V, attended the funeral.

It is extremely appropriate that her Corsican secretary, M. Pietri, who had always stood between her and importunate members of the public, should lie buried at the entrance to the vault—this at her special request—which shows her appreciation of a faithful servant and, incidentally, her own greatness of heart. It is as if he still stands guard over the privacy of his imperial charges.

The ex-Empress purchased Farnborough Hill mansion in 1881, and added a wing in 1883. In 1887, the Roman Catholic Memorial Church of St. Michael's was built. Close by is St. Michael's Abbey, founded eight years later, which is staffed by the Benedictine order. During the First World War a wing of the Empress's home was used as a hospital for wounded officers. The spire of the abbey on Farnborough Hill could be seen through the trees high above the railway outside Farnborough station. Except for the 15th-century church of St. Michael, most of the churches in and around Aldershot are comparatively modern, the whole area having come into being largely as the result of military development since Crimean War days. This is not the case, however, as regards Farnborough parish church, which dates back over 700 years: in it is to be seen a 13th-century mural painting of St. Eugenia, and the Empress Eugénie often visited this church to show her friends the portrait of the saint whose name she bore. She was of Spanish stock, with the striking beauty of her race, and was impetuous, outspoken and independent. When she had lost an empire and her family, she stood alone, and it is not surprising that such an interesting personality, so original in outlook, should have drawn to herself another kindred spirit in the person of Dame Ethel Smyth. Both were ardent suffragists. During the Empress's more than 40 years at Farnborough, she was frequently visited by Dame Ethel, who for 30 years lived in a cottage near the town, and later at nearby Woking.

Dame Ethel used to sing in the choir of the abbey church at Farnborough, and was always an independent, uninhibited type of musician who not only composed, but conducted. She records that Gustav Mahler was far and away the finest conductor she ever knew. With the passage of time since her death in 1944 at the age of 86, it has become clear that she will be remembered more for the quality and virility of her prose than for her music.

Farnborough has always been regarded as the home if not the birthplace of British Aeronautics. The Empress Eugénie was always interested in 'Colonel' Cody's flying activities. Over the surrounding downland, aeroplanes have carried out their daily practice and aerobatics for over half a century, and 'Farnborough Week' each September is attended by people from all over the world.

In 1952 my son and I saw the preview of the Farnborough Show from the hilly slopes near the tank training grounds, beyond the post office at Crookham, and had an excellent view of the take-offs and the stunts. It so happened, on the last day of the show, that a 'plane exploded in mid-air, killing the pilot, and parts of the engines and fuselage hurtling through the air killed a number of people near the place where we had sat a few days earlier.

10
Stoke Charity, Wield and Priors Dean

THESE THREE VILLAGES have given me especial pleasure over many years.

Stoke Charity is one of the three parishes—the others being Hunton and Wonston—all within a mile or so of Sutton Scotney.

The miles of cornland between Micheldever and the high ground near Popham Beacon always remind me of Tennyson's lines:

> Long fields of barley and of rye
> That clothe the wold and meet the sky,

for here the sun from out of wide skies shines on fine fields of golden grain all around. The tiny village—a cottage or two, a farmhouse with clipped yews in its garden, a 16th-century rectory, a Norman church in a meadow with the Bullington stream running through, and a background of high trees, presents an idyllic pastoral scene. Though it nestles in a quiet and remote corner, it can be seen from miles away, even from the train as it runs between Micheldever and Winchester.

Surely Stoke Charity, with its sweep of view extending from Stratton Park across Micheldever to Popham, has 'everything', including a gracious name. Its peace and old-world charm are incomparably portrayed in Mrs. C. Fox Smith's poem:

Stoke Charity: A Hampshire Place-name

Of all the names of ford and town,
Hamlet and bridge and furzy down,
That make sweet music to the ear
By troutful Test and Itchen clear,
The Clatfords and the Sombornes twain,
Freefolk and Farley Chamberlayne,
Shy Bransbury and St. Mary Bourne,
The ford dead Rufus passed forlorn,
The Candovers, the Worthys three,
The sweetest is Stoke Charity.

'Stoke Charity!' The tall elms shade
The grey old church the Normans made;
The yew-tree lifts its noon-dark head
By mounds where sleep the quiet dead;
Through mellowed panes the sunlight passes
To splash with gold the graven brasses
Of knight and lady, son and daughter,
Who went their ways as went the water
That turned, years past, the vanished mill
Whose mouldering wheel has long stood still.
A kindly name—a kindly place,
Where life still keeps its peaceful pace,
Where nothing day by day is found
But man's and nature's homely round,
But joys and sorrows, hopes and fears,
And passing of unstoried years,
Toil, rest and slumber—all the same
As when old furious Cobbet came
This way, with generous heart aflame,
Drew rein and paused awhile to see
How fared it with Stoke Charity.

Today, as then, the willows shiver
All green and grey along the river
Where in the pools Jack Heron fishes
And through the weed the moorhen swishes,
And in the bank the bright-eyed vole
Peers shy and watchful from his hole:
The whole wide valley fills and glows
With dawn-fires and with sunset rose;
In meadows bare to wind and sun
The mad March hares rejoicing run,
And gathering plovers flock and fly
Soar, turn and gleam with plaintive cry:
Season by season brings again
The former and the latter rain,
And Spring's first swallow oversea
To England—and Stoke Charity.

(Reprinted by permission of *Punch*.)

The bellcote of the church has a tapering spire. The interior is light and beautiful, and there is an aura of golden serenity about it which reaches perfection at harvest festival-tide. The wide chancel arch is Norman, as are the north arcade and the Purbeck marble font. A double squint enabled lepers and others to see the altar, and there is an archaic pre-Reformation carving of the 'Mass of St. Gregory', in which the risen Lord, pointing to the gaping wound in His body, appears to Gregory and his assistant whilst celebrating Mass, revealing His real presence.

One of its three bells dates from 1420.

Wield

I shall never forget my first impression of Wield. I was on my way home from one of my first long walks when 13 years of age. Three things stand out vividly in my memory—the hospitality of a kindly old lady who invited me to tea in her thatched cottage; the little Norman church with its diminutive wooden bellcote; and the old-world look of this farming village, which bore evidence of the hurdle-making for which it was famed. Its wells were reputed to be 300 feet deep.

Wield consists of Upper Wield, high up in the hills north-east of Alresford, on the way to Medstead and Preston Candover, and comprising the church, Church Farm, Wield House, post office, chapel, school (now closed), the green, and a number of thatched cottages; and Lower Wield, a prosperous-looking hamlet with five farms, several cottages and an inn, on the way to Bradley and Bentworth.

Wield church is of flint and plaster, and was restored in 1884. It had a west tower which was demolished in 1810 when two of its three bells were sold. During my visits prior to 1930, the west door was in use, and the wall paintings and the royal arms over the chancel arch were indistinct, but in 1932 the Norman south door, which had been blocked up during last century, was reopened, and the interior of the church again restored, with excellent results. In 1962 a charming little angel playing a musical instrument was uncovered on the west wall above the gallery. Squints on either side of the chancel arch provided a view of the chancel and altar. There are memorials in the church to the Wallop family (Earls of Portsmouth), who had associations with Wield for over six centuries prior to 1945. A member of the Terry family from Dummer—friends and near neighbours of Jane Austen at Steventon—was perpetual curate here from 1803 to 1848.

Priors Dean

Tucked away in the valley among quiet hills near Colemore, Newton Valence, Oakhanger and Hawkley, is the tiny village of Priors Dean. The dripping wet lane from Hawkley, cut deep into the steep hills and so narrow that for nearly a mile two vehicles cannot pass each other, is overhung with trees and hedges, and only occasionally, when one comes out into open country, can a glimpse be caught of the huge beech hangers mantling the hillsides. Sometimes a flock of sheep may be seen grazing on the slopes of the downs. There are few buildings in Priors Dean—the church, the tall manor farmhouse of mellowed red brick with its stepped chimney-stack, farm buildings, a cottage or two, and the solitary *White Horse* inn a mile or more away, practically constitute the entire village, but its charm is enduring.

The farmhouse, formerly the manor house of the Tichbornes, is at the foot of the hill, not far from the plain, plastered 13th-century church which has ancient roof timbers and also an aged timbered porch over its Norman north doorway, a two-tiered spired bell-cote capped by a weathervane, and a large, venerable hollow-trunked yew in the churchyard. Inside the church are memorials to the Compton and Tichborne families.

I remember reading about Priors Dean in *Hampshire Days* years after I first discovered this sequestered village, and thinking how faithfully Hudson had conveyed the scene and the sense of remoteness in his unforced, crystal-clear prose. Edward Thomas, too, captured the spirit of the tall manor house, the quaint little church and the ancient yew in his poem, *The Manor Farm*; and in another of his poems, *Up in the Wind*, the fields and unfrequented lanes round the *White Horse* inn are vividly described.

11
Basingstoke to the Berkshire Border

OUT OF THE hazy recollections of early childhood survives the memory of a visit to Sherfield and the journey home by trap in the gloaming, made darker by overhanging trees round Pyotts Hill, and a little eerie by low-flying bats, so characteristic of Hampshire country lanes on summer evenings.

Sherfield is the first real village on the Reading road after one leaves Basingstoke. The parish is wooded, and on three sides is bounded by rivers—the Loddon and two tributaries, the Little Loddon or Bow Brook, and Petty's Brook. The spired church, practically rebuilt in 1872, lies beyond a meadow, amid evergreens, and is reached long before one comes to the extensive village green. On it, not very long ago, a few geese and a pet swan roamed, a goat or two were tethered, and cricket was played. In days gone by hundreds of geese were reared on such greens as this up and down the country. They were usually plucked twice a year, both for their down, and to provide quills for pens. Many were sold to itinerant dealers who drove them away on foot, and the feet of the birds were tarred with pitch so that they could stand up to the journey.

The rectorial roll, like that of Newnham, goes back six or seven centuries. There is an old watermill and two meadows (the Lammas lands) by the Loddon, a pond, and several ancient farms which used to have moats round them.

Hartley Wespall is a peaceful village in deep country well away from the Reading road. Hartley mill is also on the Loddon. The 14th-century church was restored in 1869, and two of its three bells are of pre-Reformation date. The spired tower is set into the north wall, and the exterior of the west end of the nave reveals the fantastic, yet symmetrical, shapes of its timbered structure where one would expect a window. There are quiet byways and a raised path by the village pond, where leisurely cattle often congregate and slow up progress just as they used to do in the rustic lanes of Ellisfield.

Turgis or Stratfield Turgis is small and scattered and, like its neighbour Sherfield, has a green. The parish's association with the Stratfieldsaye estate is commemorated in the *Wellington Arms* hotel. The church is situated at the end of a country lane off the Reading road, and adjoins a farmyard. The chancel was rebuilt of brick after a fire in 1792. There are some 14th-century features, and an old stone font, yet although restoration has taken place at various times, and as recently as 1901, the building retains its old quaint look. Its country setting, box-like bell-cote and dormer windows are most appealing. In the quiet churchyard is the grave of John Mears, groom to the Iron Duke.

Stratfieldsaye is reached by a lane off the main road between Turgis and Heckfield. The park, 1,500 acres in extent, was the nation's gift to Wellington. Its trees—Wellingtonias, cedars, tulip trees, Waterloo beeches and an avenue of elms a mile long—are striking. Wellington's charger, Copenhagen, lies in a paddock, having deservedly been buried with military honours. The House, overlooking the Loddon which flows through the park, contains engravings, portraits, busts, plate and souvenirs of the Duke and other famous personalities. In those most interesting of royal memoirs, *My Memories of Six Reigns,* Princess Marie Louise, an enthusiastic admirer of Napoleon, recalls how delighted and thrilled she was when she visited this famous house, which she regarded as an historical museum.

The 18th-century brick church, reopened in 1966, is in the form of a Greek cross, the four arms being of equal

length. The churchyard is surrounded by trees which make
the edifice look dark and lugubrious. The squat octagonal
tower has a cupola, and the church registers date from 1539.
Inside are memorials to the Pitt family (later Lords Rivers)
and the Dukes of Wellington, and a gallery pew, complete
with fireplace, table and easy chair, which the Iron Duke
used during services! Facing Heckfield Common is the
Wellington Monument, erected by his son.

Though Heckfield church was much restored during the last
century, the plastered battlemented tower still shows its
early 16th-century origin. Two of its five bells are very
old, dating from 1336 and 1420. The Purbeck marble font
(1350) and the Crusaders' Chest (1199) are noteworthy.
It was at Heckfield that a former prime minister, Neville
Chamberlain, died in November 1940, and there is a
memorial to him in the church. The road from Hound Green
and Mattingley, with a high wall on the near side, leads to
the churchyard. Hazeley Heath and its inn, the *Shoulder of
Mutton,* a mile or so from Mattingley, are reached by
winding hilly lanes.

Bramshill Park, near Hazeley Heath, lies back from the
road between Heckfield Common and Hartley Wintney,
amid a square mile or so of country famous for its Scotch
firs, the original planting of which was contemporary with
the building of Bramshill House, a fine early Jacobean
mansion. Many people associate it with the Mistletoe Bough
legend, but Marwell Hall (near Owslebury) where, according
to tradition, Henry VIII and Jane Seymour stayed, makes
a similar claim, as do some other places. It tells of a young
bride who, playing hide and seek on her wedding night,
hid in a chest, not knowing that it had a spring lock, and
being unable to get out, died. Bramshill was the home of
Joan Penelope Cope who, at the age of 12, in 1938, wrote
and published her *Memoirs.* In her book (charmingly written
and illustrated by the author), she recounts the Mistletoe
Bough story, and gives an account of the North Hampshire

Mummers. There are three coloured reproductions of her paintings, including one of Bramshill House, and numerous sketches, two of which are of the house. The final chapter is her adieu to Bramshill in 1935, when it was sold to Lord Brocket. The Cope family had lived there for 240 years. Later it became Bramshill Police College.

How well I remember my first visit (1915) to Eversley. I was with my uncle John, and it was the only cycle ride of any distance that we went together. Bramshill, in Eversley parish, is bounded by the river Blackwater which forms part of the Berkshire border, and is the principal tributary of the Loddon, which is quite close. The rectory, like many Hampshire vicarages, was a rambling old house covered with creepers and ivy, as was the crenellated tower of the brick church which has a plain nave and two chancels. We found much of the beauty in the parish—the village pond, a picturesque farmhouse nearby, and the Common which is moorland clad with gorse and heather, and once famous for gypsies.

Charles Kingsley, an Evangelical clergyman, was curate here in 1842, and, at the wish of his parishioners, was appointed rector two years later (after a short period at Pimperne in Dorset), a post he held until his death in 1875. His funeral was a national occasion, and he was buried in Eversley churchyard. He was a poet, naturalist and novelist, and liked walking and fishing. There are allusions to Hampshire in his books *Chalk Stream Studies* and *Yeast*; also in *Water Babies,* most of which was written at the *Plough* inn at Itchen Abbas, and part at Eversley. He loved not only the Itchen, but the Test, and under the pseudonym of 'Whitbury' in *Two Years Ago* describes the charm that Whitchurch had for him as an angler, and how he enjoyed staying at the *White Hart*. Mrs. Kingsley described the local population in her day as 'heath croppers from time immemorial and poachers by instinct and heritage', but the gypsies loved her husband and called him their 'Patrico-rai' (priestly king).

Yateley is also on the Blackwater, near the Berkshire border. In 1957 the Yateley Textile Printers started to make tablecloths, curtains and other materials, which gained a reputation for quality, workmanship, and originality of design: the work was undertaken by girls disabled by infantile paralysis and spinal complaints, and visitors from outside parishes were invited to exhibitions of their handicraft. The church, off the large green, is a long building, with a handsome shingle-spired bell-cote on a fine base of upright timber, and a Norman north doorway. It contains 15th-century work, a crystal communion cup or bowl, and musical instruments (four clarionets, a bassoon, and a piccolo), which used to be played by the band.

Hartley Wintney (of which parish Hartley Row, on the Odiham road, forms part) is nine miles from Basingstoke. This rapidly-growing place, still reminiscent of stagecoach days, has two large greens—the Cricket Green and Phoenix Green—alongside the main road. The rich foliage of its oaks is mentioned in Cobbett's *Rural Rides*. Off the A30 are other greens—Murrell's, Dipley, and West Green. Everywhere are wooded hills and parklands. The old church of St. Mary is cruciform, and dates from the 12th century, but is seldom used except as a mortuary chapel. It has a graceful pinnacled tower, and in its secluded situation is a joy to look at compared with the nondescript bell-turret and red brick church of St. John, completed in 1870, which lies back from the green on the London road.

As one who is interested in records of longevity and who has had a long association with medical work, it gave me pleasure when a tablet to the memory of Mrs. Eleanor Lloyd was placed in St. John's church in 1962. She died at Hartley Wintney in 1960, a few days before her 106th birthday, having lived there for 80 years. She remembered talking to two great-uncles, Sir Thomas Hastings, who was on H.M.S. *Undaunted* when it took Napoleon to Elba; and Sir Charles Hastings, who founded the British Medical Association in 1832. Her great-grandfather was 100 years old when he died, and his eldest daughter nearly one hundred and four.

Fleet, formed out of Elvetham, Yateley and Crondall parishes, began to grow in 1880 when Aldershot had been in existence a quarter of a century. Whilst Aldershot is for those on the active list, Fleet is largely a residential district for the retired, and is noted for its pines, laurels and rhododendrons. Fleet pond, 130 acres in extent, is cut in half by the railway, and when the Second World War began, it was drained so as not to show up as a landmark to enemy aircraft. The modern parish church, like those of Cove, Crookham, Ewshott, and Hawley (formerly part of Yateley), has no special historical features.

Elvetham Park, between Fleet and Hartley Wintney, is a beautiful estate, originally in private ownership, which has changed hands twice in recent years since it was taken over for commercial purposes. The stone-spired church, built in 1841, contains earlier memorials as well as a 13th-century piscina. The reredos of Our Lord, the Madonna, and the archangel Gabriel is as strikingly painted as those in Lyndhurst parish church and at Minley. The former Elvetham House had associations with Queen Elizabeth I. The parish is five square miles in area, and the river Hart runs through Elvetham Park. This river gives its name to Hartford Bridge Flats—the plateau on the London side of Hartley Wintney—which served admirably for stagecoach speed contests.

Minley church is in Minley Park: its altar-piece portraying the Crucifixion, the Nativity, and the Ascension, is most beautiful. So also is the glass Madonna in the Lady Chapel of Crookham church.

12
Basingstoke to Odiham, Winchfield and the Surrey Border

LEAVING Basingstoke by the *White Hart,* an old posting inn on the London road, we journey through a long, shaded avenue of chestnuts and sycamores, and descend the Common Hill to Black Dam, which until recently has seldom been without swans on its marshy waters. Here the Basingstoke bypass branches off. We ascend Wellock's Hill and pass the London Lodge of Hackwood Park before reaching the Hatch. This name may derive from the trout hatchery which used to be there, but more likely refers to the 'hatch' (a wicket-gate) or to an opening in the road where the Lyde flows through the garden of the *King's Head* inn. A side road leads past Mapledurwell Cob Tree (a noble horse-chestnut, standing where three lanes meet) to Up Nately, where, at the crossroads, another lane ends in a pleasant cul-de-sac, with a manor house, a farmhouse, and cottages commanding a sweeping view over the downs to Mapledurwell. Fenced off from the road to Greywell is the wayside church of Up Nately, built of flint and brick, and entered by a Norman north doorway: the nave and chancel arch are also 12th-century, but the small battlemented tower, chancel and vestry date only from 1844. The plain glass windows make for light within, particularly the east window which looks out on to the downs towards Greywell. A mural tablet near the lectern reads: 'Here lyeth ye body of Joan Wither, eldest daughter of William Wither of Andwell, Esq., and of Joan [his wife], who dyed within ye 5th [year] of her infancy Janua. ye 8th, 1649'. On the wall of the gallery above the font is the coat of arms of George IV, 1829, and at the foot of the pulpit steps is a brass to the memory of Canon R. F. Hessey, who was vicar of this parish and of Old Basing from 1864 to 1911, and a priest of patriarchal appearance, who was much loved and whose preaching was greatly admired: both the pulpit and lectern were re-erected by parishioners as a memorial.

Up Nately used to be known as Nately Eastrop to distinguish it from its neighbour, Nately Scures. Nately Eastrop farm and canal bridge are situated in picturesque seclusion at the entrance to the woods, in a lane off the Greywell road just outside Up Nately village.

Continuing uphill through open country, with a marl pit in mid-field, there are wide views of the thickly-wooded estate of Greywell Hill, and of cornfields stretching away to Upton Grey. It is good to see how much unspoilt countryside there still is in Hampshire. Years ago each village had its own chalk pit, but now most of them are unused and over-grown. There is one on the left as we near the top of the hill, at the bottom of which a bridle path wanders away to Five Lanes End; further on, a lane turns off by another chalk pit on our right, to Greywell mill. Yet another lane with the gentle white and mauve flowers of yarrow by the roadside winds over the crest of the down to Upton Grey.

Many wild flowers grow on the verges, and horse-chestnut trees form an avenue at the approach to Greywell (locally called Grewell years ago, and in Tudor times famed for its Grewell silks). Just past a penthouse, a path from the lychgate leads to the churchyard, well away from the road, and to the old church, close to meadows and to the rippling Whitewater which, with tall grasses and rushes on its banks, intersects the village, and lends charm to the scene. The fine rood screen and the staircase up to it, like those at Chilbolton, are noteworthy, and so are the font and Transitional doorway. The interior is sunny and tranquil.

One side of Greywell street is flanked by cottages and fine old houses with large gardens. Simple pleasures sometimes provide the most enduring of memories: one such occurred in the summer of 1950 when we attended a garden fête in the grounds of Cedar Tree House. It was a warm sunny afternoon, and the atmosphere of friendliness, the beautifully-kept garden, and the scent of aromatic plants and herbs made the day delightful. I recall particularly the green cones of a 200-year-old cedar of Lebanon: as I write, one of them (now bronzed), as beautiful in shape and as tightly wrapped as a wasps' nest, lies in front of me. At the *Fox and Goose* inn, a road carries straight on past the old wharf, and by several old cottages to Hook Common.

Past the little bridge over the Whitewater, the road becomes hilly and leads to North Warnborough, with its row of 16th-century timber-framed cottages, the overhanging first floors of which are supported on projecting beams: the casements date from a century later. I have been struck by the beauty of the gardens everywhere, but I miss the sight of the old watermill on the corner of the Hook—Odiham road, which years ago was converted into a private residence, and largely boarded off from public view. Foundations of Roman roads, also tesselated pavements (as at Thruxton and Abbotts Ann), have been discovered in this village. Near the approach to North Warnborough from Greywell, a signpost points to Upton Grey by a lonely road over the down, and a few yards away we ascend a little hill, and can take our choice of the left-hand turning for Odiham, or the one on the right for Long Sutton, chiefly notable for the Lord Wandsworth agricultural college and, close to the road, a heavily-timbered church dating back to 1200, with a typically small wooden 'Hampshire' bell-cote rising out of the centre of the nave, a Norman font, a 13th-century nave and chancel; also a chalice from Elizabeth I's reign, and ancient chests, as at Heckfield, Linkenholt, and Warnford. The church's glory, however, belongs not only to the past, for recently a war memorial vestry has been built by local members of the British Legion.

Odiham (originally Woody-ham) was pronounced 'Ojjum' by old country folk years ago, and is called 'Odium' today. For centuries it was a royal demesne, but markets and fairs are no longer held there. It is a quiet and attractive little town which has a beautiful High Street, unusually wide verges and buildings which admirably display the architecture of each of the four centuries since the *George* hotel was first licensed in 1547. This well-preserved coaching inn has a panelled dining room with a handsome chimney-piece and Tudor beams. Behind some of the old buildings and Georgian houses—seldom two alike—are lovely old-world gardens of rare charm and fragrance. King Street has timbered red brick Tudor cottages, with latticed windows peeping out from gable ends.

The fine old parish church which lies modestly in a precinct nearby, has a spacious nave and aisles, and a Saxon piscina and remains of Norman choir columns. It was rebuilt about 1500. There are two old galleries at the back, and in a turret of the battlemented tower, which houses a peal of six bells, hangs a prayer bell dated 1538. An old brass depicts a young babe in swaddling clothes. There are some interesting modern memorials, too, one to a verger who served here from 1897 to 1943, and another to a churchwarden with 57 years' service. There are two pre-Reformation mass clocks (sundials) on the buttress of a wall, also eight scratch dials. Nearby are tombstones of two French officers, Napoleonic War prisoners, who died at Odiham. Many were incarcerated in the chalk pit outside the town, and Frenchman's Oak on the Winchfield road marked the limit of their parole. Outside the churchyard are almshouses founded in 1623, and, beyond the churchyard railings, are the old stocks (dating from 1376), a whipping post and a pest house for isolating victims of the plague.

Odiham chalk pit is probably the largest in north Hampshire, though perhaps not so big as one or two in south Hampshire, e.g., that on Portsdown Hill. This chalk pit, near Odiham camp, has been associated in my mind with aircraft activities for 60 years. A clump of trees, 'The Firs', on Beacon Hill, over 400 feet above sea level, is the scene of a prehistoric burial ground; beacons were lit here to signal the approach of the Spanish Armada.

William Lylye, whom readers of George Borrow's *Lavengro* will remember from his enthusiastic references to *Lilly's Latin Grammar,* was born at Odiham, but died of plague in London in 1522. Robert May's Grammar School, Odiham, and John Eggar's Grammar School, Alton, were both founded in the 17th century.

The handsome memorial on Gospel Green in the High Street keeps fresh the memory of those who were killed in two world wars. It blends well with its surroundings.

Odiham would never countenance a railway station in or near the town. Winchfield station is two and a half miles away, a little nearer than Hook station, which is probably more easily accessible. The fork at the foot of the High Street forms a quaint junction, with an old-world bakery on the corner.

Bearing left, the road out of the town, past the *New* inn by the humpback bridge over the Basingstoke Canal, leads to Winchfield station and Hartley Wintney. There is still plenty of water in the canal, and aquatic plants and arrowhead leaves float on the surface. Moorhens paddle fussily, as though they had been interrupted.

Many flowers, including chicory, heather, oxeye daisies and agrimony grow on Odiham Common (which is kept very tidy by one who obviously loves his work), and the oak trees in the background give a sense of permanence. Meadow-sweet adds beauty and a gentle aroma. A mile out of the town, we turn right at the signpost for Winchfield church. The way is well wooded, with oak and holly trees

shading it, and a grove of silver birches heightening its loveliness. Cow parsley grows alongside the road, also wild mint
and silverweed, with convolvulus mantling the hedges,
and there are massive coronets of tall flowering hogweed.
Eventually farm buildings and cottages on the outskirts of
Winchfield come into view. Tall 'fireweed' (that irrepressible
variety of willow-herb—the rose-bay) flourishes here, with
a patch of gorse and a clump of broom with blackened
seed-pods. The sough of the leaves of many oaks is like the
very breath of summer.

I recall the dedicated service of the Rev. A. W. Hopkinson
to this parish as I approach the church. Its beautiful Norman
chancel arch and south dôorway (finely carved and most
impressive) remind me of the exquisite Norman architecture
of Kilpeck church in Herefordshire. The semicircular chancel
arch is only six feet wide, and if the circle were completed
in imagination, it would include the whole of the visible
chancel, with the altar and small sanctuary stained glass
window forming a wonderful centrepiece. The arch and
its supporting pillars form a doorway into the chancel and
sanctuary—an unforgettable picture as viewed from the
nave. Five tiny Norman lancet windows leave the interior
rather dark, yet not so much as to dim its loveliness. A brass
in the chancel is dedicated to the memory of Charles Frederic
Seymour (1818-97)—a friend of John Keble—who for 41
years was Rector of the parish and restorer of the church in
1851. The church walls are of stone and flint, and the large
tower, of stone and plaster, is pinned in a number of places.

Father Hopkinson was Rector here for nine years from
1909, and during the latter half of this period he combined
the duties of priest-in-charge of the adjoining parish of
Dogmersfield with those at Winchfield. He walked over the
fields from his rectory (which is as beautiful as Odiham
vicarage) to ring the bell and say mattins and evensong
daily. He was for long a lone worshipper on weekdays, but
his parishioners working in the fields or at home thought of

him, knowing he was remembering them in his prayers. Gradually his example and influence were felt, and others joined in the services. A woman graduate of the University of Liverpool once visited his little church to study its architecture, and in his autobiography, *Pastor's Progress,* he states that she found what she thought was 'a mad parson having a service all by himself'. A few years later she became a devoted churchwoman, and served overseas as a missionary. This book reveals that he was a steadfast Tractarian, a good man and a reasoning theologian, who wrote fine prose not only about church dogma and saintly characters, but about such diverse visionaries as T. E. Lawrence, Thomas Hardy, Winston Churchill, Dorothy Sayers, and the Rev. Christopher Tatham (author of *We the Redeemed* and *Power from on High*). For those interested in delving deeper into Father Hopkinson's philosophy there are three other books of his which followed at two-yearly intervals after the publication in 1942 of *Pastor's Progress,* viz., *Pastor's Psychology, Mysticism Old and New* and *About William Law* (an 18th-century mystic). The first two bore a shepherd's crook on their wrappers, and no shepherd ever served his flocks more faithfully. In 1901 he married a daughter of Canon J. E. Millard, a former vicar of Basingstoke and joint author of Baigent and Millard's *History of Bastingstoke,* published in 1889. Father Hopkinson died in 1960, aged 85, at Wareham in Dorset, where he served in a part-time capacity for a number of years following his retirement from full-time duties elsewhere.

Returning to Odiham, the road bearing right at the foot of the High Street leads to Rye Common and Farnham. A fine avenue of oaks, preserved by public subscription in 1932, made a handsome approach to Odiham from the Farnham road, which is bordered by commons and extensive woods as far as Dogmersfield and Crondall: it is regrettable that nine or 10 years ago, a number of these magnificent trees were felled in the interest of road widening.

Things of beauty from the past are not only the Suffolk thatched barns, but the old tile-roofed variety built with ships' timbers: one such is the Elizabethan barn of 17th-century Little Rye Farm, near Odiham; another is the bottle-shaped chimney of the old hop kiln at Hillside Farm in the vicinity, whose rounded brickwork is as pleasing to me as that of any windmill or rustic bridge. Farmsteads and barns were often built in a circular fashion, giving them a satisfying and symmetrical appearance, some of which are near South Warnborough and Hurstbourne Priors. The old village ponds by reason of their circular formation, and the semicircular chalk dells, too, have a beauty peculiarly their own.

Two miles outside the town, Dogmersfield College may be seen in the distance from the Farnham road: formerly Dogmersfield House, the home of the St. John Mildmay family, it was a Roman Catholic training college for teachers until 1973, and is now occupied by Daneshill girls' preparatory school. In 1963 a chapel was built adjoining the college as a memorial to Brother Simon, a teacher and headmaster who died in 1958. The style of the building is simple, but the work has been carried out with fine craftsmanship. The interior is most attractive—windows run the entire length of the walls and the chapel is flooded with daylight.

Two lakes in the park were originally fishponds. Further on, a road leads to Dogmersfield parish church, built in 1843, to replace an older one demolished in 1806, and another whose situation had proved inconvenient. It contains various memorials and brasses, but the 16th-century chalice and paten cover are by far its oldest possessions, with the exception of a bell dated 1420.

The Basingstoke canal runs through the parish, which includes Pilcot and its old watermill. The right-hand turning off the Farnham road leads to residential Crondall. The large and much-restored church, dating from 1170, with

massive piers, a fine chancel arch and two ornamental
Norman doorways, is very dark inside. An 18th-century
pitch-pipe is on exhibition there. A red brick tower, built
in 1659, dominates the landscape. An avenue of limes leads
to the west door.

Away to the left of the Farnham road are lanes leading
to Crookham and Church Crookham, with tobacco planta-
tions and sheds for drying and curing the leaves of the
plants, which often grow to a height of eight feet by late
summer. At Grove Farm are several acres of hopfields, which
bring the annual invasion of family pickers each September.
The hops are dried in the local kilns.

It is nine miles from Odiham to Farnham, and the
second half of the journey includes a steep gradient, Jackals
Hill, which in recent years has come prominently into the
news because a large animal—not the one whose name it
bears, but rumoured to be a puma—is reported as having
been seen locally at various times. Ewshott is the last
parish on the Hampshire side of the Surrey border, and lies
off the main road, not far from Jackals Hill. Itchel Manor
was once famous for a ghost which was heard but not seen.

A characteristic of several of the parishes between here
and Blackwater—Fleet, Cove, Hawley, Crookham, Minley,
Elvetham and Ewshott—is that their churches were all built
during the last century.

William Cobbett (1762-1835) was born at, or in a house
adjoining, the *Jolly Farmer* inn, Farnham, and is buried
in Farnham churchyard.

George Sturt (1863-1927), who wrote under the *nom
de plume* of George Bourne, was also born at Farnham. His
earlier books mainly concern his gardener Fred Bettesworth
and his wife. Chief among them are *The Bettesworth Book*,
Lucy Bettesworth, and *Memoirs of a Surrey Labourer*,
which contain the philosophy and wisdom of hard-working
old country folk who, despite their skills, lived on the
poverty line all their days. *Change in the Village*, published

in 1912, is more generalised, but the books written in the last seven years of his life—*William Smith, A Farmer's Life, The Wheelwright's Shop*, and the posthumously published *A Small Boy in the Sixties*—are biographical or auto-biographical, dealing more particularly with human contacts arising out of his own life and those of his forebears as Surrey wheelwrights. Sturt, as a recorder of village life, is to Surrey what Alfred Williams (in *A Wiltshire Village*) was to his county, and Flora Thompson (in her trilogy, *Lark Rise to Candleford*) to north Oxfordshire.

Farnham Castle, outside the town, a dominating feature of the landscape as one approaches the town, was for long the residence of the bishops of Winchester.

13
Tunworth Down, Weston Patrick and Upton Grey

THE SHORT ROUND TRIP from Mapledurwell to these villages—a journey I made on foot in mid-August 1965—covered much typical Hampshire countryside. Leaving Mapledurwell by Nunnery Hill, I struck out into open country, and at the signpost, turned left for Tunworth Down Farm. The lane was shaded by oak and ash and thorn, and golden bracken, hazel nuts and maple keys heralded the approach of autumn. Robin's pin-cushions gleamed on the wild rose bushes, and honeysuckle crowned the hedges, its scent unrivalled among wayside flowers. Passing a path which led through Ragmoor Wood to Devil's Ditch, I noticed two houses inscribed 'Lovely Cottages, 1946', which recalled memories of that year's Grand National winner, and of our elation in Liverpool at the news that this steeple-chaser, trained on Tunworth Downs, had won the gruelling race.

Wild mint, self-heal, and the curving cup-like formation of the flowers of the wild carrot were a change from the familiar knapweed, 'fireweed' and woody nightshade of the verges. Just beyond a lin-hay alongside the road is Tunworth Down Farm and racing stables. At Tunworth crossroads, I continued up a chalky lane through a lonely wood to Hay Down. There were high banks on one side of this narrow track with an occasional old-fashioned lay-by to enable carts to pass. The oaks were ivy-clad, and the maple trees had thick jungle-like trailers of traveller's joy hanging in festoons from a height of 10 to 15 feet. The tiniest of

shaded cliffs with chalk scooped out of its face, its whiteness marked only by a few rusty stains and exposed roots
of beeches, is an unchanging feature of this enchanting lane.
It is a gentle climb to the top of Hay Down, delicate patches
of harebells, whose pale blue complemented the mauve
tints of scabious, gracing the chalky banks in which flints
are embedded. Wheat and timothy grass stood six feet tall,
and several holly and yew trees—one 35 feet high—seemed
strangers here, wild pigeons taking flight from their branches
with a loud flapping of wings. From a small plantation of
Scots pines crowning the hill, I could see Weston Patrick
church in the valley. There were clumps of toadflax in the
hedge, and knapweed and brambles in abundance, as I
descended the hill by a little lane, and drew near to Weston
Corbett Place and the walled buildings of the manor farm.

In my grandfather's time, I had often heard talk of two
cottages here called 'The Case is Altered', burnt down in
1936. This curious name appears on an old wall map in
Basingstoke Museum, and may have referred to a wayside
ale-house here a century and more ago. How it came to
be so named is uncertain: it may have no local significance
as the name is not unknown elsewhere. Mrs. Mary Keene,
who lived there for years and died in 1964, was married
at Weston Patrick. If ever there was a dedicated Christian,
she was one. Not only was she verger and bell-ringer for
25 years, keeping the church spotless, stoking the boiler
for services, and blowing the organ; but she made dresses
and toys in aid of church funds, and served on various
village committees. She was always there when help was
needed. No wonder Weston Patrick was proud of her and
erected a tablet to her memory in the church she loved and
served so faithfully over many years.

The road from Weston Corbett to Ellisfield passes over
the old level crossing by the derelict station of Herriard.
Further on, 80 yards beyond a signpost to Ellisfield, is a
grassy mount in a copse on the edge of Herriard Beeches,

known as the blind gypsy's grave. It has been there longer
than even the oldest inhabitants can remember, but
someone still visits it occasionally and places flowers on
it. When I saw it in 1965, its small wooden cross was simply
inscribed 'In memory of Harriet. R.I.P.', but a year later,
the words 'Keep out' had been scrawled across it.

Weston Corbett parish has had no separate church since
the end of the 16th century, when it was in ruins. Its
population in 1801 was ten, and in 1901 it was eleven!
It is now part of Weston Patrick. I noticed the pale yellow
flowering heads of the great mullein as I made my way
along a winding lane leading to Weston Patrick church, which
was rebuilt in 1868. Though small and compact, it has a
south aisle and a nave, and on the ornate little bell-turret
is a miniature spire. The north doorway is practically all
that remains of the older building, but there is a silver
chalice and paten cover dating from 1568, and the centre
of an altar cloth (1682) on the wall near the door. Adjacent
to the churchyard is the manor farm, from which a lane runs
down to the Upton Grey road.

Upton Grey, just over a mile away, is a gem among Hampshire villages. Pictures of the handsome half-timbered
cottages and the willows reflected in the 400-year-old village
pond used often to appear in the newspapers. The 12th-
century church has a plain red brick tower and a Norman
tower arch, and lies on a grassy slope off the hilly road to
Tunworth and Greywell: it is an oddly-shaped structure
with a gallery, and the raised north aisle was built in 1731
for the people from Hoddington House and later presented
to the church by a Lord Basing, to whose family (the
Sclaters) there are several memorials. Hoddington was a
manor in Canute's time. The narrow nave, dark chancel
and altar are the original Upton Grey portion of the edifice.
A tablet above the Norman nave states that Charles Edward
Beaufoy, who died in 1846 in his 15th year, was 'blest
with fine understanding, intelligence far beyond his years,

conduct and manners most amiable and prepossessing'. From a distance, an excellent view of the church, church-yard and lych-gate on a flank of the down, presents itself.

David Seth-Smith, well-known years ago as the broad-caster, 'Zoo Man', used to live at Upton Grey, and another resident since the turn of the century, Charles Holme, founder and first editor of *The Studio,* who restored manor houses, farms and cottages in this village, giving them great rustic beauty, is still remembered.

Off the 'top road' to Greywell, just beyond a row of horse-chestnut trees, is a much overgrown bridle track, with wild Canterbury bells and blue vetches two to three feet high poking out from dense hedgerows, which winds its way laboriously to Five Lanes End—a clearing where bridle paths from Upton Grey, Bidden, Ragmoor, Greywell, and Mapledurwell meet. The descent to Mapledurwell is by Down Lane, always exuberant and varied in its wild flowers, and one is rewarded by a fine view of the church and green in the valley below.

14
Winslade, Tunworth, Herriard and Lasham

IN 1965 I WAS IN Basingstoke, and wished to go from there to Winslade. As the bus did not leave for an hour, I decided to walk and see the country at close quarters. One cannot identify all the trees and wild flowers when rushing along in a bus or car; the only way to do so is to wander at leisure.

The real country started a mile outside Basingstoke, when I reached the Hackwood Lodge at the junction of the Alton and Tunworth roads. Hackwood House, once a home of Lord Curzon, and of members of the Belgian royal family during the First World War, lies in the park behind the long brick and flint wall skirting the Alton highway. Forest trees—oaks, limes, sycamores, and beeches, with masses of traveller's joy hanging from them at a height of over 30 feet—shade the road. The forest trees in the park are dense and afford cool shade in summer. White campions, bladder campions and cranesbill brighten the verges, and as these widen, clumps of bracken appear, and the tall graceful spires of agrimony and mugwort thrive. Before the Alton bus passed, I had reached Winslade churchyard, which was covered with Canterbury bells, milfoil and wild thyme; the pathway to the church door was a mass of harebells. Lord Curzon was churchwarden here when he lived at Hackwood, but there is no memorial to him in the church, which is small, rectangular, and cemented practically all over, except for a slated roof: it has no separate chancel. In the east window are the pale, watery colours of medieval and 16th-century Flemish painted glass. The little slatted bell-cote is surmounted by a fine weathercock. One hundred and forty yards away, the rail-less track of the old Alton Light Railway is still clearly discernible.

Leaving the Alton road, I turned left into a lane bordered with convolvulus and ladies' slippers: beyond were a few Southdown sheep with black faces, which belonged to a farm near the rectory. (My grandfather sometimes drove us in his trap to the rectory when we were children: the rector came over specially to Mapledurwell to christen me.) The rough, flinty road became a muddy lane beset with nettles, but smiling barley on one side, dense bracken in the wood on the other, and the gentle pungent smell of wild thyme, made me glad I had left the busy main road. A hedgeless lane runs off alongside a cornfield and comes out near Hackwood Farm, but I carried straight on and took the track which leads to the manor farm and church at Tunworth. The wood became denser, but the lane, shady and stony, remained unchanged, with nettles galore. I had a feeling that this memory would linger, just as I did over 40 years ago when I looked up at Ashley church from a tracery of shadows in the lane below, and knew that the recollection would be permanent. Such impressions occur whenever I am in the presence of Saxon churches, which seem to cast their spell on me. A car stood outside a cottage near the manor farm, and the owner passed the time of day. I remarked that it was many years since I last passed that way, and that I had been refreshing my recollections of Winslade. My new friend dissuaded me from making the remainder of my journey on foot, and most kindly gave me a lift through peaceful lanes to Mapledurwell. Such old-world courtesy is rare, and all the more appreciated when one receives it.

The 'little, lost Down church' of Tunworth is hidden away behind an enclosure of thatched mud walls on three sides, with an approach darkened by beeches. The porch was

restored in 1908 in memory of Julia C. Jordan who loved
this church and parish: I can appreciate her feelings. Nineteen
men are on the 1914–18 roll of honour, and 14 on the
1939–45 list, and in each of these wars all but one returned
home. Inside the church, near the door, is a curious old
alms box, rather grotesque in appearance—a square box
on an ornate pedestal surmounted by a large central knob
and smaller ones, the mouths of two carved faces forming
slots. Although it was rebuilt in 1854–55, I have the con-
viction that this is a Saxon edifice; indeed the masonry and
jambs in the thick walls suggest a pre-Conquest origin. The
church was still lit in 1965 by lamps and candlelight—three
of the candles are on long poles. The little rustic bell-cote is
spired. There is a deep sense of peace in this quiet churchyard. The fallen beech leaves beside the walls are like a
sinking cushion under the feet, and there is a paraffin lamp
in the old lantern by the church path. Outside in a field
I saw a piebald mare who nodded her head approvingly in
answer to my greeting. The banks were starred with large
celandines and rich with luxuriant pink mallows as I passed
the post office.

   Tunworth is as much the next village to Mapledurwell
as are Up Nately, Old Basing, and Upton Grey, but while
some villages are closely linked with their neighbours, others
seldom grow to know each other well. Some are joined by
a farm and cottage development, while others meet only at
lonely distant boundaries where there are hundreds of acres of
arable and meadow land, and this applies to the scattered
parish of Tunworth and to the closely-knit village of Upton
Grey. Scabious, knapweed, chicory and traveller's joy abound
in the lanes, and the view over the downland country
stretches away to the horizon. Years ago I called at Tunworth
post office for view cards, and the post mistress asked me
if I were related to the Princes of Mapledurwell. Answering
in the affirmative, I asked how she had guessed. She said,
'I was sure you were related to Old Mr. Prince. The likeness

is unmistakable'. Her words filled me not only with happiness, but with pride, for I loved my grandfather above all men. She also mentioned that, a long time ago, I had called at her shop as a boy. I said, 'How is it that you can call these things to mind after so many years?' She replied, 'Strangers so seldom call at these out-of-the-way places, and when one does, it stands out in the memory'.

In the old days when people had to walk everywhere, they sometimes took short cuts over fields, by unfrequented rights of way, and through woods, to save time. One day I lost my bearings in a remote part of Tunworth after a long walk, and wondered if there might be a near way home, so I asked an old labourer whose trousers were 'yarked up' with straps or string, and who was hoeing in the fields: 'Can you please tell me the nearest way to Mapledurwell?' He rested from his labours for a few moments and thought deeply, but was obviously puzzled. I said I thought it should be this side of Old Basing and the London turnpike, and mentioned the name of a local farmer, when he suddenly came to life and exclaimed, 'Oh, you means Mapperty-well' (the pronunciation which used to be given to it by the old inhabitants in my early childhood), and, following his directions, I was soon on the right track for home. It is easy for a child to lose his way in the lanes and bridle paths round Tunworth, and not everyone in Mapledurwell knows the turnings at Five Lanes End leading to Ragmoor, Upton Grey, Bidden Farm, and Greywell.

If I had kept to the main Alton road at Winslade, I should soon have reached Herriard, a scattered parish whose chief features were the extensive park and the flint church alongside the road. This dates from 1200, but has been restored from time to time: surprisingly, the tower and north aisle were added only 90 years ago. When I passed by in 1966, the roof of the nave was being tiled and battened; new roof beams replacing the old beetle-ridden ones. Inside there is much to admire—fine woodwork, pre-Reformation windows (which, like Winslade, contain medieval painted glass), and a Transitional doorway and chancel arch. Along the road, houses are few and far between, and this applies to an even greater extent to Lasham (pronounced Lassum), a sparsely-populated parish, after which there is no other village or hamlet before reaching Alton. Lasham church, recognisable by its shingled steeple, celebrated in 1967 the centenary of its rebuilding. In it is a sepulchral slab dating from 1698. The registers go back a century or more before that. The village pond is fed with water from local springs.

15
The Alton Light Railway

APART FROM SOMETIMES noticing the short train which often stood in the sheltered bay of Basingstoke station looking down on Station Hill, my first sight of the Alton Light Railway in action was in 1910, at a distance of several miles, from a meadow adjoining the garden of Hungry Lodge Farm overlooking Mapledurwell. The long frontage of forest trees in Herriard Park had at its centre two tall majestic fir trees which lorded it above their fellows and were visible for miles around. They could be seen to advantage on the horizon from the London turnpike road between Huish Lane and Dickens Lane, two miles from Basingstoke. At certain times of the day, puffs of smoke appeared and reappeared in small clearings on the outskirts of the park as trains passed through at a leisurely 15 to 20 miles an hour, or even as low as 10 miles where warning notices necessitated a restriction at level crossings, field gates and cattle grids.

In the 1890s there was talk of having a railway service direct from Paddington to Portsmouth, and of making a line from Alton to Portsmouth through the Meon valley. To make a through connection, what better plan could have been evolved than to construct a line between Basingstoke and Alton? This scheme took three years to complete, and the railway was opened in 1901.

There were three intermediate stations at Cliddesden, Herriard, and Bentworth and Lasham: two had windmills which drew water from wells, whilst Herriard had a well specially built, which was 300 feet deep and worked by an

oil engine. Cliddesden station was one and a half miles from
that village; Herriard station a mile or so from Herriard;
and Bentworth and Lasham station two miles from Bentworth and half a mile from Lasham. The line was a single
track for most of its course. Cliddesden and Bentworth
and Lasham stations each had a single platform, and
Herriard a double one so that goods vans could be shunted.
The train passed Viables Lane on its way from Basingstoke
to Cliddesden, and skirted Farleigh Wallop and Swallick
Farm as it proceeded to Winslade. For most of its way,
the railway passed alternately through open and wooded
country, in the vicinity of Burkham House (near Bentworth),
Thedden Grange, Shalden Manor, and Beech. The track was
full of twists and turns. For the latter part of the journey—
between the Golden Pot and Alton—the main road from
Basingstoke ran close to the line, and a boarded notice on one
of the railway cottages gave warning of Shalden Crossing.
Because of the leisurely speed, the journey seemed more
personal than others through the countryside, especially at
haymaking and harvest times, the passengers having unusual
opportunities of seeing unfamiliar, lonely country at close
range. An added attraction was bird-song as the little train
made its way through hedges of wild rose, elder and old man's
beard, copses of ash and willow, and woods carpeted with
primroses, violets and wild hyacinths. It was a common sight
to see rabbits scuttling to their burrows when the stillness of
their haunts was disturbed by the noise of the passing train.

The round trip from Basingstoke—14 miles each way—was
a pleasant one which usually took nearly an hour on the
outward journey and rather less on the return. In 1903
there were four passenger trains in each direction on
weekdays, six in 1914, and three from 1924 to 1932. A
goods train ran each weekday, and a cattle train on Wednes-
days. The speed was limited to 20 miles an hour, according
to the notice announcing the opening of the railway: on the
other hand, I understand that a light railway engine was

legally permitted to travel at a maximum speed of 25 miles an hour. The rail gauge was the same as that of the other lines at Basingstoke, which meant that ordinary trains could be used. Towards the end of 1916 the railway was closed, and in December of that year the rails were taken up and shipped to France for use by the Army in the field.

When the war ended it was assumed that the line would be reopened, but in 1923, a Bill was presented to Parliament proposing the abandonment of the project. This led to local opposition, the final outcome of which was that the track was relaid and the line reopened in August 1924: the excitement at Cliddesden station was such that when the first train came into sight, the Union Jack was inadvertently flown upside-down, and the 71-year-old stationmaster, Charles Bushnell, stood on the platform waving his walking-stick!

The new timetables were restricted compared with the old ones. Dissatisfaction with these timetables, which did not fit in with other schedules at Basingstoke and Alton, soon manifested itself, but by December of that year it was decided that no additional trains would be run, although cheap return tickets on certain days at half the normal fares were conceded. Competition from road vehicles greatly increased, and the railway began to sink into obscurity. The distance of the stations from the small village communities, and the relative infrequency of the train services, drove people to use the road services and to neglect the railway; the traffic dwindled, and in 1932 the passenger service was discontinued. A goods train service operated on the Basingstoke-Lasham section of the line until the railway closed down on 30 May 1936. To Mr. William Hudson, who drove the first train in 1901, fell the task of driving the last train over the branch line. That day also marked the termination of the appointment of Mrs. Violet Taylor, stationmaster at Cliddesden since the line was closed for passenger traffic. Her father, the late Mr. Bushnell, the first stationmaster at Cliddesden, had previously been platform inspector at Basingstoke for many years. The heyday of its life was the period prior to 1914, when on market days as many as 70 or 80 passengers travelled on a single train.

Part of the track at Lasham was utilised when the newer portion of the Basingstoke–Alton road, which skirts the glider airfield, was constructed. The bridges over the Winchester road, Basingstoke, and at Cliddesden, were demolished in 1961 and 1962; and in 1963 the last three-coach passenger train on the sole surviving stretch of the Alton line ran from Basingstoke station to the Thornycroft siding not far from the Worting road bridge.

In 1928, a Gainsborough film entitled 'The Wrecker' was made, in which a train crashed into a lorry at Lasham.

In an issue of the *Southern Railway Magazine* in July 1936, it was announced that a Gaumont-British film, 'Seven Sinners', taken on the Basingstoke and Alton line a month or two previously, would be shortly released, in which Edmund Lowe and Constance Cummings starred.

In 1937, another rail film, 'Oh! Mr. Porter', was made at Cliddesden station, which in its new guise with film props, bore the name of 'Buggleskelly'! That lively trio—Will Hay, Graham Moffat and Moore Marriott—were the stars of the comedy. Level crossing gates 'went west', as the old engine, *Gladstone,* with a tall, jagged-topped funnel, plunged through them. The cast, including extras and members of the local fire brigade, enjoyed the fun as much as those who saw the show at the cinemas. It so happened that a fire broke out in the kitchen of our farm that summer, and the brigade had to be called in. As it chanced, they were otherwise engaged at 'Buggleskelly', six miles away, when the call for help came, but it was surprising how efficiently and quickly they extinguished our small blaze, before gladly returning to duty where it was rumoured that something stronger than water was flowing plentifully!

16
Windmills and Watermills

WINDMILLS HAVE ALWAYS beautified the hills of England and watermills its valleys: the former stood in the open on high ground, whilst the latter usually lay sheltered in flat country by the side of rivers. When one thinks of Hampshire's downs, it is only natural that windmills should have crowned them, but only a handful still stood (and those mostly falling into ruin) when I was a boy. Except for those at Chawton, Grately and Upper Clatford, they were all in southern Hampshire—at Burlesdon, Chalton, Denmead, Hambledon, Hayling Island, Owslebury, Portchester, and Portsmouth. There is only one windmill on the Isle of Wight, that at Bembridge, dating from 1700, which ceased to be used in 1913: it is now owned by the National Trust, and some of its original wooden machinery could still be seen in 1972. The most valuable and interesting account of Hampshire windmills is contained in two articles by A. Keeble Shaw in the *Proceedings of the Hampshire Field Society,* Volume XXI, pt. 2 (1969) and pt. 3 (1960). Most 20th-century books about English windmills contain no mention of existing Hampshire windmills or what remains of them, apart from the reputed Smugglers' Mill, Langstone—a tidal mill without sails for many years which used both wind and water. There were other tidal mills at Ashlett (since 1958 the headquarters of the Esso Sailing Club); Beaulieu (which closed in 1942); the 15th-century Eling Mill; Emsworth (Quay Mill), and Fareham (known variously as Cams, Bishop's and Clarke's Mill—though these may overlap as does the City, Soke, or Town

Mill at Winchester). There were three tidal mills in the Isle of Wight—East Medina and St. Helens (both of which were demolished about 1946-47, and Wootton (which worked until 1941, when it changed over to diesel engines).

Windmill Hills survive at Alton, Lower Wield and Nutley in the north, and at Chalton, Hambledon, Hayling·Island, and the New Forest in the south. There is Windmill Down near Hambledon, Windmill Fields at Newton Valence and Bentworth, and Windmill Farms at Priors Dean, and not far from Tangley and Hurstbourne Tarrant, but as Hampshire is a county of watermills rather than of windmills, I shall devote the remainder of this chapter to them.

Watermills were existence long before windmills.

The nearest watermill to our home at Mapledurwell was at Andwell, on the Lyde, which joins the Loddon a short distance below Hartley Wespall Mill. Andwell Mill (mentioned in the Domesday Survey) was busy up to 1905, to which time my recollections of harvest times at Addison's Farm go back. The huge steel wheel which faced the meadow had long been silent when I sketched and photographed it in 1929, and the purling sound of running water could be heard most of the way from the Priory Farm bridge to Waterend.

Old Basing has two watermills on the Loddon—Barton's Mill in the shadow of the railway viaduct, and the Lower Mill which we knew as Smith's Mill, on the Newnham road near the foot of Pyotts Hill. At the far end of the Newnham road, three miles away, was Lyde Mill, tall and upstanding among the trees: though in the heart of the country, it is now a block of flats! Hook Mill, on the Whitewater, near the *Crooked Billet*, is in restful contrast to the incessant traffic on the A30 which runs so near to it. Mansbridge's (Wellock's) Mill, Old Basing (which was near the foot of Wellock's Hill and opposite Black Dam, which its stream fed) has vanished, and so have two mills at Eastrop, on the

15. Andwell mill and the river Lyde, 1929.

16. Mansbridge's mill, foot of Wellocks's hill, Old Basing, 1930.

The Street, Mapledurwell, looking towards 'Jasmine Cottage'. (*Left to right*: 'Rose Cottage', 'Jasmine Cottage', 'Addison's Cottage', Addison's Farm). (*Watercolour by Julia Waterhouse, 1929*)

The church and green, Mapledurwell. (*Watercolour by J. W. Milliken, 1934*)

St. Mary's Church, Old Basing, 1962. (Pages 44-45)

Peacock Corner, Old Basing, about 1930. (Page 45)

The Broadwater, part of the Basingstoke Canal, Old Basing, about 1930. (Page 54)

The Bolton Arms, Old Basing, 1926. (Page 45)

St. Michael's Church, Basingstoke, 1908. (Page 48)

The interior of Nately Scures Church, about 1925. (Page 71)

Looking towards St. Lawrence's Church, Winchester, 1967. (Page 82) (*Photo: Andy Williams*)

The Market Place, Ringwood, 1967. (Page 146) (*Photo: Andy Williams*)

(*above*) Mr. George Lailey, the bowl-turner of Bucklebury, Berkshire, 1950. (Pages 157-158)

(*below*) Mr. Lailey outside his hut on Turner's Green, 1950. (Pages 157-158)

(*opposite above*) South Warnborough, from a watercolour painting by J. W. Milliken, 1929. (Page 211) (*Photo: Roy Chamberlain*)

(*opposite below*) 'An old Hampshire mill', based on the mill by the quayside at Christchurch, from a watercolour painting by A. F. de Bréanski, about 1910. (Page 135) (*Photo: Roy Chamberlain*)

The Pond, Upton Grey, about 1930. (Page 116)

Greywell Mill, 1964. (Pages 135-137) (*Photo: Ena Wells*)

Buckler's Hard: east side, about 1930. (Pages 144-145)

'Candy' and 'Riddle-me-ree', 1961. (Pages 159-160) (*Photo: Basingstoke Gazette*)

Winchfield Church in the snow, 1964. (Page 108) (*Photo: Ena Wells*)

The buried church at Chilton Candover, about 1930. (Page 195)

The Blind House, Shrewton, Wiltshire, 1965. (Page 164) (*Photo: Ocean Pictures Ltd.*)
New Alresford, 1967. (Pages 197-199) (*Photo: Andy Williams*)

ferry from the Isle of Wight arriving at Portsmouth, 1967. (Pages 250-251) (*Photo: ady Williams*)

1ay Street, Lymington, 1966. (Page 142) (*Photo: Peter Rosser*)

Communion Plate of All Saints' Church, Deane Tazza, 1551; Flagon, 1694; Chalice, 1569; Paten cover, 1570. (Page 202)

Ellisfield Church, about 1930. (Page 193)

17. Lyde mill, Newnham, 1931

outskirts of Basingstoke, one of which was barely noticed by the passer-by, even in its heyday.

Longbridge Mill at Sherfield straddles the Loddon some way back from the Basingstoke—Reading road, and is a pleasant reminder of the leisurely past. Pilcot Mill, Dogmersfield, with its wheel, mill-race and silent pond, evokes nostalgic memories: so does the overshot wheel of West Meon Mill and the pretty undershot wheel—without its mill— in a country lane at Hunton. Anstey Mill, between Holybourne and Alton, was burnt out about 1947, and tragically five children died in the fire: they were buried in Holybourne churchyard and have a memorial there. I understand that the mill worked up to the time of its destruction, and that the unburnt machinery is still there. Upper Neatham Mill, which lies within Holybourne parish and between Lower Neatham and Anstey Mills, ceased to work some years ago, and is now a farmhouse. Lower Neatham Mill, the furthest of the three from Alton—all on the river Wey—was grinding by water power with stones until about 1962, and stone-ground wholemeal could be bought here, but I believe that modern machinery has since been installed. The ancient tithing of Neatham (1,100 acres) was at one time more important than Alton, and in pre-Conquest days had its own market. Now it consists of a mill, farmsteads and a handful of scattered cottages.

Watermills which are now private residences include those at Andwell, Bedhampton, Dipley, Durley, Fordingbridge (Town Mill), Froyle, Goodworth Clatford, Hawkley (Hocheleyne, an ancient mill of the bishops of Winchester), Headley (the one near Liphook), Horsebridge, Isington, Longparish (Lower Mill), North Warnborough (Castle and King's Mills), and Bere Mill, near Whitchurch. There are probably others which have been converted into private houses from among old watermills up and down the county: Abbot's Worthy, Allbrook (near Otterbourne), Bickton (a hamlet near Fordingbridge), Boarhunt, Bramley (Lilly Mill),

Breamore, Bullington, Cheriton, Droxford (now demolished), Fawley, Fleet (the old Brooke Mill), Greatham, Hartley Wespall, Holtshot (Heckfield), Kimbridge (near Mottisfont, where the Dunbridge stream joins the Test), Knapp (on the Avon), Liss, Mottisfont abbey, Nursling, Overton (Northington Mill, which once belonged to Izaak Walton; Quidhampton and Town Mills), Ovington, Poland (near Odiham), Romsey, St. Cross, Shawford, Sopley, Southampton (Wood Mill, St. Denys), South Stoneham (West End and Barton Mills), Sutton Scotney (which was thatched, but is no longer extant), Testwood (Totton), Throop (on the Stour near Holdenhurst), Titchfield abbey, Twyford, Wallop, Warnford (paper mill), Wickham (built from the timbers of the *Chesapeake*, an American frigate), and Winchester (the College, Durngate and Wharf Mills, and the City Mill which is also called the Soke or Town Mill, now a National Trust hostel). When I saw Durngate Mill in 1967, it was in the process of being converted into a private residence.

Among the prettiest are Dipley Mill, near Mattingley, which can be seen to best advantage from the low wall of the bridge on the road to Hartley Wintney—a gem at all times of the year—and Bere Mill, which is equally and most beautifully cared for: Henri de Portal's earliest paper mills were at South Stoneham and Bramshott, but later (in 1712) he acquired Bere Mill, and six years later, took over Laverstoke Mill, two miles upstream, obtaining his first order for the manufacture of paper for bank notes in 1724. Laverstoke Mill became the headquarters of the new industry, and here the Bank of England notes are manufactured and watermarked by a secret process: Portal's large factory is at Town Mill, Overton. Bere Mill ceased to work in the middle of last century. In 1962, when H.M. Queen Elizabeth II attended the celebrations of the 250th anniversary of the founding of Laverstoke Mill, she also visited lovely Bere Mill and walked across the narrow plank bridge over the river Test close to the trim mill-house.

Isington Mill, near Binstead, the home of the late Field-Marshal Viscount Montgomery, conjures up the image of giant oast-houses in Valhalla! It was rebuilt and enlarged nearly 25 years ago, but retained the sluice gate and plank platform reaching out over the river Wey, but handsome and luxurious though it is, I prefer to recall it as it was nearly 50 years ago, when Douglas Snowdon made a charming water-colour sketch of the old grist mill from rising ground behind it, for Clive Holland's book, *Unknown Hampshire*.

Other watermills in idyllic settings were those at Bossington, Fullerton, Houghton, Longstock, and Timsbury, on the Test or its tributaries; Sheet Mill on the Rother, with Ellis's Mill close by, near Petersfield, and three delightful thatched fulling mills at King's Worthy, Alresford and Easton.

The Silk Mill at Whitchurch, a Georgian building with traditional small window pane divisions of that period, is still used for winding and weaving, but the Town and Lower Mills, which were working between the two world wars, have long ceased to do so.

The Town Mill at Andover lies athwart the river Anton in the background of Bridge Street, and can be seen from the bus station. The Old Mill is not far away, but in a more secluded setting.

Itchen Abbas Mill, a tall brick building, stood gaunt and solemn among the sedge and long grasses which infested the wide expanse of the Itchen, and graceful, slow paddling swans on the placid waters accentuated the loneliness of the scene. I was puzzled when I saw no sign of the mill when passing through the village in 1967, and wrote to the rector, who informed me that it had been pulled down in June 1966, having been inoperative for seven years, and that the owner had kept the waterwheel. I was also surprised to learn that its correct name was 'Avington Mill, Itchen Abbas'. Not far away, but nearer to Martyr Worthy, is Chilland Mill.

Two modernised and eminently practical mills are those at Bishop's Waltham and Botley.

The old wheels gathering moss, their slats rotting or rusting away, the pent-up water of the mill-races held permanently at bay, and the silent mill-pools beyond, all have a sad beauty. 'Ichabod' is writ large on their picturesque ruins.

Terry Hunt's photographs (taken between the wars) of mills on the Loddon—Sherfield, and two at Old Basing—and of Gailey Mill and the Old Mill, both at Kingsclere, were excellent pictures of these rustic mills.

The water-colours of Wilfrid Ball, painted during the early years of ·the century, capture the unique rosy tint of old red brick, whether of mills, farmhouses, cottages or bridges.

In my own home, pride of place goes to a water-colour by A. F. de Bréanski, entitled 'An old Hampshire mill', based on the mill by the quayside at Christchurch, but idealised and reset in more tranquil and pastoral surroundings.

Lastly, a valedictory about Greywell Mill, always a great favourite of mine and one near home. Many watermills are half-hidden from view by trees, but Greywell Mill, on a secluded reach of the river Whitewater, in open country away from the village and the straggling road to Up Nately, is a most attractive feature of the landscape.

The Whitewater is a quiet little trout stream, 12 miles long, rising in Bidden Water, Upton Grey, and flowing close to Greywell church; past the King's Mill and Castle Mill at North Warnborough, to Poland Mill and to Hook Mill near the *Crooked Billet*, past Dipley and Holtshot Mills, on to Riseley Mill in Berkshire, ultimately emptying its waters into the Blackwater at Swallowfield, which itself joins the Loddon there.

A forerunner of Greywell Mill is mentioned in Domesday Book. The present picturesque though somewhat dilapidated building did yeoman service up to 1933, when it suddenly came to a halt owing to a major mechanical breakdown, never to be repaired. It used to grind the local corn, locust beans and horse beans, and had a good reputation among farmers as far afield as Herriard for the quality of its flour. The charge for grinding a sack (four bushels) of corn, which took an hour, was a shilling. Local firms made the machinery for the mill—Mulford Brothers of Greywell Wharf (the wheel), and Gower's foundry at Hook (some of the metal gears, and also the brass bearings). The gears and machinery were removed when the building showed signs of subsiding, and together with some of the milling tools, were presented to Basingstoke Museum. The old millstones are gone, but the giant wheel of elm was still visible (1965), though rotting away in its narrowed covered-in compartment at one end of the mill, whose roof is higher than that of the adjoining mill-house. The front of the old buildings is mirrored in the clear, peaceful water which, sluiced off, froths down into the narrow channel below the wheel, and flows underneath and on through the garden. The millstones were not made of solid blocks, but comprised a dozen or more separate stones, and the mill had two sets, the one in use, and the other being dressed, i.e., grooved and roughened, kept in reserve.

Greywell pumping station, built in the late 1920s, delved to a considerable depth and drew heavily on local water supplies, including the river Whitewater. It emptied wells 60 feet deep at Mapledurwell, nearly three miles away, of much of their water, which was slow in replenishing itself.

Greywell Mill came into national prominence in 1955 when 'Charlie Moon', starring Max Bygraves, was filmed. The mill and the rush-laden and flowering banks of the broad stream, were the subjects of charming film shots.

I visited the mill in the late summer of 1965, and met with great kindness from Mrs. Mary Dean. Her husband,

Donald Jabez Dean, the last miller, lived there for 59 years, and has been a watercress grower since the mill stopped working. Mrs. Dean showed me pictures and photographs of the mill, and souvenirs of those four memorable days when the film unit was on location there, and talked of the days prior to 1933 when the machinery of the mill set up such a vibration that crockery on the dresser in the mill-house did a constant war-dance! She also permitted me to wander at leisure along the lengthy stretch of riverbank, where I noticed figwort, scented purple willow-herb, wild mint, agrimony, and meadow-sweet. Ducks and swans paddled gently in and out among the reeds. There were blackberries, elder trees and wild rose bushes in the hedges; oxeye daisies and silverweed alongside the path; tall ragwort and flowering reeds six to eight feet high at the far end of the still waters, and, best of all, hundreds of bulrushes. The cooing of wood pigeons and doves, and now and again the sudden scuttle of a moorhen or the querulous rustle of other wild fowl among the rushes, were the only sounds in that peaceful place.

Alas! by the following summer, the mill-house had lost its tenants, and was uninhabited.

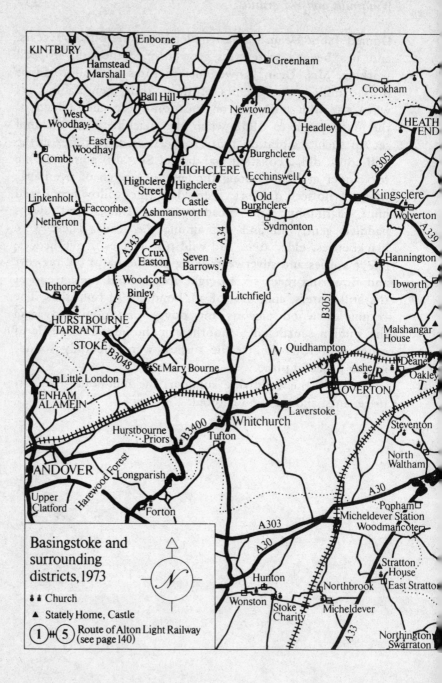

Basingstoke and surrounding districts, 1973

♦♦ Church

▲ Stately Home, Castle

(1) ⊬⊬ (5) Route of Alton Light Railway (see page 140)

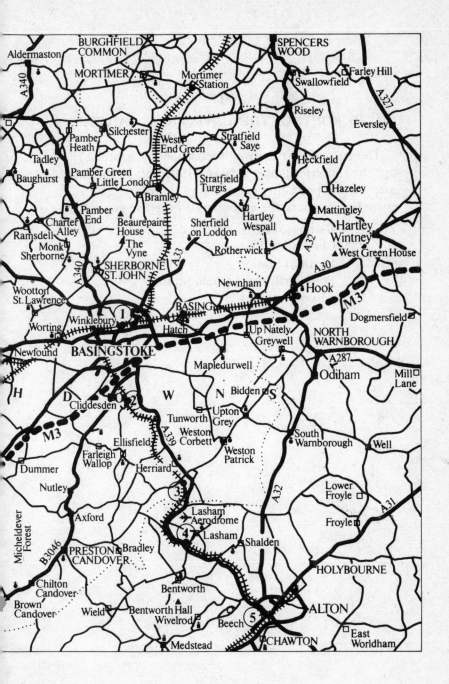

A NOTE
ON THE ROUTE OF THE ALTON LIGHT RAILWAY

The Alton Light Railway (described in Chapter 15) operated intermittently between 1901 and 1936. The map on the preceding pages shows the route it took, encircled numbers corresponding to the five stations:

1. Basingstoke Station
2. Cliddesdon Station
3. Herriard Station
4. Bentworth and Lasham Station
5. Alton Station

17
The New Forest

THE NEW FOREST occupies about a tenth of the Hampshire mainland, and consists of wooded country, open spaces of heath and rough grazing land, and villages with pasture land under cultivation. I visited it a number of times over the years, by cycle, coach, and car. In 1923, my uncle Hugh and I spent two days on the round journey from Basingstoke, staying overnight at Christchurch, where the priory church and its tower stood out against the sky beyond the dark, sombre ruins of Twynham Castle on the banks of the Avon. Behind the high altar is the reredos representing the Stem of Jesse showing the genealogy of Christ, and there are quaint, grotesque carvings on the miserere stalls. The circular turret or north tower is a gem of Norman architecture, and for columns and pillars it ranks third to Winchester cathedral and Romsey abbey in imposing strength and grandeur. The Shelley memorial, a fine bas-relief, is near the west doorway. The Avon joins the Stour at Christchurch, both entering the English Channel at Mudeford (pronounced Muddy-ford). A local glen bears the amusing name of Chewton Bunny!

On our second day we cycled near to Hordle where we saw the incongruous tower at Sway (218 feet high, with a spiral staircase of 330 steps), completed in 1885. Andrew Peterson (1813-1906) was a wealthy barrister, a retired Indian judge, who sought to demonstrate the strength and durability of Portland cement. During a slump he employed for six years, and at good wages, local labourers who worked from the inside, without scaffolding, pouring concrete into frames for the walls and the tower's 13 storeys, an interesting experiment which established the soundness of his principles. Some people designated it 'Peterson's Folly', but it showed the far-sightedness and kindliness which animated this pioneer of the uses of concrete.

We pressed on to Lymington, a small seaport, market town and borough over 800 years old, once famous for its salt industry, and later for boat building. The parish church on the main street has a tower with a curious cupola on top. We liked the look of the quaint old shops and inns, the boats and jetties, and saw a ferry-boat setting off on its four-mile journey to Yarmouth in the Isle of Wight. Wishing to see as much of the Forest as possible, we scouted round and eventually found Boldre church, whose heavy, embattled tower and long nave leant down low in a quiet corner of the county, surrounded by oaks. It was at Royden Farm in Boldre parish that Hudson wrote the opening and concluding chapters of his *Hampshire Days,* though he called it Roydon House.

We then rode on to Lyndhurst, the capital of the Forest, where ponies roamed free and unharmed in the streets. What appealed to me most was the exquisite fresco of the Ten Virgins, by Lord Leighton, R.A., behind the altar, his own gift to the tall, steepled parish church built in 1863. The thatched cottages on the edge of Swan Green are among the prettiest in the Forest. Another beauty spot near Lyndhurst is Emery Down, and at Beaulieu Road annual sales of forest ponies are held.

The 'Lion of Hampshire' (Romsey abbey), has a heavy tower with a staircase turret and polygonal belfry. There is a Saxon rood on the west wall of the south transept. The abbey, which was sold to the inhabitants of Romsey in 1538 for £100, dominates this small market town like a huge hive.

On our way from Romsey to Winchester, we passed Ampfield church, built in 1839, in which there is a memorial window to John Keble who ministered there. He called Ampfield Wood his 'cathedral'. We soon reached Hursley,

a quiet village in those days, with dignified cottages built
in a semi-ecclesiastical style, grouped round the handsome
church with its impressive tower and spire, and its wide
nave and aisles. John Keble, author of *The Christian Year,*
and a leader of the Oxford Movement, was vicar of Hursley
for 30 years. The centenary of his death was commemorated
in 1966, by which time Hursley church had lost its spire.
A gentle character and country gentleman, Richard Cromwell
—the antithesis of his father Oliver—was lord of the manor
and lived here for some years: those who called him
'Tumbledown Dick' had their sense of values mixed. He
died in 1712 at the age of 86, and is buried in the chancel
of the church. Sir Isaac Newton also died at Hursley, at
Cranbury Park.

William Rufus's body was conveyed from Minstead to
Winchester on the cart of a charcoal-burner (who may have
followed the route we had taken via Copythorne, Romsey,
Ampfield, and Hursley, though he is said to have rested the
night at Chandler's Ford). In a dip of the road we passed
the mud walls of Pitt Village, and before reaching Winchester, saw across the sunny Itchen water-meadows, the
cloistered buildings of St. Cross Hospital. It was too late
in the day for us to request the wayfarer's dole (a horn of
beer and a piece of bread) at St. Cross Hospice, for the day's
ration would long since have been exhausted, so without
further ado, we left the city by the Basingstoke road. Outside
Winchester I caught sight of the ancient church of Headbourne Worthy on a slightly raised island alongside a stream,
but did not stop to examine its Saxon remains—a typically
narrow doorway, a mutilated crucifix, pilasters, and the
so-called 'long and short work'. The little building and its
weather-beaten boarded bell-cote containing three pre-
Reformation bells, breathe the spirit of antiquity.

A mile further on is the quiet village of King's Worthy
whose church has a 15th-century plain square tower, its
only old portion. The only village on the 16-mile stretch

between King's Worthy and Basingstoke is Popham, whose population during the last century and a half has seldom exceeded a hundred. Its church and open gable-end bell-turret stood out against the sky in those days, but was damaged by a land-mine during the Second World War, and had to be demolished in 1946.

We pushed on to Kempshott Hill and Basingstoke. We passed the town hall and looked up at the clock which confirmed that we had covered the 18 miles from Winchester in an hour and a half. In less than 20 minutes we were home.

In later years I made special journeys to Brockenhurst, Beaulieu, Buckler's Hard, Minstead, Ringwood, Fording-bridge, and Lyndhurst. Brockenhurst was easily accessible by rail, and my wife and I were good walkers and revelled in the scenery of the Forest. The spired church stands on a slight elevation, and in the churchyard is a venerable yew tree and the gravestone of 'Brusher' Harry Mills (so named because he used to brush Lyndhurst cricket ground between innings), who died in 1905, aged 67: it depicts the old bearded man catching adders, and the inscription states that he 'for a long number of years followed the occupation of Snake Catcher in the New Forest. His pursuit and the primitive way in which he lived, caused him to be an object of interest to many'. Parts of the church are Norman, some may even be Saxon. We walked the six miles to Beaulieu, and saw the Palace gateway, abbey house, the cloisters, the large domus (lay brothers' quarters), and the parish church (formerly the refectory) with its pulpit built into and approached through the wall. The monks' mill at Beaulieu lies on the Beaulieu River which runs from near Lyndhurst to the causeway on the Solent where once was 'the ancient and powerful town of Lepe', the port for Cowes in the Isle of Wight. The Cistercians were noted agriculturists, those at Beaulieu particularly so. Buckler's Hard, its single street running down to the water's edge, had long been familiar. Its shipbuilding yards were famous for the wooden ships associated with Nelson's victories, and the *Agamemnon,* one of the several built here which fought at Trafalgar, gave its name to the present yard. Very appropriately, a maritime museum contains exhibits reminiscent of those days when ships were built of forest oaks. Miss Elizabeth Goudge once wrote that at Buckler's Hard there was 'the loveliest small chapel'. This occupies a room in a terraced cottage on the left as one looks down the slope: it was once a cobbler's shop, later a schoolroom, and ultimately converted into a place of worship by the Rev. P. F. Powles, curate and vicar of Beaulieu from 1880 to 1939, who held services here for the cottagers. A bell hangs outside. The room was dark and quiet, but its calm beauty was enchanting —the wooden panelling, the altar and blue sanctuary lamp, the gentle tints of its frontals and flowers, the candlesticks, the crystal cross and the statue of the Virgin. A silver plaque states that the cross and altar are a memorial to Lady Poole (whose ashes lie beneath it) and to her only son who died in 1933, a year before his mother. The chapel, in memory of a young R.A.F. pilot killed in 1918 while flying over the Solent, was dedicated in 1935 by the Bishop of Winchester.

Minstead church, with a pinnacled tower, is curious in shape. It has a rare three-decker pulpit, and one of its galleries is double-tiered. The squire's high, curtained pew, with chairs, fireplace and separate entrance, is not only a disfigurement, but a relic of the pretensions of local landowners in past centuries who showed little of the humility of the church's founder. The mortal remains of Sir Arthur Conan Doyle, previously buried in the garden of his Sussex home, were re-interred in Minstead churchyard in 1955.

My wife's enthusiasm for *The White Company,* which describes life in the 14th century at Beaulieu Abbey (founded by King John in 1201) and its dependencies (St. Leonard's grange, Sowley Pond, the ironworks, and Exbury),

led to a deep interest in Hampshire, and, conversely, my
affection for the county had kindled a special interest in
this book. The *Trusty Servant* inn stands outside the churchyard, its painted sign showing the old familiar figure in
Winchester College. The Rufus Stone at Stony Cross, near
Castle Malwood, is in Minstead parish. Just as one associates
other parts of the New Forest with bluebells, foxgloves and
kingcups, Minstead may be remembered for its wild daffodils
in springtime.

Ringwood is a pretty little market town with a row of old
thatched cottages near the railed-off pond. It is still famed
for 'Ringwoods'—woollen gloves knitted by craftswomen
in the villages round about. When I went inside the towered
13th-century church on whose walls are paintings of the
Keble family, I noticed in the porch a reproduction of the
late Margaret W. Tarrant's painting of 'The Lord of Joy',
a copy of which also hangs in the children's corner in Mapledurwell church.

Three miles from Ringwood is Ellingham, in the churchyard of which lies Lady Alice (Dame Alicia) Lisle, executed
in the Bloody Assize of 1685 for sheltering followers of the
Duke of Monmouth. Inside the Early English church are her
family's canopied pew, a Flemish painting, and an iron
frame for an hour-glass. Originally there was a rood loft
above the rood screen, but a wall was erected between
the screen and the roof, and entirely covered by tablets,
texts and a Royal coat of arms (1671). Outside is a handsome
old porch, and above its outer doorway, a painted sundial.

Bransgore church and Thorney Hill chapel, both in
wooded country, may be comparatively modern, but are
beautifully furnished, and worthy of a visit. Hinton Admiral
is in forest country, too, its church, 18th-century, but much
restored, as is Burley church, built in 1839. Milton's church
tower is 17th-century, and Milford church contains Norman
work. The 13th-century church of Sopley stands on a bank
of the Avon out of floodwater's way, its spired tower giving

it a striking appearance. Spanning that fine salmon river at Fordingbridge is the ancient seven-arched bridge with its background of timbered inns and old houses which, with the 700-year-old parish church, constitute the town's chief architectural attractions.

Bramshaw, Harbridge and Ibsley churches were modernised in the 19th century. Bramshaw has a 13th-century nave, west window and blocked-up south doorway. These villages, with their charming cottages, emphasise the inherent beauty of the Forest, which has an enviable tradition of good thatching, witness Swan Green cottages, and thatched hostelries such as the six-centuries-old *Cat and Fiddle* at Hinton Admiral, the *Sir John Barleycorn* at Cadnam, and the *Royal Oak* at Fritham. Deep forest goes particularly well with thatch, and so does river scenery. At Ibsley, the thatched roofs and porches of cottages alongside the Avon bear comparison with those of any other river villages. There is even a thatched chapel on a hill at Poulner, a mile or two north of Ringwood.

In the north-west corner of the New Forest where Hampshire drives a wedge between Wiltshire and Dorset, are several villages usually neglected by the tourist. All lie in the valley of the silvery Avon and its tributaries. Martin has a much-restored 12th-century church with an octagonal spire, and an ancient market place near which is the pleasantly-named Sweetapple's Farm. Rockbourne is a pretty downland parish whose ancient barn has two fine wagon porches and a chapel under the same roof, also a church with a Norman arch. Its chancel and wide east window are most attractive. South Damerham (or Damerham, pronounced Damrun), on a hill, has a towered church dating back to 1130, and a tenor bell of 1666 bearing the realistic inscription' 'I was cast in the yeere of plague, warre and fire'. Whitsbury, like Rockbourne, has a long straggling village street, and appeals to the archaeologically minded because of its Roman and Saxon earthworks, camps and ditches. The modern church, built in 13th-century style, stands on a hilltop and—most unusual for any country church—has nine bells, though one is housed in a loft. Hale church, in Hale Park, was erected in 1715, and, like Wickham church, contains a plethora of memorials: the village is on a hill, near to the pretty water-meadows of Charford, the scene of a battle in 519 between Britons and Saxons. There is no church here or at Woodgreen, which is a modern village.

Breamore's attractions are many and varied. There are tumuli on the Down and a mizmaze (85 feet in diameter) in a wood; a pretty mill over the Avon, village stocks, and a 10th-century church—probably the most complete specimen in Hampshire—which is a veritable treasure-house. It is built of stone and flint in herring-bone fashion, is remarkable in shape, and has lancet windows and a high roof, from the centre of which projects a small bell-cote set on a much broader timbered base. Above the doorway in the porch is a carved Calvary with faded paintings forming a background. Inside the church are traces of other wall paintings; evidences of its Saxon origins (rough quoins or corner-stones and pilaster strips), and a curious old inscription over the south transept arch which translated reads: 'Here the Covenant is made plain to thee'.

To the south-east of the Forest are several villages well worthy of a visit. Fawley is remembered for its Norman church, heathland scenery, a small quay on a creek of Southampton Water, and for the part which it and neighbouring Calshot played in the plight of refugees from volcano-stricken Tristan da Cunha a few years ago. Dibden's Early English church sustained serious damage during the Second World War, but the burnt-out nave and chancel, also the old font which was smashed when crashing bells fell on it, have happily all been most beautifully restored. The former altar rails were reputed to have been made of yew from a tree which stood in the churchyard.

Eling has its attractions—a 15th-century mill and a church with a Saxon arch, and artistic paintings and furnishings—and so has Exbury on the Beaulieu river, with a Norman font in its restored 13th-century house of worship. Both Calshot and Hurst Castles were built of stone from Beaulieu Abbey.

18
The Sherbornes,
Ramsdell and Baughurst

IT WAS A CLIMB from Basingstoke station to the outskirts of Sherborne St. John, but one was rewarded by commanding views of the surrounding countryside from both the Aldermaston highway and the direct road which meets that from Old Basing. White campions, St. John's wort and many other flowers brighten the hedges near Park Prewett hospital, built just before and during the First World War. New estates and factories have shot up everywhere in this outlying sector of Basingstoke. Noticeable in the valley is Sherborne St. John church tower, its copper-sheathed spire glinting green and amber as the sun's rays fall on it. There are many 14th-century features, a 12th-century south doorway and Purbeck marble font, and chained volumes of Foxe's *Book of Martyrs* in the church, which was extensively restored during the last century. The lardy cakes of this village had a high reputation years ago and were much sought after.

Monk Sherborne is situated at a considerable distance from the main road to Aldermaston, and is reached by winding lanes between high hedgerows past the *Mole* inn. Some 26 years since, I had occasion to ride over to inquire about new ladders for fruit picking, but nothing resulted, though I recollect that previously a family of ladder makers from Southampton way used to go round our villages: the senior member, who was reputed to be a centenarian, called on prospective customers and referred those who wanted ladders, which were made to order, to his 'lads', one of whom was in his seventies! The village has retained more of an old-world appearance than its much larger neighbour, Sherborne St. John, and the old heavy-timbered Norman doorway, porch and bell-cote of the ivy-covered 12th-century church impart an ancient look to the edifice which suits the name of the parish. A holder of the Victoria Cross, the Rev. Geoffrey Harold Woolley, was vicar here from 1923 to 1928.

Between Monk Sherborne and Ramsdell is the hamlet of Charter Ley, which used to be called 'Chatter Alley'. Ramsdell, a mile or so away, was formerly in Wootton St. Lawrence parish, but became a separate entity in 1868. Its flint and stone church, built in 1867, is peacefully situated amid trees—firs, beeches, Spanish chestnut trees, and an aspen in the churchyard—and a tapering spire tops the tiled roof of the clock-tower. Ramsdell is noted for its century-old industry, which produces three-quarters of a million hand-made bricks annually, of far greater durability than the cheaper machine-made variety. Those engaged in the work are kept busy all the year round, the clay being dug from the pit in the summer, and the bricks fired in the kilns in the winter. On the countrified route to Baughurst there are walls of hurdles, and rosebay and bracken are plentiful. Most prolific among the forest trees are the oaks, and I rejoice that Baughurst prefers to remain rural and has not sacrificed its splendid tree population.

When the Rev. H. G. Studdert-Kennedy (brother of the well-known padre, 'Woodbine Willie' of the First World War) was Rector from 1945 to 1959, I had occasion to trace the baptismal dates of my mother and three of her brothers who were born in Baughurst, and he was most friendly and helpful in going through the registers in the vestry with me. He had served in India for 29 years prior to returning to England. Baughurst church of flint and stone was built in 1845. The font and chancel screen are 15th century, and minor portions of the earlier church were

incorporated in the present building. A stone spire surmounts
the narrow octagonal tower which contains five bells cast
in 1775. Cottages in Baughurst are as tidily kept as any in
the county.

In 1954 I had a chat with Mr. Leonard West, who has
a long tradition of thatching going back several generations,
mentioning Mr. Norman Goodland's book, *My Father before
Me*, which concerns Mr. West's father and his forebears. He
informed me that Mr. Albert Frank West, the central figure
of the book (boy and man) was clerk and sexton at Baughurst church for 40 years before his death in 1953, at the
age of 78, and that his father before him held the joint
office for a like period, and died in 1919, aged seventy-six.
Mr. Goodland's association with this well-known north
Hampshire family of thatchers and hurdle-makers began
nearly half a century ago, he having been adopted by Frank
West, who was also a member of the local parish council
for 50 years, and captain of the church bell-ringers. *My
Father before Me* preserves for posterity an authentic picture
of what life was like for the thatcher, the village carrier,
and the agricultural labourer in north Hampshire from about
1870 onwards. Those were the days when Joseph Arch
(who died in 1919 at the age of 92) was in his prime and
fighting to found the National Agricultural Labourers'
Union (in 1872), which, within two years, had close on
90,000 members. If you know Basingstoke and the country
round about, it should not be difficult to recognise most
of the sketches and tail-pieces provided by Frank V. Martin
for the book, which include Baughurst church interior and
the churchyard, Manydown House, Basingstoke town hall,
and the station railway bridge. The fictitious place-names
are only thinly disguised.

In 1954, Leonard West was not only carrying on the
family tradition of thatcher and hurdle-maker, but the office
of parish clerk and sexton at Baughurst church. His son,
Alwyn, is now in the century-old craft of his forefathers.

When one hears so often that thatching is dying out, it is pleasant to read in a church magazine for February 1965 that a father and son from Hannington were then thatching a house in Rotherwick.

In the 17th and 18th centuries there was a large and influential Quaker community in the district, the meeting house and burial ground being at Brown's Farmhouse, Baughurst.

The famous pianist, Solomon, spent some time as a child prodigy practising for concerts, in the Baughurst home of his patron and teacher, Mathilde Verne (1865–1936), who also used another local cottage as a summer school for training her pupils.

At the far end of Baughurst village is Heath End and the *Cricketers* inn, just inside the Hampshire border.

19
Old Basing
to Aldermaston and
Bucklebury Common

FROM UNDER the single arch of the railway bridge between the river Loddon and Cowdrey Down, Swing-Swang Lane climbs to the crest of the hill after crossing the Basingstoke—Reading road, and looks down on Sherborne St. John in the distance, where my maternal grandmother was born in 1835. The cricketing tradition in this village—as in others in Hampshire (the birthplace of the game)—was strong, and I remember with pleasure John Arlott mentioning the local team when broadcasting a commentary on a Test match.

Off a lane on our right leading to Bramley is the Vyne, a spacious red brick mansion which was built by Lord Sandys, who entertained Henry VIII here. Especially impressive are the chapel and the great staircase. Since the Civil War, it has been owned by the descendants of Chaloner Chute, a famous lawyer who was Speaker of the House of Commons when Parliament assembled under Richard Cromwell early in 1659: unfortunately this office proved so great a strain to his health that he died less than 11 weeks later.

At Bramley, the Little Loddon or Bow Brook joins the river Loddon. The late Norman church, discernible by its red crenellated tower, contains ancient wall paintings (including a fresco of the murder of Thomas à Becket), stained glass and brasses. Like Sherborne St. John church, it has a Brocas chapel to the memory of a family who lived for almost five centuries prior to 1870 at Beaurepaire, an old mansion—damaged by fire in 1941—surrounded by a moat and a wooded park. Other buildings of architectural interest in Bramley are the 16th-century half-timbered manor house, farmhouses and cottages.

The scattered village of Pamber includes Pamber Forest (beloved by Hudson when he stayed at Silchester), and also Pamber End, where Mr. Sims, the last of the local makers of wooden rakes, carries on his trade. West Sherborne (Pamber) Priory church is approached from a lane off the Aldermaston road, and its only near neighbour is a farmhouse. It has a massive tower which resembles that of Wootton St. Lawrence, but it is only part of the original Benedictine priory. There are two fonts, one Norman, the other Tudor. I used to clamber up a heavily-buttressed staircase above a narrow doorway to the left of the main entrance, from which I could look down into the dark nave. There are large lancet windows, also high circular ones, chantry arches, a 14th-century oak effigy of a knight in armour, cross coffin lids, a piscina, mural paintings, an aumbry and a consecration cross. There is admittedly a somewhat elephantine look about the church, inside as well as out.

I have so far said nothing about Hampshire charities—too numerous to mention—which have old and interesting origins inextricably interwoven with the history of England, but I should like to single out one, the Adam de Port Charity, 1471, commemorative of a donor who lived 300 years earlier, because it is associated with the ancient priory church of Pamber, and, incidentally, because the name of its founder, who was Lord of Mapledurwell early in the 12th century, is so closely linked with my home village in its most historic days. The Charity Commissioners are now drawing up schemes for the amalgamation of such funds, with the object of providing sums which can be used to help old people in emergencies. In Henry II's reign, Adam de Port gave to Pamber priory 'all tithes of all my mills in Sireburn' (Sherborne). For many years, however, the priory was from time to time burdened with debt. Henry V granted it to his college at Eton, but Eton neglected it, priors and monks were expelled, and jewels and relics carried off. In 1461, Edward IV gave the priory to the Hospital of St. Julian or God's House, at Southampton, an Act of 1471 confirming this. This was tantamount to making Queen's College, Oxford, responsible for the care of the building and for providing one honest priest to say Mass and the Offices daily. On each New Year's Day, a solemn dirge was to be sung for Richard, Duke of York, and for the souls of Henry de Port and others buried there. The Act also directed that 23s. 4d. be distributed annually to the poor—this is the Adam de Port Charity—eleven poor persons to receive 2s. each, and the twelfth, representing Judas Iscariot, 1s. 4d. It is nicknamed the Apostles' Charity.

Returning to the main road, we pass the *College Arms* inn on the way to Tadley, which is a go-ahead and rapidly-growing community with several churches and chapels, and large modern shops. It was known locally as 'God-forsaken Tadley' in the last century, but possessed a good choir which visited villages for miles around at Christmas-time: the choir sang outside farmhouses and cottages as far afield as Mapledurwell, which is 10 miles away. Tadley's prize-winning silver band, founded in 1875, is as well known today as the choir was in its day. The village used to have a considerable gypsy element in its population, and there are still some besom makers there who send their brooms all over the country. Services are still held regularly in the old parish church of St. Peter, but in recent years the accent has been on building the new church of St. Paul.

Not far away, but over the Berkshire border, is Alder-maston. A long, steep hill runs down to the old-world village, which fans out from the triangular green. A hundred yards down the street is the Aldermaston Pottery, where one can have the pleasure of seeing excellent pottery made, which is fired in the kilns and cooled in cupboards on the ground floor of the shop, and stored on shelves there and in the large room above. Craftsmen mould the soft, wet clay into symmetrical shapes on potters' wheels, and finish their work by hand-painting and glazing. You can purchase practically any article which pleases you, and the design and finish of the work are all that could be desired—most satisfying, and a joy for everyday use.

Aldermaston church, the Kennet valley, and the beautiful old red brick houses and cottages near the *Hind's Head* retain their perennial charm. It is a pleasant journey past the fine old mill and mill-house—now a guest house in its waterside setting—through flat countryside and water-meadows, to the busy Bath road between Theale and Woolhampton, some of whose hostelries still have a stagecoach look about them. Here we leave the Newbury road for Midgham Green and go by way of the woods to Bucklebury Common.

In the old days, I often rode through Aldermaston on my way to Turner's Green to buy treen (wooden bowls, cheese dishes and bread platters, candlesticks and a mushroom-shaped coffee table), all of which were made of elm wood and turned by George William Lailey. Treen (a word derived from 'trees') was in general use in the Middle Ages among ordinary folk, before the advent of pewter, and even later among poor people. In 1927, H. V. Morton's book, *In Search of England,* brought Mr. Lailey and his work to the notice of a wider public. Earlier still, L. Salmon, in *Untravelled Berkshire,* devoted a chapter to Bucklebury, in which he relates that during the last century, a number of families were busy making bowls on the Common, and that one of Mr. Lailey's forebears took them to London in his cart. Many a time have I seen him in his wooden shed on Turner's Green, busily chiselling out shapely bowls, working his lathe by a treadle attached to a sapling reaching to the roof. From a rough block of elm, he could cut and shape four bowls so graded that they fitted perfectly into each other. Some were used by banks as cash bowls.

Unpolished and unvarnished, each bowl had a line of yellow turmeric round the rim, and was signed by him with his carpenter's pencil. Most of his work had to be collected personally, yet he had orders from all over the world. He continued working until well into his eighties. Among his most treasured possessions was a letter from Marlborough House, saying that Queen Mary was interested in his workshop and a great admirer of craftsmanship in all its forms.

Blacksmiths formerly made the tools of the bowl-maker's trade, but Mr. Lailey told me that he made his own. When he died, his lathe and tools went to the Museum of English Rural Life at the University of Reading.

Mr. Lailey was born on 22 June 1869, and died on 18 December 1958. His grave, marked by a simple wooden cross bearing his name, is situated to the right of the main path going up to the chapel in the cemetery on Bucklebury Common. Thus the last of the bowl-makers has passed on, leaving no successor. The old shed has gone, too. His friends will long remember this happy country craftsman and the kindly twinkle in his blue eyes.

20
Oakley to Hannington, Wolverton and Ewhurst

OAKLEY (including Church Oakley) had been familiar to me long before 1914, when the spread of modern housing began to make itself apparent, because it lay off the road from Basingstoke to Whitchurch. It is, however, inseparably associated in my mind with a charming incident which occurred as recently as 1961. At home in the Wirral peninsula of Cheshire, my wife and I had seen in the *Hants & Berks Gazette* a captivating photograph of a skewbald Shetland mare, 'Candy', standing 34 inches, with her tiny 20-inch high foal, 'Riddle-me-ree', aged nine days, in an Oakley meadow. We had visions that when on holiday at Basingstoke that summer, we might see the fluffy grey foal. On a Saturday evening three months later, we were in Basingstoke, waiting for the Old Basing bus to appear, when another, labelled 'East Oakley', suddenly drew up. On the spur of the moment we boarded it, moving off almost immediately. Twenty minutes later we reached our destination, a beautiful old farmhouse, and on confiding our hopes to the owner of the ponies, she gladly acceded to our request and drove us in her car to see the Shetland and other ponies in a meadow some distance away. Hearing her voice, the spirited young animals came frisking down the field at a gallop, to be petted by their mistress, and welcomed by us. We could not help falling for 'Riddle-me-ree', but were equally entranced with 'Candy' (who had pulled Cinderella's coach in an ice pantomime in London), and with a little white pony, 'Sugar-Plum Fairy'. As we talked to them and stroked them in the gently failing light, the scene seemed to take on an almost magical quality. Our hostess's kindness gave us great joy and a memory we shall always cherish.

Near the railway viaduct, which is not far from Oakley station, a long hilly side-road climbs from Clerken Green through both wooded and open country to remote Hannington. On the green are two village ponds, a roofed well, and a farmhouse close to the old-world church, whose double-tiered pagoda spire gives it an oriental look. In the pre-Norman building are several pillars of solid chalk, on which there are Crusader crosses. There is a 12th-century north doorway, and work from each of the succeeding centuries is apparent in its arches, windows and pulpit. Each time I return, I recapture the old charm it has always had for me. It retains, as far as I am concerned, the very essence and all the typical features of an ancient Hampshire village. Like Tadley, Hannington has its own silver band.

By continuing hilly lanes through woodland and deep country, we come out on to the Kingsclere road at Wolverton. In the park of Wolverton House is a small lake where swans hiss at the approach of strangers. The Georgian church, rebuilt in 1717, lies in a dip of land beyond, and only the top half of its heavy red brick tower is visible from the road. If it was not designed by Sir Christopher Wren, his influence is reflected in its style, and in any case it was built during his lifetime (1632–1723). Inside the church are box pews and much carved oak.

The next village, if it can be so designated, is Ewhurst, consisting only of a few buildings—Ewhurst House (which became the property of the first Duke of Wellington in 1837), the church, a farm and a cottage or two. The small church is of flint with an open bell-turret, and was rebuilt in 1872 by the Plowden family (formerly of Ewhurst House) on the site of its early 14th-century predecessor. The house with its park and lake is secluded, and a quiet country lane leads to the Kingsclere–Basingstoke road.

Two miles or so from Basingstoke there used to be a lonely clump of pines over a Quaker's grave in the middle of a field on the crest of Rooksdown, but this vanished about 60 years ago (1913). It was a landmark and commanded a fine view of the surrounding country before the Royal Canadian Hospital at Park Prewett and Rooksdown Hospital were built, during the First World War. The older generation pronounced it Park Privett. When my grandfather was measuring land not far away, I was able to tell the time of day from the clock on the now dismantled tower of Basingstoke town hall three miles away as I scanned the landscape through a pocket telescope.

21
W. H. Hudson

W. H. HUDSON (1841-1922) was a great field naturalist
and the author of a number of books, written in most
pellucid prose, about the southern English countryside—
*Hampshire Days, Afoot in England, Adventures among Birds,
Birds and Man, The Book of a Naturalist, A Traveller in
Little Things, Dead Man's Plack, Birds in Town and Village,
Nature in Downland* and *A Shepherd's Life.*

Several of them record observations of life and of nature
in Hampshire, and through these books and also through
pamphlets written for the Royal Society for the Protection
of Birds, he sought to preserve wild life. To this end he
escaped for short spells, whenever his financial circumstances permitted, from the drab surroundings of a London
boarding house which his wife kept, to the country, and
when in Hampshire resided in remote villages: Fawley and
Boldre, Bransbury, Silchester, Itchen Abbas, Hurstbourne
Tarrant, Martin and Selborne.

Hudson, being a lover of the New Forest, preferred
southern Hampshire, and once remarked that when in Christchurch, he was on the threshold of the county richest of
all in wild life, which continually called him back from all
others to its heaths, forests and rivers. He stayed at Rollstone
Farm, near Fawley, and at Royden Farm, near Boldre. He
walked and cycled, but often stood or sat motionless observ-
ing wild life in the Test Valley or in Harewood Forest, near
Longparish, where he stayed at the *Crook and Shears,* an inn
off a shady lane, where anglers resided. Near Bransbury was
Longparish station, 'a smartish step' from the village of that

name, and not far from there and the *George* inn is Harewood Forest. A wide avenue from the Andover road narrows as it enters the wood, in a copse of which at some distance from the road is Dead Man's Plack, a stone monumental cross erected in 1826, alongside a lonely overgrown path. The cross is in memory of Earl Athelwold, who was murdered by King Edgar so that he could marry his dead friend's wife, Elfrida. *Dead Man's Plack* tells how Hudson sat down in the shade of oaks in the forest, and pondered the ancient story until it came to life as related in his short book. Into it he wove an account of life a thousand years ago at nearby Wherwell, where Elfrida's reputed grave is to be seen.

For beauty of thatched cottages, majestic trees, and crystal streams, Wherwell may be rightfully acclaimed the queen of Hampshire villages. The cockatrice windvane, formerly on Wherwell church spire, is now perched on a house.

The Test and the Dever (the Bullington stream in its upper reaches) which meet at Wherwell, run either side of Bransbury Common, which is rich in wild life, birds as well as flowers, including the snipe and redstart: even the hoopoe has been seen here. How Hudson must have revelled in the Hampshire countryside all the way from St. Mary Bourne, Hurstbourne Priors, Longparish, Forton, and Bransbury to Wherwell—a string of lovely villages and hamlets on the delightful Test and its tributaries.

Hampshire Days is one of his most down-to-earth books so far as humankind and nature study are concerned. The late Mrs. Shering (a former proprietor of the stores on Silchester Common) who, as a young woman knew Hudson when he stayed at 'The Pines', the home of her aunt, Mrs. Lawes, on the Tadley road, not far from Pamber Forest, used to talk to me about him. She herself lived there later on. Mrs. Lawes's husband, James Lawes, was the village carrier. He had previously worked for many years as a shepherd at Martin, but was crippled in one foot and rode to his fold

in a donkey cart. He used to hobble along with his sheep
on the downs between Martin and Pentridge, and, eventually,
as a result of his lameness and infirmities, left Martin to
live at Silchester. Hudson has written that early in life
Lawes caught a chill through long exposure to wet and
cold in winter, which brought on rheumatic fever and a
malady of the thigh finally affecting the whole limb, making
him lame for life. There is little doubt that James Lawes
and 'Caleb Bawcombe' in Hudson's *A Shepherd's Life* are
one and the same person. In the churchyard of the neighbouring Hampshire border parish of Mortimer West End—
which, strange to say, is in the diocese of Oxford!—lie the
mortal remains of James Lawes and his wife: metal crosses
on their graves, which I saw in 1949, stated that he died
on 26 March 1914, aged 84, and Emma Agatha Lawes
on 5 May 1921.

I knew that Hudson had given the fictitious name of
'Winterbourne Bishop' in *A Shepherd's Life* to his favourite
village, to put the curious off the scent. This inspired me
to try and discover its real identity, so one summer morning
in 1938, I set out on my cycle towards the Wiltshire market
town of Devizes. From here, I rode through three delectable
villages—Potterne, West Lavington, and Tilshead—and on
over the rolling downs of Salisbury Plain, but as I neared
Maddington and Shrewton, I could not bring myself to
believe that either of these villages, despite a few cottages of
decorative flint and a dry Winterbourne by the side of the
road, fitted the author's description, though a year or two
later I came to realise that nearby Orcheston St. Mary and
distant Martin might tie for the honour. As I pedalled along,
past the Round House or 'Blind House'—a tiny stone gaol
opposite the *Catherine Wheel* inn at Shrewton, I had almost
given up hope of identifying 'Winterbourne Bishop',
when, all of a sudden, I saw a notice 'Local postcard
views' in the window of a Dickensian-looking grocery store.
On an impulse I entered the shop, and was soon in deep

conversation with the proprietor, Philip Henry Bond. He showed me views of the village landmarks and of the surrounding downland countryside, even mentioning the *Bustard* inn as a probable means of identification, and I refreshed myself with lemonade and bought some of the cards. He told me that there had been some letters on the subject of 'Winterbourne Bishop' in his local weekly paper, and inviting me to join him in a cup of tea, he led me through quaint old rambling passages into his cool kitchen, whilst his wife, Blanche, obligingly took over his duties in the shop. He then produced newspaper cuttings setting out the viewpoints of various correspondents, and narrowing down the field to two villages which might fairly lay claim to the coveted title. His enthusiasm matched mine, and made me more determined than ever to solve the mystery which, incidentally, was a second reason for my journey into Wiltshire. I could not have met anyone more kindly, helpful and informative. Later on I learned that he once had plans to train at Kelham for the priesthood if only his health had been good enough, and I believe he realised that in him I had actually found the 'Winterbourne Bishop' I had been looking for!

Still 42 miles to go before reaching home, I rode off in the direction of Stonehenge, four miles away, promising to write after the holiday was over. This I did, enclosing a copy of *A Shepherd's Life,* and he most kindly sent me the treasured Hudson cuttings. So began a friendship which has never flagged from that day to this. Many a happy hour have I spent in the company of my good friends at Shrewton. Philip frequently acted as deputy organist at a number of local churches, including Winterbourne Stoke, and, of course, Shrewton, which W. H. Hudson once attended (see his *Afoot in England*). We met each year, at Salisbury, Andover, or his home, when, as often as not, we took our music to one or more of five country churches— Rollestone, Maddington, Shrewton, Orcheston St. George, and Orcheston St. Mary—all of which can be visited on a walk of under three miles, and then joined in organ and flute sessions, our theme song the minuet from Handel's *Berenice*. It was always a wonderful experience, and I look back on that first pilgrimage to Wiltshire as providential.

At Silchester House, close to the Bramley road, is a turret clock where four members of Father Time's family chime the quarters, he himself striking the hours on a fifth bell. Visitors are always fascinated to hear the 'Silchester Quarters' and to see the clockwork figures emerge. Mr. T. H. Hartley, who lived at Silchester House and died in 1966 at the age of 88, made this and other turret and church clocks.

One and a quarter miles from the village stores on the Common is the Early English church of Silchester, off a leafy lane which can be very muddy at times. In it is a beautifully-carved oak screen, and also stone coffin slabs, two aumbries, and two piscinas. Close by is a lonely farmhouse. A field on the way from the Common to the church was excavated at the turn of the century, and the remains of a Roman city (Calleva) and an early Christian church were unearthed. It was strange to see in later years, after the soil had been replaced in 1901 to a depth of several feet, a plough making furrows in the soil where, not so long before, an ancient city had been uncovered. The Roman walls are a mile and a half in circuit, and the city 120 acres in area.

Hudson once said that he knew quite a dozen villages on the Itchen, which he loved even more than the Test. In the summer of 1900 he resided for 10 weeks by the Itchen. Sir Edward and Lady Grey—to whom *Hampshire Days* is dedicated—were deeply interested in bird life and its preservation, and placed their summer cottage or fishing lodge on the outskirts of Itchen Abbas at his disposal. Six months after Hudson's death, the cottage was burnt to the ground.

In *Afoot in England,* Hudson records that he stayed at 'The Rookery' in Hurstbourne Tarrant, a farmhouse where,

80 years before, Cobbett enjoyed 'free quarters' with his friend, Joseph Blount. Hudson had been unceremoniously turned away from the *George and Dragon* by a woman who resented his inquiring for lodgings at a time when the 'shooting gents' occupied all the available accommodation. In this village he observed the cirl bunting, and visited Combe (on which he expatiates so delightfully), Crux Easton, the villages of the Clere country, and Wolverton. Inside Silchester church were Red Admiral butterflies which could not get out. In *Afoot in England,* he delivered a diatribe against thoughtless women there who wore plumes in their hats; yet, though his head was filled with thoughts of butterfly nets and ladders, he apparently did no more about releasing the innocent prisoners than they! My thoughts at this juncture inevitably turn to a man of different outlook, the late William Repton who, under the psedonym of 'C de B', wrote *A Naturalist and Immortality,* an 18-page monograph on Hudson's writings. He was a disciple of A. R. Orage, a Jainist, and had a deep appreciation of the Upanishads. It was always a pleasing prospect to take the road to Riseley, Swallowfield, and Arborfield—through which the slow-moving Loddon flows to meet the Thames—on my way to his home at Winnersh in Berkshire, and to listen to the refreshing talk of this wise and kindly man.

I was specially interested in Hudson's references to Crux Easton being a hilltop village, its church, erected in 1775, not much bigger than a cottage, and to the abundance of spindlewood trees on the lower slopes of the hill. There is a long barrow nearby which is of archaeological interest, and also one at Woodcott. It was at Seven Barrows, near Beacon Hill on the Earl of Caernarvon's estate, that the de Havilland brothers, Frank and Geoffrey (whose parents lived at Crux Easton) bought two sheds which Mr. Moore Brabazon, later Lord Brabazon, had erected, and where they carried out much of their pioneer flying from 1909 onwards.

I came to know those steep lanes round sparsely-populated
Crux Easton, Woodcott and Ashmansworth when visiting my
friend, the Rev. A. H. Bishope Lunn, who held all three
livings conjointly from 1940 to 1961, when he retired
from active service at the age of ninety. He died on
30 August 1967. The chalk masonry of Ashmansworth
church, the chancel separated from the nave by a wall on
which there are old paintings high up, with two squints
on either side of the narrow Norman arch, the little altar,
and the tub font, combine to emphasise the age-old
appearance of this 12th-century building. Cobbett stated
in *Rural Rides* that the wells at Ashmansworth were over
300 feet deep. After descending the slippery hangers in
the region of Hindhead, he concluded that Ashmansworth
lane was not the worst piece of road in the world! What
I still remember best, apart from the long, tiring climb to
Ashmansworth, the fascinating church and the good
company of the vicar, was the way my machine cleaved
the air on the homeward journey past the *Three-legged
Cross* inn at Crux Easton, and the lonely little church of
Woodcott with its Belgian carving, and an ancient yew
in its hallowed acre, the breeze lifting my flapping jacket so
high that my coat tails must have resembled wings as I
flew down to the plains heralding the approach to Whitchurch miles away.

Between 1903 and 1910, when Hudson was gathering
material for *A Shepherd's Life,* he stayed on a number of
occasions with Mr. William Easter at his handsome old
thatched farmhouse—Harris's Farm—in the main street of
Martin, which I visited in 1945. Mr. E. H. L. Poole, who
lived there, showed me over it: he it was who proved
almost conclusively in the *Times Literary Supplement*
(23 June 1945) that Martin and Hudson's 'Winterbourne Bishop' were one and the same place. I also
talked to Mr. Easter, who was then 73 and remembered
Hudson well.

By the side of the road was a winterbourne—a stream which dries up during the summer months—and in the churchyard a fine yew tree. Thus can Martin, like Orcheston St. Mary, lay claim, under Hudson's deliberately-veiled description, to being 'Winterbourne Bishop', his favourite village. With his eye for a beautiful landscape, Orcheston St. Mary, in Wiltshire, may qualify for the distinction, as there is a Bustard House not far away; but the fact that James Lawes ('Caleb Bawcombe' in *A Shepherd's Life*) was for most of his long life a shepherd at Martin, and that there was a Bustard Manor in East Martin, is strong support for Martin's claim to the honour.

Incidentally, Martin (like South Damerham) was transferred from Wiltshire to Hampshire in 1895, and both are in the diocese of Salisbury. Alongside the road from Salisbury to Blandford is a signpost which reads 'Ancient Church, Martin (Winterbourne Bishop)'. The Rev. Lovell Pocock, who left Martin early in 1967, mentioned in his farewell letter in the parish magazine its lovely and ancient church, saying he was proud to have lived in the village of William Lawes, 'a shepherd of the Wiltshire Downs', the village of W. H. Hudson's *A Shepherd's Life*, and would carry away memories of the Downs, the sheep, the attractive cottages, the bells, the floodlit church, the village school, the kindness of the Martin people, the Sunday worship and the happy determined congregation. William Lawes ('Isaac Bawcombe' in Hudson's book), who died in 1886, is buried in Martin churchyard.

Hudson first came to know Selborne in 1896, and the concluding chapter of his *Birds and Man* was the result. In *Hampshire Days* he mentions further visits in 1898, two in 1901, and a lengthier one in 1902. Sometimes he stayed at the *Queen's Arms* hotel there, but in 1898 he was accommodated at a cottage in Woolmer Forest—which occupies three-fifths of the extensive parish of Selborne— by a landlady, born in 1822, whose mother (1781–1867)

remembered Gilbert White, she being 12 years old when
he died. Her husband, John Newland, was the 'horn-blower'
or trumpeter of the 'Selborne mob' when they stormed
the local poorhouse in 1820: his grave lies between the
porch and the famous yew tree in the churchyard, and is
marked:

T
H E
T R U
M P E
T E
R

In 1902, Hudson made the discovery that even more
beautiful than the view from Selborne Hill was that from
Noar Hill (696 feet), and that a delightful walk separated
it from Wheatham Hill, the highest point (800 feet), from
which the many-hued foliage of the hanger country, Woolmer Forest, and the South Downs beyond Petersfield to
Sussex, could be seen to excellent advantage. He also
explored the villages of Blackmoor, Colemore, Empshott,
Farringdon, Froxfield, Greatham, Hartley Mauditt, Hawkley,
Kingsley, Newton Valence, Oakhanger, Priors Dean, Privett,
East and West Tisted, and the two Worldhams. The mere
recapitulation of their names brings back memories of a
unique part of Hampshire—the hanging woods with their
precipitous slopes, huge clumps of beeches clinging by
roots protruding from the surface to seemingly frail and
unstable chalk foundations. To see these forests swaying,
and to hear them in the turmoil of a gale are things to
remember: so also are the sheltered, sunken lanes connecting some of these villages.

Hudson and T. E. Lawrence admired each other's accomp-
lishments, though they probably only met at artists'
studios when one or other's portrait was being painted;
but Hudson deeply valued Edward Thomas as a friend,
one of the most lovable beings he had ever known. They
met occasionally in London at the 'Mont Blanc' restaurant

where other writers and poets gathered. A few days before
his sudden death in 1922, Hudson had undertaken to write
an introduction for a collection of Edward Thomas's essays
entitled *Cloud Castle and Other Papers*, and an unfinished
fragment was found among his papers: this, nevertheless,
formed the foreword to the book, which was published
later that year.

While I do not concede that Hudson's letters are as good
quality prose as his books, they are outspoken and revealing,
throw light on views expressed in the books, and help in
identifying places. They also breathe his freedom of spirit,
having been written from remote villages where he really
'lived', and complete our quintessential picture of the
full man.

22
Sir George Dewar
and the
Hampshire Highlands

SIR GEORGE DEWAR was not only a prolific author of books on Hampshire, but a fisherman and sportsman who wrote about angling and wild life in the north-west corner of the county which he immortalised in his vivid descriptions. I have always enjoyed his guide, *Hampshire with the Isle of Wight,* and the vignettes by J. A. Symington which adorn it. The *Victoria County History of Hampshire* describes practically every village and hamlet, yet a diminutive book by Sir George, *The Pageant of English Landscape,* contains the only prose which conjures up for me the pastoral scene of the Lyde and Loddon rivers within a two-mile radius of Andwell Mill. There is a high standard of writing in his *Wild Life in Hampshire Highlands* and *Life and Sport in Hampshire*; and *The South Country Trout Streams* is most interesting.

He spent a good deal of time at Doles House and Wood, up above Hurstbourne Tarrant, and dedicated *Wild Life in Hampshire Highlands* to his elder brother who lived there, where they so often roamed and shot together. He first resided at Enham Place, Knight's Enham; subsequently at Church Oakley and, after his wife's death, at Abbotts Ann. If he had mentioned place-names oftener in his other books, they would have appealed to me even more, for I prefer descriptions to be associated with places, rather than generalised. *The Glamour of the Earth,* and more particularly *The Faery Year,* are crammed with observations about bird and plant life. *The Leaning Spire* is a collection of short stories about country characters for the most part, first published in 1911. *Nature: The Supreme Problem* goes further afield than Hampshire, but there is a good chapter on 'Gilbert White, The Man', and references to Richard Jefferies. A footpath guide by R. H. Brown, entitled *Hampshire Highlands,* published in 1947, states that the National Trust bought Doles Wood and made it a bird sanctuary: that would have delighted W. H. Hudson. Incidentally, there are some ornithological observations by Sir George in Kelsall and Munn's *The Birds of Hampshire and the Isle of Wight.* He died in 1935 at the age of 72, and he and his wife are both buried at Knight's Enham.

The remote village of Combe is tucked away in a fold of valley in the opposite direction from the panoramic view of Berkshire from the gibbet on Inkpen Beacon. The present gibbet—the fourth—erected in 1950, commemorates the hanging on 7 March 1676 of a man and woman for the murder of two of her young children.

Inkpen Beacon, Walbury Beacon, Combe Hill, and Sheepless Hill, each nearly a thousand feet, are the highest hills in Berkshire.

In *Afoot in England,* Hudson tells of a Londoner who liked quiet places, but soon returned to town as he could not abide the 'tingling silence' of Combe. I can supplement what Hudson wrote about its blithe old vicar. He was the Rev. George Pearson, who died in 1910 at the age of 83, and had been inducted to the living in 1856. He was a man who preferred quietude and achieved serenity, yet he was not only steadfast, but outspoken. Three Sundays running he was locked out of his church, having rebuked his churchwardens for spending more on their persons on market days than they paid their ploughmen for a week's work. Years ago I remember copying out in a cottage at Combe a very full newspaper account of the old man's life during his 54 years' ministry there. His early days at Combe were times of prosperity and good prices for farming produce.

The population of the village rose to 400, but at the time
of his decease it had fallen to a quarter of that number,
and had at one time even been as low as fifty. The church
is ancient, and the font is believed to be Saxon.

I recollect how, on my earliest visit, some of the older
inhabitants maintained that Combe was in Hampshire,
pointing out that their postal address was Combe, Hants,
via Hungerford, Berks, yet it had been transferred for civil
purposes, to Berkshire in 1895. In 1910 the living was
annexed to the Wiltshire rectory of Buttermere in the
diocese of Salisbury, but in 1933 was united with Faccombe,
and returned soon afterwards to the Winchester diocese.
When the fourth volume of the *Victoria County History of
Hampshire* was published in 1911, Combe was included
in its survey of villages, thus upholding the contention of
the old inhabitants who clung tenaciously to their traditional
origin and heritage. Sir George Dewar has recorded that the
villagers of Hurstbourne Tarrant regarded Combe as 'quite
the end of the world'!

The ascent to Combe gibbet from the leafy village of
East Woodhay is a testing one for the cyclist, but the view
at the crest is the finest and most expansive in north
Hampshire. My itinerary usually included either the Clere
country (Kingsclere, Highclere, and Burghclere), and the
Hampshire highland villages of Combe, Linkenholt,
Faccombe, Netherton, and Vernham (or Vernhams) Dean;
or Ashmansworth, Crux Easton, Woodcott, Hurstbourne
Tarrant, Litchfield, and home through Whitchurch and
Basingstoke. Vernham Dean and Linkenholt have fine Tudor
manor houses, and their churches each have Norman doorways, that of Vernham Dean the more elaborate. In the
stonework surrounding two windows in Linkenholt church
are fossilised sea-urchins ('shepherds' crowns'). Like its
neighbour at Faccombe, Linkenholt retains the Norman
circular or tub font from an older building. Faccombe
also possesses some good windows, whilst those of East

Woodhay are even more interesting, some ancient, some modern. William of Wykeham and Bishop Ken were rectors here, and they are commemorated in one of the windows. At one time, bishops of Winchester had a palace at East Woodhay.

As I look back on visits made to this unforgettable country, I recall not only the incomparable views from Combe Hill and Inkpen Beacon of the Kennet valley—a patchwork quilt of many colours on the Berkshire plain below—but the bracing air and country scents of the isolated villages and hamlets, which compensated me for the energy expended in climbing those steep tracks leading to 'the hills of God'. To rest awhile and enjoy the prospect from the crown of the highest hill was in itself sufficient reward, but there was another treat in store—the cooling wind on those rapid descents from the highlands to the valley far below, when the wheels of my machine kept up their continuous hum with little slackening of the invigorating pace for miles.

23
The Jane Austen Country

THE COUNTRYSIDE between Oakley and Ashe, with Deane on its periphery and centring on Steventon (where Jane Austen was born in 1775), was the scene of her life for the first 25 of her 41 years. For the most part, it still remains unspoilt. The railway from Basingstoke to Winchester passes through Steventon, the nearest station on that line being Micheldever, four miles away. The most direct route by road to Steventon from Basingstoke is to turn left at the *Deane Gate* inn, about half-way to Whitchurch. In Jane Austen's day, the Basingstoke coach to Winchester picked up passengers at the *Wheatsheaf*, near Popham Lane; whilst the Basingstoke coach to Andover did so at the *Deane Gate*. The park flanking the Whitchurch road near Deane village and church, with the dense foliage of majestic trees shading the meadows, is as unchanging as was the quiet, uneventful life of the authoress. Measures taken to deal with possible invasion during the long years of the Napoleonic wars made little impact on so inland and pastoral a spot as Steventon, judging from her novels.

She seldom described in detail the Hampshire countryside at least from the point of making it identifiable, yet she loved it and must have been steeped in it. Seldom even in her letters does she refer specifically to place-names, but all her books were written in Hampshire. She had a natural talent, poise and self-control; was not a member of any literary circle, and it is astounding that she ploughed her lonely furrow without being beholden to others. Neither did she travel. Her special gifts were delineation of characters and motives, a gentle irony, and a faithful study of the manners of her time. Her writing was as exquisite and precise as her needlework: everything she did, whether it were singing or playing the piano or drawing, was characterised by those qualities. For her to have received the wholehearted commendation of Sir Walter Scott and Lord Macaulay in her short lifetime is sufficient evidence of her exceptional gifts as a writer. Later, Lord Tennyson went so far as to rank her next to Shakespeare.

Steventon old rectory was her birthplace, but it was demolished in 1826, nine years after her death, a pump in a field marking the site. She was one of eight children, and two of her brothers became admirals. Jane's father, the Rev. George Austen (1731–1805) coached students who resided at the rectory, and she received her education (which included French, Italian, Latin, and English literature) from him. He was actively rector of Steventon for 40 years and titularly for another four, but, strange to say, is not commemorated in the church. He was married at Walcot church, Bath, in 1764, and it was in the crypt of that church that he was buried 41 years later. His son, James, officially succeeded him as rector of Steventon in 1805, but had actually taken over the care of the parish four years earlier, when his father retired to live at Bath.

As one approaches Steventon church, the façade of the south wall presents an unusual appearance, for three windows form a triangle above the entrance door, and above them is the small, neat, crenellated tower, with a gentle steeple rising from its roof. One of the three bells dates from 1380. Inside the church there are 13th-century wall-paintings above the rood screen, and a tablet records that Jane Austen worshipped here: it was erected in 1936 by her great-grandniece, Emma Austen-Leigh, who, a year later, wrote a brochure, *Jane Austen and Steventon.*

Nowadays Steventon, still a quiet little village, is united with the adjoining parish of North Waltham and with

Dummer. Friends of the Austens lived in neighbouring
villages—the Lefroys at Ashe rectory (three members of the
family were incumbents there); Mr. Holder at Ashe Park,
the Bramston family at Oakley Hall, the Terrys at Dummer,
the Bigg-Withers at Manydown Park, the Harwoods at Deane
manor house, the Lloyds at Deane parsonage, the Portals
at Laverstoke and Freefolk, Lord Portsmouth at Hurstbourne
House, the Dorchesters at Kempshott, the Boltons at Hackwood, the Chutes at the Vyne, and the Digweeds at Steventon manor house, monuments to which family are in the
church. All of these places were within reach of each other
by carriage, and Jane Austen attended at least one Assembly
ball at Basingstoke, which she greatly enjoyed, though in
those days roads were muddy and in poor condition, many
literally cart tracks.

Stephen Terry, who was a year older than Jane and outlived her by 50 years, writes in *The Diaries of Dummer*
of her winning smile and ready wit. She and her sister,
Cassandra, always her confidante, sometimes stayed with
their friends, the Lloyds (mother and two daughters), after
they removed to Ibthorpe, a hamlet in the parish of
Hurstbourne Tarrant, on the death of the Rev. Mr. Lloyd.
Her brother James was married to one of the daughters
at Hurstbourne Tarrant church.

Jane Austen lived successively at Steventon (1775–1801),
Bath (1801–5), Southampton (1806–9), and Chawton
(1809–17). She died, probably of Addison's disease, at
8 College Street (a gracious Georgian house) in Winchester,
whither she had gone for medical treatment, and was buried
in Winchester cathedral near the tomb of its founder,
William of Wykeham. Her gravestone is a plain inscribed
slab on the floor of the north aisle. Her mother outlived her
by 10 years, dying at the age of 88; she and Cassandra
(1773–1834) are buried in Chawton churchyard.

The large red brick 'cottage' (a misnomer, for it is a
fair-sized house) at Chawton, just outside Alton, was the

home of all three for eight years, and during almost the whole of this period Jane worked continuously on her novels, all of which, except *Northanger Abbey*, which was published posthumously in 1818, were either written or revised in their final published form here. The house was purchased by Mr. T. Edward Carpenter, who conveyed it to the Jane Austen Society in memory of his soldier son, who was killed in Italy in 1944, aged twenty-two. It was opened in 1949 by the Duke of Wellington, president of the Society, as a museum, and contains such relics and mementoes as her writing desk, piano, furniture, a patchwork quilt, a handkerchief which she herself had worked, and a lock of her hair. There are also pictures and photographs. Only part of the house—her drawing room, in which she wrote or revised her books—is at present occupied by the museum. Her donkey cart is preserved in an outhouse.

Chawton church was destroyed by fire in 1871, and the new building is very graceful, with an imposing avenue of trees leading up to it. Inside the church is a 16th-century painting of the Crucifixion. Nearby, in the park, is Chawton House, in which a brother of the novelist (who changed his name to Knight) and his descendants used to live.

Jane Austen's reputation and popularity have increased with the passage of time, and during 20 years' attendance at selection committee interviews of prospective medical students at a university I have been impressed by the number of young women applicants who expressed a great admiration for her works.

24
Round and about Selborne

SELBORNE, named after the Bourne which flows through the village, is five miles from Alton and from Liss. The road from Alton is mostly though open country, whereas the approach from Liss is more leafy and well wooded, along narrow hollow lanes which are apt to drip water as a result of rainfall from the ridges of majestic beeches which hang on to the surface of the steep hills rather than take root deeply in the soil. The huge hangers (or hanging woods) afford a magnificent shelter—a spectacle in itself—to the large scattered village in the valley. Selborne, a place of great natural beauty rich in flora and wild life, is famous for its association with the immortal Gilbert White (1720-93). Thatched cottages are numerous, and many of the landmarks mentioned in *The Natural History of Selborne* (published in 1789) can still be seen—'The Wakes' (the large house near the church, which he inherited and in which he spent over half his life—now a museum), the Sundial, the Zigzag (the diagonal climb by easy stages to the top of the 300-foot hanger), the Wishing Stone, the Long Lythe, the Short Lythe, Wood Lane, Gracious Street, Selborne Street (which runs practically parallel with the hanger), and the Plestor (the children's playground outside the churchyard). The water supply which flows from a lion's mouth into a trough in the village street, bearing the date 1894, is a memorial to him.

Sir George Dewar wrote of Selborne's 'sylvan loveliness', and W. H. Hudson, a bird watcher and nature lover after White's own heart, visited it at various times. The latter's

Naturalist's Calendar is not so well-known as *The Natural History,* but is equally factual. White was a prolific letter-writer, especially when his correspondents were two such kindred spirits as Pennant and Daines Barrington. The eldest of 11 children, and a bachelor all his life, he was educated at Basingstoke Grammar School under the Rev. Thomas Warton, vicar of Basingstoke, and professor of poetry at the University of Oxford, who had two famous sons—Joseph, headmaster of Winchester College from 1766 to 1793, and Thomas, also professor of poetry at Oxford, poet laureate and author of *The History of English Poetry.*

Gilbert White never became vicar of his native Selborne, but his grandfather, who bore the same names, held that office for 46 years. Apart from the time when he was junior proctor at Oriel College, Oxford (of which he was a Fellow for 50 years), he was successively curate at the Hampshire villages of Swarraton, Selborne, Durley, Faringdon, and Selborne (for a second time). He was a plain, bewigged, unpretentious man, shy and retiring, of small stature, but of giant repute. A little book has even been written about his tortoise, 'Timothy'! It would be presumptuous to comment on his *Natural History of Selborne*: a bibliography larger than the present volume was compiled years ago about his few writings, and I will content myself by remarking that several of these are very desirable by reason of their notes, format and illustrations. Memorials to Gilbert White and several members of his family may be seen in Selborne church, one of which records that his forebears hailed from the ancient family of that name at South Warnborough. His little headstone in the churchyard, close to the chancel, modestly reads: G.W./26 June/1793. In the south aisle of the church is a very appropriate stained glass window showing St. Francis preaching to the birds, 82 species of which are portrayed. The building is a mixture of Traditional Norman and Early English styles of architecture; the font is old, and the tower plain.

The beautiful village of Newton Valence, beyond Selborne hanger, is reached from Gracious Street. It has a 13th-century towered church, and a tub font, and in the churchyard is a noble yew like those at nearby Selborne, Priors Dean, Farringdon, and Liss (St. Peter's). The large village pond, like that at Lasham, is fed by underground springs, and is said never to run dry, which is far from being the case with some other Hampshire village ponds I know. As Newton is high up, excellent views of the surrounding countryside, including Priors Dean and Colemore, can be seen.

The small parish of Empshott is also on high ground, and may be approached from Selborne or from Hawkley. The church of the Holy Rood lies above leafy hedges in a lane off the Alton road. Its font is dated 1190, its chancel is 13th century, and there is a rood screen. The shingle-spired belfry is vertically panelled with timber and glass.

Hawkley Hanger, much beloved by White, Cobbett and Hudson for its extensive views, is as famous as that of Selborne. White has related how a large slice of the hanger collapsed in 1774, leaving a cliff as naked as the white face of a village chalk pit. For me the highlight of *Rural Rides* is Cobbett's account of his ride—or rather his walk—down Hawkley Hanger, which is in the best descriptive and conversational style of George Borrow. He, like Borrow and White, was a lover of horses, and a seasoned rider. I can visualise all three mounted on horses of varying stature—Borrow, a magnificent, imperious, fearless figure on his Andalusian stallion; Cobbett, the rugged, breezy, forthright critic of the agriculture and national economy of his day, nearly as tall, spending long days in the saddle of his sturdy cob; and lastly, White, a lowly five feet three inches, all eyes and ears, travelling to visit friends, on a pony of proportionate size. He infinitely preferred this to the stagecoach, which always induced travel sickness in him.

The old mill at Hawkley is now a private residence, and with the waters of the Rother in the foreground still holds beauty for lovers of erstwhile watermills. The hollow lanes which run up and down between fields on a higher level often result in muddy roads, but with pleasantly overhanging trees and hedges, they can best be enjoyed from an open car. Though Hawkley church dates only from 1861, there are old features, such as the 12th-century font and a 14th-century alabaster panel of the Betrayal. The building is unusual in that it has a high gabled tower crowned by a spire, reminding one of the similarly-shaped, but smaller towers of the Saxon church of Sompting in Sussex, and the 12th-century church of Newnham, in Hampshire. It would be hard to match the hanger country round Hawkley, Empshott, Selborne, Newton Valence, Froxfield (including Stoner Hill), and Steep.

The river Rother rises at Greatham, where there are the ruins of a 13th-century church, and divides the residential villages of East and West Liss. The parish church of St. Peter in ancient West Liss has a heavy spire on its Norman tower, and Woolmer Forest enhances the landscape. Not far from Greatham is the quiet village of Bramshott on the river Wey, within easy access of Waggoners Wells and Hammer Pond, beauty spots noted for their woodland glades and lakes: the former was purchased for the nation in 1919 in memory of Sir Robert Hunter, and in recognition of his work for the preservation of public open spaces. Bramshott church, with its wooden steeple, is in a pastoral setting on rising ground, and is a combination of several old styles dating from 1220. It has been completely rebuilt, but has preserved its 14th-century octagonal font. Grayshott parish is 600 feet above sea level, and its modern church, like that of Greatham, is also spired.

A beautiful village in the vicinity, east of Woolmer Forest, is Headley, close to the Sussex and Surrey borders: its church has been rebuilt, but the tower has been standing for six centuries. Liphook is famous for its *Royal Anchor* hotel, a coaching inn for 500 years, which is shaded by a fine old chestnut. Pepys knew it well, and Lord Nelson also stayed there. The wild windswept grandeur of the gorse-clad heaths round about has been admirably caught in some of Wilfrid Ball's paintings.

In 1966 I took the opportunity of rediscovering Steep church, late Norman, but much restored, the wooden bell-turret of which reminded me very much of that of Weyhill. It is in a quiet country lane, off which large sand-pits were being extensively excavated. At Sheet, not far away, the handsome spire of the church (1869) and a splendid specimen of an old English watermill complete with overshot wheel—both of which stand near the busy Portsmouth road at the approach to Petersfield from the direction of Greatham—leave a vivid impression of the beautiful village.

For old times' sake, remembering one glorious springtime when Easter was late, and there was a profusion of pink prunus blossom around Steep, I returned to Basingstoke by the winding road up tree-shaded Stoner Hill (which has been called 'little Switzerland')—in the parish of Froxfield. Here there are two 19th-century churches of pleasing appearance (St. Peter on the Green and the parish church of St. Peter). The latter has an octagonal spire which gives the impression of being much older: arches from a former church on Froxfield Green are incorporated in the structure.

I took the opportunity of revisiting Priors Dean and Hawkley, passing a rough country road leading to Oakhanger, a hamlet beloved by Hudson. Colemore church's dedication to St. Peter-in-chains is unusual for a country parish: its thick walls are of flint and rubble, and its 12th-century font of Purbeck marble. There is a Gothic chancel screen, rood loft stairs, and an ancient bell (1420). Before joining the Gosport road, I followed the old familiar narrow country lane to East Tisted. The most striking characteristics about its church, rebuilt in 1846, are its impressive tower, parts of which are older, its south doorway being 14th-century work. Inside are numerous ancient monuments to the Norton family, one of which is an early 16th-century effigy of Richard and Elizabeth Norton, with their 17 children, all kneeling, which, however, is outshone by that of Sir Thomas Whyte and his wife Agnes, with their 19 children, in South Warnborough church.

25
Itchen Abbas
and Viscount Grey

THE NEAREST WAY from Basingstoke to Itchen Abbas
is by the Winchester highway to King's Worthy, where
a countrified road leads to Alresford. After the climb up
Kempshott Hill, it is a relief to leave the busy main road,
and disappear up quiet hilly side lanes to the downland
parishes of Dummer and North Waltham.

On the left, at the back of beyond, is Dummer, a peaceful
old-world village which consists of manorial houses, farmhouses and cottages in the shady heart of the country, high
up on the downs. George Budd founded the celebrated
flock of Hampshire Down sheep. The name of the village
is also that of an old family who lived here for centuries.
In the Regency years, life of local high society was unbridled,
and acquired an unsavoury reputation because of the excesses
of the Prince of Wales (later George IV), who lived for
hunting at Kempshott House, which he occupied from 1788
to 1795. Dummer has long been noted for its large houses—
Dummer House, Dummer Grange, and Kempshott House—
and for the large wells belonging to them, some of which
were 360 feet deep: a fourth can still be seen in the village
street. The wooden bell-tower of the old church peeps out
from a wooded corner close to a picturesque manor house
at a junction of country lanes. A glance at the interior will
be sufficient to make the visitor stay and look around.
The old-fashioned gallery with a balustrade in front, under
the belfry, probably accommodated the minstrels in the days
before harmoniums and organs created an innovation from
which local musicianship never fully recovered. The edifice

is mentioned in Domesday Book, but the nave is 12th-century and the chancel a century later. The heavy posts supporting the bell-tower, and the preponderance of timber throughout, impart a sense of solidness and cosiness as well as of antiquity to a building whose dark interior prior to 1961 was lit by oil lamps. The arched, panelled 'ceiling over the rood' is most unusual; the pulpit is 15th-century.

George Whitefield (1714-70)—a brilliant preacher, a leader of the Calvinistic Methodists, and a lifelong friend of John Wesley, despite their doctrinal differences—was curate here for a few weeks, and in that short time endeared himself to the villagers so much that they wept when he left. Wesley preached at Dummer in 1739, and frequently at Basingstoke between 1739 and 1763. It was appropriate that the poet, Sir John Betjeman, who has an eye for individuality and for the beautiful, should have introduced this ancient church to television viewers in 1960 to represent 'D' in his alphabetical series of talks illustrating differing styles of ecclesiastical architecture in this country. He did a similar programme about St. Cross in the summer of 1966.

On the right of the Winchester road is North Waltham village, out of sight and sound of the noisy highway, on the far side of a hill, and reached by straggling lanes from the A30 on which lie the *Sun* and *Wheatsheaf* inns on the outskirts of Dummer and North Waltham parishes respectively. Although Jane Austen lived in the adjoining village of Steventon, North Walham is not specifically alluded to in her letters or in her works, though muddy Popham is referred to in the former: rather is it from memorials in Steventon, North Waltham, Dummer, Deane and Ashe churches to members of families she knew, or from the reminiscences of a sportsman, Stephen Terry (1774-1867), *The Diaries of Dummer,* edited by A. M. W. Stirling, and published in 1934, that we can piece together a picture of life in those days.

In December 1965, Harvey Bolton of North Waltham, probably Hampshire's last carrier, gave up the family business with which he had been actively associated since 1897. The hooded vans of the carriers, which were not unlike covered wagons, provided the only public transport to many such outlying villages before omnibus services were introduced between 1916 and 1923.

The story of North Waltham has been well told in Mr L. F. Hewey's interesting little book issued in 1966 on the occasion of the centenary of the rebuilt church, whose shingle spire can be seen from the village green.

Just past the *Wheatsheaf,* Popham lane branches off from the Winchester road, over Popham Beacon (on which there are groups of tumuli) to Andover, Stockbridge, and Salisbury. Beyond Popham, on the Winchester road, lies Woodmancote (a lovely name), off the beaten track: I shall always remember it best as it was when my young friend, Jack White, and his team-mates were busily engaged from sunrise to sundown steam-ploughing or scarifying its fields in 1915. We both went on Army service not long afterwards, and were not to meet again until the summer of 1920, the year before he was killed.

Outside Stratton Park, whose lodges mark the extent of its boundaries, lanes of beeches lead to Micheldever and Stoke Charity. A side road opposite runs off to East Stratton village and war memorial (on the site of the old church demolished in 1878): the new edifice was built 10 years later. Its shingle spire was re-sheathed in 1966. Stratton House was the home of the Baring family (Earls of Northbrook) until 1930, when it became a girls' school: Northbrook and West Stratton are hamlets near Micheldever. Further on is the *Lunways* inn, an old posting house and the only tavern between the *Wheatsheaf* (near Popham lane) and King's Worthy, whose village and flint and rubble church lie between the direct road to the city and the Winchester by-pass, begun in 1935 and opened in 1940. Here the fields

are low-lying and well watered by the Itchen. Swaying
clumps of tall buddleia lend beauty and fragrance to the
chalk embankments.

The little church of Headbourne Worthy on the quiet
city road is one of the oldest in Hampshire, and lies so low
behind hedges that it can easily be missed. Its Saxon crucifix,
pilasters, long and short work, and small arched doorway,
quietly proclaim its ancient origin.

The road to Alresford from King's Worthy winds through
Abbot's Worthy—where there is a pretty mill—and beyond
the water-meadows of Martyr Worthy is the village church,
and that of Easton with its tent-like tower. Further on is
Itchen Abbas church, rebuilt in 1863, which retains its
Norman chancel arch and west doorway. Outside the village
and close to the river Itchen stood Sir Edward (later
Viscount) Grey's fishing cottage. It was here that W. H.
Hudson and other friends of the Greys were occasionally
invited to stay. One such summer is mentioned in *Hampshire
Days,* and in the descriptive, but nostalgic, prose of Sir
George Trevelyan's *Grey of Fallodon.* Unfortunately, Lord
Grey's diaries—the *Cottage Book* (which was privately
printed) and the *Fallodon Green Book*—were not available
in a wider circulation: quotations from these private diaries
in the appendices of Sir George's biography of Grey whet
the appetite for the complete record. The death of Lord
Grey's first wife, Dorothy, in 1906, and later the gradual loss
of his sight at about the time when his cottage was burnt
to the ground in February 1923, were a great grief to him.
The fire also enveloped the bird sanctuary in the old chalk
pit. His Fallodon house had met with a similar fate in 1917,
but had been rebuilt. The little chalk pit in the bird sanctuary precinct, together with 'Grey's bridge'—a plank bridge
with a single rail, just above river level—and the lane
approach from Gages Close on the Alresford road had
changed little when I last saw them, and the hum of insects
and the songs of many birds were a reminder of the old

days. The rector of Itchen Abbas informs me—1967—that the chalk pit still exists, but that the little plank bridge over the Itchen has been replaced by one of concrete. Lord Grey was not only a great nature-lover, but a fine writer about bird life, angling and chalk streams, to witness, *The Charm of Birds, Fly Fishing* and *Fallodon Papers*. His love for angling began when, as a Wykehamist, he fished the Itchen at Winchester.

In 1961, his private railway station at Fallodon in Northumberland, derelict and overgrown, with its name just discernible on the platform, on the edge of the adjoining woods, was a saddening sight.

An attractively-illustrated monograph by Seton Gordon, *Edward Grey of Fallodon and his Birds,* is a graceful tribute to a happy side of the great politician's life and the pleasure he derived from his beloved birds which became quite tame in his presence. Although it was pathetic that his life should have been overshadowed in his later years, anyone who knows of his idyllic companionship with his first wife, and, much later, with his second wife, that very gracious Wiltshire lady who was formerly Pamela, Lady Glenconner, will realise that nevertheless, life conferred on him great boons. Both women had beauty, character and charm. You have only to read Lady Glenconner's book, *Edward Wyndham Tennant* (1897–1916), to realise what an adorable personality she possessed, and her kindly nature is also revealed in her other books, *Shepherds' Crowns, The Sayings of the Children, Village Notes,* and an anthology, *The White Wallet.* She had outstanding qualities as a wife, mother, lover of nature, and as a writer of both prose and poetry. She was also deeply interested in symbolism, mysticism and immortality, and in this respect resembled the wife of another enthusiastic angler, Gwen Plunket Greene. She died in 1928, Lord Grey surviving her by five years.

Whenever I am in Salisbury—even on a fleeting visit—I make time to pause before the mural tablet to the memory of

Lieutenant Edward Wyndham Tennant just inside the door of the north porch. The sculptured likeness in marble is a reproduction from the painting by Sargent of this young soldier who was as handsome of heart as of face: the inscription tells of his spirit of friendship and service to his men in the trenches in France. He was also commemorated on a village hall at Amesbury, close to the Avon bridge, between the wars.

Itchen Abbas, Itchen Stoke and Ovington churches were rebuilt only a century ago. That at Itchen Stoke stands on a slight eminence above the road, and was built in the Sainte Chapelle style with a large rose window and numerous lancet windows, its only antiquity an early 16th-century brass which probably came from the old church in the grounds of Itchen Stoke House. In this parish is the site of a former village—Abbotstone—whose large farm I found to be secluded, self-contained and most picturesque: close to one of the barns was a waterwheel. Near to Itchen Stoke I followed paths by the river, or narrow roads over tiny bridges in the park, and remember photographing the old watermill and mill-house at Ovington and the spired church, which has a late Norman font of Purbeck marble.

The crystal-clear Itchen beautifies all the villages through which it flows, and particularly Avington Park in a wood of which is the Gospel Oak under which St. Augustine is reputed to have preached. On the edge of Avington Park is the red-brick towered Georgian church with old-fashioned box pews, a gallery and a double-decker pulpit with a domed tester which has a figure of a pheasant on top—all in wood—and high windows. It is an excellent example of the architecture of the period, but has little appeal for me because of its boxed-in appearance. There is an old barrel organ in the church, in which practically everything dates from 1771.

Charles II once resided at Avington House, in front of which there is a large lake. A pretty sight years ago was the roofed well alongside a quiet road. Cobbett in his time thought highly of the beauty of Avington village, and so did Hudson.

26
Mapledurwell to Alresford

IF ONE WISHED to avoid the heavy traffic of the London road—the A30—at Hatch, and the Basingstoke by-pass in journeying to Cliddesden, a pleasant and little-frequented way could be taken through country lanes from Mapledurwell to Polecat Corner, where Hackwood Farm lies well back from the winding road to Tunworth.

Deer may sometimes be seen in Hackwood Park, but they usually keep their distance. Further on is a chalk cliff alongside the road where a brick bridge, built in 1821, links the forest on either side. Tall avenues of trees in the park, Paradise Walk and 'the Cathedral' are matched by the sylvan beauty of Springwood. Descending to Hackwood lodge and crossing the Alton road, it is not far to the *Golden Lion* inn, and from there runs the Alresford road to Cliddesden, whose pretty cottages and *Three Horseshoes* inn, hidden in a quiet cul-de-sac, retain their old-world atmosphere. Cliddesden station, outside the village on the road to Ellisfield, has been derelict for 40 years, like the other two stations—Herriard, and Bentworth and Lasham—on the line between Basingstoke and Alton. Cliddesden church has an open gable-end bell turret. The north wall doorway is all that remains of the ancient edifice mentioned in Domesday Book. It stands near the village pond at the foot of Farleigh Hill, which was formerly used for motor-cycle rallies. The steepness and awkward curves at its worst gradients must have presented problems for the contenders, and as for the pedal cyclist, woe betide him if his brakes failed on the descent from the crest of the hill, for it always had the reputation of being the most treacherous for miles around. Farleigh Hill commands the finest sweep of view of the north Hampshire countryside, as far afield as Berkshire, but to see this entails a 300-foot climb from Cliddesden.

Farleigh Wallop is a scattered parish, and its church, of flint and stone, is reached by a green lane and stands in a lonely, peaceful place, for the fenced-off churchyard is in the middle of a field. It was rebuilt over 200 years ago, and contains many memorials to the Wallop family (later Earls of Portsmouth) who formerly lived at Farleigh House. It is cruciform and contains many heraldic monuments, floor slabs and mural tablets. Fairly recently, local craftsmanship has provided a reading desk here, also pews and panelling at Dummer church. The battlemented tower was built in 1873, and as it is on a site as high as Farleigh Hill, nearly 700 feet above sea level, it is more open to the winds of heaven than any Hampshire church I know, including its namesake, Farley Chamberlayne on Farley Hill.

Two miles off the Alresford road is Ellisfield, nearly as high up as Farleigh. Whichever way it is approached—whether by the hilly lane from Cliddesden; by the wooded route from Herriard; or from Farleigh, by cottages bearing the curious name of Bedlam Bottom—it presents a pleasing picture. With its pond, its narrow, winding, leafy lanes and its splendid views of the countryside, the village has a prosperous air. The church, much restored less than 100 years ago, contains portions of an older building, and a handsome altar and east window.

Returning to the main road, I am reminded of a scorching hot day in the rainless summer of 1921. I had walked my bicycle up Farleigh Hill—the highest in the district, higher than its neighbour, Kempshott Hill, and much harder to climb—and was admiring the view, when I got into conversation with a young fellow who had an intelligent face and friendly manner. He was strolling behind a herd of cows on their way home to the farm, but was obviously well-informed, and had a mind of his own. We fell to talking about townspeople and country folk. He thought that the town boy was one up when it came to book knowledge and life in towns, but that what the country lad lacked in that respect was compensated for by his special knowledge of the country and by a natural cunning. A countryman's life in those days was often very secluded. Consequently, he was thrown on his own resources, and acquired a practical knowledge of life and work from his own observations and experience. What he knew he acquired at first hand by experience, rather than at second hand from books.

From the wooded country on the plateau, I descended to Nutley, whose 19th-century flint church, with an open gable-end belfry, was demolished in 1955 owing to its dangerous state. The small parish could not raise sufficient money to repair it, and so worshippers have to go to Preston Candover for church services. On through another hamlet, Axford, to the river country of the large residential village of Preston Candover, where there are many attractive old cottages and a fine avenue of tall luxuriant trees. The spired church built about 80 years ago, after the old one was burnt down, has a Saxon stone coffin over its doorway. A short harvest-home service is held annually in the saloon bar of the *Purefoy Arms* inn. Mummers perform at Christmastide in the village, which is a focal point for lonely parishes such as Bradley and Wield.

The country is more open and less wooded at Chilton Candover, but there is an avenue of yew trees, three-quarters of a mile long, said to have been planted in 1200. In a meadow on the far side of the road is the 'buried church', underneath the open stone floor of a church demolished in 1876. It had become completely overgrown, and almost forgotten until 1928, when it was unearthed, revealing a vaulted flint crypt dating from the 12th century, measuring 14 yards by four, with an apse and round chancel arch, and containing an altar, a font of the same date, and stone coffins from a century later. Steps lead down to it, and there is a solid timbered door inside the entrance. The interior is dark but well preserved. It was regarded as a 'seventh wonder' at the time when it was rediscovered, fantastic articles appearing in the local press, some even suggesting that it was originally a Mithraic temple! It is most unusual for crypts to be built under country churches. Black's *Tourist's Guide through Hampshire* (1859) states that Chilton Candover's small ancient church was then in good repair, but Kelly's *County Topography of Hampshire* (1875) records that it was in ruins and that services were performed at Brown Candover. Several other local churches were pulled down not many years before—Northington in 1838, Brown Candover in 1844, and Swarraton in 1848 or 1851. The 'buried church' at Chilton Candover could well be used for worship if it were ventilated, lit and heated, but it could only accommodate a small congregation. A service was held in 1966 above the crypt in the open air, when a large number of people attended.

Brown Candover, further down the road to Alresford, lies in a pleasant, well-watered district. Its spired church, built in 1845, by the first Lord Ashburton, houses relics from the old church at Chilton Candover, an altar from Northington's old church, and a well-preserved brass (1520) of a lady and gentleman arm-in-arm. Many Hampshire worthies are similarly commemorated in its churches—e.g., Bramley, Bramshott, Dogmersfield, Havant, Kimpton, King's Somborne, Mapledurwell, Monxton, Nether Wallop, Odiham, St. Cross, Thruxton, West Tytherley, and Whitchurch.

Between Brown Candover and Alresford the land rises. I was much surprised when I first saw the handsome tower of Northington church crowning the slope of the hill. It is a fine building, and was completed posthumously in 1889 at the expense of the fourth Lord Ashburton, replacing the

church demolished 50 years earlier. Nevertheless it struck
me as most unusual to find such a splendid edifice in a
country village of the size of Northington, and reminded
me of another large modern church—Privett—whose steeple
rising to a height of 160 feet or more, appears incongruous
in its country surroundings, and which W. H. Hudson found
jarring. Not all modern churches struck a discordant note,
however, for he was captivated by the handsome tower
of Blackmoor church, set among the conifers of Woolmer
Forest, not far from Selborne.

An old painting of Swarraton church, with its squat nave,
a lofty spire surmounting its pinnacled tower, shows how
charming it looked among tall trees and water-meadows.
When it was pulled down no new building took its place,
but a stone cross in the old churchyard commemorates
the site. Gilbert White was once curate-in-charge here, and
another great lover of the country, Edward Thomas, described this area—Swarraton, Abbotstone and Godsfield—as
'the airy highlands of Hampshire'.

Old Alresford was noted for its pond, a reservoir
constructed in 1200 by Godfrey de Lucy, Bishop of
Winchester from 1189 to 1204, between the rivers Alre
and Itchen, to make Alresford accessible by water, and
to serve as a trade artery joining the Winchester—Southampton
section of the river, which is navigable for 14 miles—an
ambitious project for those early days, which was in a
measure successful. It is now less than a third of its
former size of 200 acres. Old Alresford church was
rebuilt in 1753, and its massive tower added 16 years
later. Admiral Lord Rodney is buried in the churchyard.
The cottage gardens and river scenery combine to make
the village beautiful. In 1965, celebrations were held commemorating the founding of the Mothers' Union by Mary
Sumner (1828-1921). Her husband, the Rev. George H.
Sumner, was rector here for 34 years, and later became
Bishop of Guildford.

Alresford (pronounced Awlsford) or New Alresford, is a quiet little town with a handsome tree-lined Broad Street, on one of whose period houses is a plaque stating that Mary Russell Mitford was born there in 1787. Most editions of her book—*Our Village*—about Three Mile Cross, near Reading, do not contain all of her *Sketches of Village Life,* but in 1947, a fuller edition was published, with all 30 of the essays about her Berkshire village and the district, illustrated with some excellent wood engravings by Joan Hassall, including pictures of 'The Mitford' (Miss Mitford's home at Three Mile Cross), and of the mill at Swallowfield. The authoress died in 1855, and was buried in Swallowfield churchyard, close to the Blackwater river, which rises near Aldershot.

Alresford is shaped like a T-square, the road on which stands the parish church forming the top, and Broad Street the vertical stroke. Fairs take place here, and it is a jolly spectacle when the merry-go-rounds and booths monopolise the sloping grass verges on Fair-day in October. The Norman tower of the church looking up the street seems to keep watch over the activity and frivolity going on in front of the quaint houses and antique shops, and the unaccustomed volume of traffic and business in the little town imparts an air of gaity, variety and movement to the scene.

Neville Chamberlain enjoyed angling in this district. Alresford and the surrounding villages are noted primarily for watercress. 'Creeses'—as they are sometimes called—are grown all over north Hampshire, in the Basingstoke district (Mapledurwell, Andwell, Old Basing, and Greywell); between Whitchurch and Andover (Hurstbourne Priors and St. Mary Bourne): and at Abbotts Ann, where rivers abound. Judging by the size of the cress beds round Old Alresford, Bighton, Cheriton, Hinton Ampner, and Tichborne, this would appear to be the largest area in the county in which watercress is intensively cultivated. Skill, experience and hard work are necessary for growing, cleansing and planting watercress, and in its cutting and bunching.

All river villages have their own special attractions. At Easton, for example, there is a fishing lodge—Fulling Mill Cottage—with whitewashed and thatched buildings at its rear, and a low footbridge just skimming the Itchen in whose tranquil waters the colourful scene is reflected. There is much of interest in the old church at Easton, which has two Norman doorways: one (the south) is curiously pillared and arched in an elaborately chevroned manner. To me its unique characteristics were the quaint roof formation of its tower and the pleasing effect of the slatted windows poking out on all sides from its steeple. There is also a rood screen staircase and a doorway to the rood loft, a 13th-century piscina, a vaulted chancel with horseshoe arch, and a memorial to Dame Agatha Barlow, once a nun, whose husband became a bishop: their five daughters all married bishops, and their son was for 48 years rector of this parish. Sir Philip Sidney, that great-hearted Elizabethan poet and scholar, was lord of the manor of Easton.

I must mention several other villages in the Alresford area. Hinton Ampner, high up on a hill, has a church with Saxon remains—two pilaster strips and long and short work— two Norman doorways, one of which may be Saxon, and a double piscina. There is a Roman villa near the village, and a former rector, Canon Milner, excavated a long barrow (75 feet in length) dating from the Neolithic Age. Kilmeston church was restored three times in 33 years during the last century, and in the process was enlarged and altered, but it contains a 13th-century font, also a piscina. Beauworth— with which Kilmeston is united—has a church, built in 1838, which, like its neighbour, is without a separate chancel. In 1833, some boys discovered 6,500 coins in mint condition at Beauworth. At the *Fox and Hounds* inn on Millbarrow Down is a deep well worked by a treadmill, and a recent innovation is a thatched petrol pump!

Bramdean, which was of importance in Saxon days, and Milo the Porter, seneschal of the royal castle of Winchester, who held Woodcote manor from William the Conqueror, are mentioned in Domesday Book. Woodcote manor is the subject of a novel, *The Old Manor House,* by the 18th-century writer, Charlotte Smith (1749–1806), of Brookwood House, equidistant from Bramdean and Hinton Ampner. Close to Woodcote House (a mansion among woodlands, built in 1611), a Roman villa with tessellated pavements and a collection of coins were discovered in 1823, after a shepherd encountered obstruction near the surface of the ground when folding his flock.

I had long admired in photographs the little parish church of Bramdean before I actually saw it, and found the reality even more charming in its woodland surroundings. Its chancel dates from 1170, and the slim, tapering bell-cote, and broad south transept added in 1853, seemed to me exquisite. Hinton Marsh (Hinton Ampner) is strictly speaking the permanent source of the Itchen, supplying the watercress beds there, but water-courses from the higher ground near Kilmeston and at Bramdean—where the road is sometimes flooded—augment the flow of the river in wet seasons. The miniature Stonehenge alongside the road is a collection of sarsen stones assembled by a local resident in 1861, and has no special or historic significance. On Bramdean Common is the 'Gypsies' Church', a little building called the Church-in-the-Woods, which can be seen from the road when the trees are bare. It was erected in 1883: an endowment keeps it going and in repair, and services are held in the afternoon on alternate Sundays from June to October, but gypsies have long been forbidden to camp on the Common, and, therefore, there are no more gypsy congregations. The people who do attend are a few from the surrounding districts, and some who come from places further afield. Every year there is a harvest service, which is generally crowded.

Fifteen hundred men perished in the battle of Cheriton (or 'Alresford Fight') in 1644, many of whom were buried in Cheriton churchyard, in which there is a grove of yew trees. As the 13th-century church is on an eminence, the line of the flat tower against the sky is memorable: gaunt and unrelieved, it looks as if it realised the folly of men.

As famous as any Hampshire village is Tichborne, a name which probably derives from De-Itchen-bourne. Its church has Saxon features (the chancel and the pillars of the nave), a Norman font, and a 15th-century door and staircase leading to the rood loft. The brick tower dates from 1703. The Roman Catholic Tichborne family have since the Reformation used the north aisle as a chapel and mausoleum.

The Tichborne Dole commemorates a charity endowed in Henry II's reign, when Lady Tichborne, who was said to be on her death-bed, was promised by her husband as much land as she could crawl round while a torch burned, for the benefit of the local poor: she won 23 acres! In carrying out the bequest, which takes the form of flour, a large bin and sacks of flour are placed in front of Tichborne Hall each Lady Day, and after being blessed by the family's chaplain, are given away.

Another *cause célèbre,* the lengthy Tichborne Trial, took place in the early 1870s, when there was an unsuccessful attempt to alter the family succession. That the court assessed the claimant's motives correctly and that justice was done, is shown by an extract from his notebook: 'Some men has plenty money and no brains, and some has plenty brains and no money. Surely men with plenty money and no brains were made for men with plenty brains and no money'. Eleven years after his release from penal servitude, Arthur Orton (the claimant) admitted his identity, and three years later, in 1898, he died in poverty.

Exton, Soberton, Beauworth, and Kilmeston were all well known to Cobbett, and in his references in *Rural Rides* to 'the hard country round about Tichborne' and to 'the little hard iron village of Cheriton', he was presumably thinking of the two subjects always uppermost in his mind at that time—the soil and the state of agriculture.

27
Basingstoke to Whitchurch

FROM THORNYCROFT'S engineering works, on the out-skirts of Basingstoke before the First World War, the two miles to Worting are now a continuous suburb of the town: indeed a road sign indicates that Worting is now part of Basingstoke. Industry has laid a hand on the village near the well-lit tunnel over which runs the railway line to Win-chester. The pretty little church of St. Thomas à Becket, with a slim spired bell-cote, lying snugly back from the Whitchurch road, is not old.

Traveller's joy entwines itself round the hedges on the way to Newfound. When I recently passed through this hamlet, which is in Wootton St. Lawrence parish, there were fewer thatched cottages than there had been a few years ago, and the avenue of beeches which used to afford welcome shade or shelter had been thinned out. Cornfields and meadows spread out on each side as Church Oakley is approached. Manydown Park and Wootton St. Lawrence, with its massive towered church and beautifully ornamental Norman south doorway inside the porch, lie a mile or so off the main road. The Rev. Charles Butler, author of *The Feminine Monarchie*, and vicar here for 46 years, was buried in the church in 1647. Outside the churchyard is a large village pond.

Beyond Oakley station and the viaduct are Clerken Green and the *Beach Arms* hotel: the Beach family used to live at Oakley Hall, now a school. The pinnacled tower of Oakley church, with a sturdy staircase turret, is in the park and visible from the road.

A mile further on, with many varieties of trees on one side and open fields on the other, is Deane. A tiny school-house and the *Deane Gate* inn, which harks back to coaching days, are the only buildings in Deane on the Whitchurch road, the village lying back from it a quarter of a mile. A notice 80 yards up a side lane from the *Deane Gate* indicates that Steventon parish starts here, but the village and church are a mile or two away. When Deane church and park were flooded in 1961, the reflection in the water accentuated the beauty of the dark evergreens and the elaborately-pinnacled tower and exterior of this church, built in Gothic style a little over 150 years ago. It called to mind a similar occurrence when the nave of Salisbury cathedral was under water and the pillars were reflected therein. Some of Deane's communion plate is old—a silver tazza cup and an alms plate (1551), chalice (1569), a paten cover (1570) and flagon (1694).

A mile away, over the hill, is Ashe corner. Off a side lane flanked by meadows, cornfields and tall trees, lies the village of Ashe. In the church, inside a cupboard let into the south aisle wall near the chancel arch, is a beautifully-carved model of a robin on its nest. It commemorates the delight which the nesting activities of the bird gave to workmen who, in 1878, were engaged in restoring the building. It had been their constant companion, had built its nest there, and brought up a brood of young ones. This robin so captured their hearts by its tameness and friendli-ness that they felt impelled to create a permanent memento of the happy association, and so made the carving which has ever since gladdened the hearts of those who have looked in to see it. The pastoral beauty of fields of waving corn seen from the windows of Ashe church during a harvest-time visit lingers in my memory. The mother of Mary Russell Mitford was born and bred at Ashe rectory, Mrs. Mitford's father, Richard Russell, having been rector for 63 years.

The Whitchurch road climbs to a point where it overlooks the large village or minor town of Overton, which, like Stockbridge, used to have a sheep fair. The long street has still a haunting look of stagecoach days. Portal's huge modern factory, the former Town Mill, looms in the distance. As I was interested in archaeological remains, I made my way in 1922 to Quidhampton Farm, which is some distance from the growing village and former market town, to see what remained of the disused small Norman chapel. It is . scarcely higher than the adjoining walls of the farmyard, and is built of flint. When I photographed it, it was simply a stable in a weed-infested farmyard. Each year Overton seems to lose some feature of its age-old attraction. Sometimes an old inn is converted into a shop or dwelling-house. For many years Overton church has had a spired tower, but 60 years ago its tower was flat. The river Test rises near Ashe Place, and another stream joins it at Polhampton, but it is at Overton that it makes its presence apparent. By the time it reaches Laverstoke Park, it has considerably widened, and in its reedy waters can be seen the trout for which it is famous. It was by no means uncommon to spot a heron fishing knee-deep in midstream, a sight which in other stretches of the river would have given seasoned anglers apoplexy! In the park are cedars, and the house can be seen from the road. Tucked away out of sight until its demolition in 1952 was the old parish church which, from 1874 onwards, was the mortuary chapel of the Portal family, who have lived at Laverstoke for over 200 years. I fancy few outsiders visited it, although its ancient history went back to Saxon days, but when my uncle Hugh and I did so in 1922, we were captivated by its quiet setting among the trees, its graceful spire, neat lychgate and the figure in the niche in the arch above the wide west door.

The road from Overton to Laverstoke is lined with horse-chestnut, lime, and willow trees, the woods sloping down to the river. Laverstoke Mill, a factory, is featureless architecturally from the road. The Test flows under it from the park on its way through Freefolk to Whitchurch.

Freefolk chapel was built just 700 years ago, and is a small unecclesiastical-looking building without a separate chancel. It has a tiny reddish box-like bell-cote, and in midsummer can elude one's vision, so screened is it by trees: cattle often add a pastoral touch to the scene. Men with scythes, thigh-deep in the river, periodically trim and cut the tall weeds and underwater vegetation. Laverstoke and Freefolk are virtually one village, not only well-watered, but well-wooded. The modern church of Laverstoke is spired, and contains a triptych, a rood screen and relics from the old church in the park. In front of the church, a crescent of thatched cottages was erected before the Second World War. Originally, this part of the village was in a hollow formed by a disused chalk pit, and the flint cottages, some of which were semi-detached, were damp and had few amenities. The new terrace was wisely built on a raised concrete ramp, and the number of dwellings increased from 14 to 18, all with indoor sanitation and electricity: eight had separate living rooms as well as kitchens. They were beautifully constructed, and the continuous thatched roofs are a showpiece from the road: the dormer windows peeping out, and an extra ridge of decorative thatch, in a different style and lighter in colour, linking the sturdy chimneys, are as appealing as the front gardens with their flowers, fruit trees and thatch-roofed wells. Their appearance would have been even more enhanced if the backs had also been thatched.

Foliage thins out as the road leaves Laverstoke, with beeches, elders and traveller's joy in the hedges, and ragwort and meadow-sweet in the fields through which the river ripples in the valley below. Mention of Laverstoke Mill inevitably brings to mind the older mill associated with the Portal family, Bere Mill, reached by a lane near the summit of the hill which overlooks Whitchurch.

The most impressive of my many visits to Whitchurch and Bere Mill was in early September 1969, when my son and I saw grey squirrels scampering like flying foxes among the tree-tops the entire length of the sequestered little lane leading gently down to Bere Mill. The river Test was flecked by the sun, and trout were clearly visible from the brick bridge and near the single plank bridge over which the Queen had walked seven years before.

The main road runs downhill, past the *Prince Regent* inn to the centre of the small homely town of Whitchurch, where five roads meet near the *White Hart* hotel.

Among my greatest literary pleasures have been the three volumes of *Kilvert's Diary* (1870–79), by the Rev. R. F. Kilvert (1840–79), edited by William Plomer, and first published in 1938–40, and the five volumes of the *Diary of a Country Parson* (1758–1802), by the Rev. James Woodforde (1740–1803), edited by John Beresford, and first published in 1924–31. Apart from details of his stay in the Isle of Wight, Kilvert says nothing about Hampshire except for a wait at the railway station of Bishopstoke (the old name of Eastleigh station) and a passing reference early in 1874 to the Tichborne Trial verdict. Although we know from Parson Woodforde's diary that he travelled through north Hampshire between 1776 and 1802 on his periodic visits to his relatives in Somerset when he was rector of Weston Longeville, Norfolk, sparse mention is made of any Hampshire towns and villages through which he passed, apart from revisiting Winchester (where he had been a scholar of the college) and solitary references to breakfasting at Whitchurch (on 1 June 1782), and at Stockbridge (6 October 1786). We do know, however, that he travelled on the Salisbury coach from the Belle Sauvage yard, London, through Hounslow, Staines, Bagshot, Hartford Bridge Flats ('the best five miles for a coach in all England'), Hartley Row, Hook, Basingstoke, and Overton, to Whitchurch, which is no longer the bustling place it was when the

Salisbury coach met the one from Oxford to Winchester
at the *White Hart*. From here the former swept on to
Andover, Weyhill and Amesbury before reaching its destination in the cathedral city. The *White Hart* has always been
a well-known hostelry, situated on the corner of the Basingstoke road at its junction with roads leading to Andover,
Newbury, St. Mary Bourne, and Winchester. It is good to
know that this 'listed building of architectural interest'
is not to be converted into shops with living accommodation
above. Thus Whitchurch will retain a historic link with its
illustrious past, and preserve an attractive building, and the
fine figure of the white hart above the balcony will continue
to gaze out benignly on the homely little town.

The fate of the late 18th-century town hall was also in
the balance between 1967 and 1972. It was hoped that its
historical interest would save it from demolition, and that
a worthy use for it would be found to justify the expenditure
necessary to restore it. Through the efforts of Lord Denning,
Master of the Rolls—who was born nearby, and lives at
'The Lawn' in Whitchurch—restoration of this distinctive
Georgian building has recently (1973) been completed.

Whitchurch has declined in importance since coaching
days. It has a mayor, but no corporation, and the railway
station is less busy than it used to be. During the Second
World War it was the emergency headquarters of the Bank
of England, members of the staff living in and around the
town, including Hurstbourne Park.

The parish church beside the road to Andover looks old,
indeed there is a Saxon tombstone inside, but it is mostly
modern. Many weathered gravestones have been placed
against the far wall of the churchyard, leaving a smooth green
plot which can easily be mown, thus greatly enhancing its
appearance. A heavy steeple dwarfs the roof of the church
and seems to weigh down the squat tower, whose peal of
eight bells makes pleasant music, in contrast to the swish of
vehicles as they negotiate the corkscrew bends in and out

of the town centre: this is so low-lying that when there is a heavy storm, water sometimes gathers to a depth of two feet on the flat Winchester road, which accumulates the drainage from the hilly Basingstoke and Newbury roads.

The river Test flows from Bere Mill through Whitchurch, close to cottage gardens and under a low four-arched brick bridge on the Winchester road near the old Silk Mill. Charles Kingsley and Andrew Lang both enjoyed the river at Whitchurch. It has three well-known tributaries in its upper reaches, the Bourne, the Anton, and the Wallop, which join it at Hurstbourne Priors, Fullerton and Bossington respectively. The Anna brook, also known as Pill or Pillhill brook, joins the Anton at Upper Clatford. Between Romsey, nine miles from Southampton, and its outlet into Southampton Water, the Test is joined by three tributaries, the Cadnam and Bartley streams, and the Blackwater (not to be confused with the river of that name which runs from Aldershot to Swallowfield). Throughout its entire length the Test is serenely beautiful, whether or not one has a thought for its incomparable trout fishing. The pictures of this lovely chalk-stream in such books as J. W. Hills' *A Summer on the Test* and *River Keeper,* C. Ernest Pain's *Fifty Years on the Test,* C. F. Walker's *Angler's Odyssey,* and, particularly, Dr. E. A. Barton's *An Album of the Chalk Streams,* give an idea of the pervading charm of the river scenery. This is equally true of the river Bourne, in Harry Plunket Green's *Where the Bright Waters Meet.*

28
Hop-growing Villages

ONE DAY I was about to start on a long walk, when my grandfather met me at the gate. He inquired how far I was going, and I said 'Bentley and Binsted'. He replied, 'God bless my heart and soul. I don't know where you get the energy to do it', and slipped some small silver into my hand for the purchase of lemonade or ginger ale, knowing that I usually took sandwiches and cake with me on my travels. He was the finest of men, and the kindest.

By bridle-paths and farm tracks I skirted Upton Grey and South Warnborough and soon reached the *Golden Pot*, three miles from Alton. In those days the country lane from the *Pot* to Froyle was not only dusty but gravelly, and when cycling in the reverse direction 16 years later, I found little change in its surface. The going was heavy, and laboriously churning my way up hill, making but slow progress, I was absently-mindedly humming a tune, when my companion said, 'Do you realise what tune you are singing?' It was 'Is my team ploughing?' from Vaughan Williams' *On Wenlock Edge* song-cycle!

The walk in 1912 was my first visit to Froyle. Facing Froyle Place, built in 1588, is the pinnacled red-brick tower of the church, which is in Upper Froyle. Much of the building is 18th- and 19th-century, and of stone. The chancel and east window (with its original armorial glazing), as well as an Easter sepulchre, are all of 14th-century date. There is a piscina in the large chancel, which is almost as long as the nave, the choir being on a slightly lower level.

Bentley is a large village and, like Froyle, is on the river Wey. On a hill crowned by hop gardens and beeches, a splendid avenue of yews leads to the Norman church, which is of stone, and has a low heavy tower. The Chief Scout, Lord Baden Powell (founder of the Scout Movement in 1907) and Lady Baden Powell (World Chief Guide) lived at Pax Hill from 1918 to 1939, and he presented to the village an open book in stone with a thatched roof, alongside the road, on which are recorded points of interest and a history of Bentley.

The Alice Holt forest, three square miles in area, which supplied oak to the government in past centuries for the building of naval vessels, is in the neighbourhood of Binsted, and is also famous for its beeches.

The Transitional Norman church of Binsted is as wide as it is long. The belfry of the square tower is supported by massive beams and heavy posts, and the building contains a 14th-century recumbent effigy of Richard de Westcote. Lord Kitchener's ancestors are said to be buried here.

Not far away are the Worldham villages, which the inhabitants pronounced 'Wurdlum', derived from its former name of Wardelham. East Worldham church, on a hill, has a spired closed-in bell-cote, and 12th- and 14th-century remains: the tall chancel and nave were restored just over 100 years ago, material from the old church being used in the reconstruction. One would not guess from the outside of West Worldham church, restored in 1888 and 1898, that it was a late Norman building with 15th- and 16th-century features: one has to go inside to see these. It measures only 44 feet by 18 feet, and has a 13th-century doorway and a 14th-century sanctus bell in a niche under the west gable. As there is no separate chancel, tower or spire, it resembles a chapel. West Worldham parish is very small, little over 400 acres. The two Worldhams, like Bentley and Binsted, are in the hop country. Arthur Young (1741-1820), whose writings on farming were well known, and whose *Annals of Agriculture* ran to 45 volumes, once described the country between Alton and Farnham as the finest 10 miles in England.

Hartley Mauditt is associated in my mind with its lonely Norman church, its Round House, its pond, and the beauty of the local countryside. The attractiveness of many Hampshire parishes is enhanced by their shapely, sometimes circular, ancient village ponds, just as chalk dells add greatly to the beauty of others. W. H. Hudson appreciated the charm of these villages bordering on Woolmer Forest. The railed-off churchyard is in the middle of a field, and remote from human habitation. The interior of the stone church has several interesting characteristics—the ornamentation of the arch of the south doorway (1190), the Norman nave and a 13th-century horseshoe chancel. Restoration took place in 1854 and 1904: in the former year the slim octagonal spired bell-turret replaced an earlier one which had lasted for 400 years. It is curious that this church, like those at Appleshaw, Corhampton, Farnborough, Mattingley, Morestead, Priors Dean, and Rotherwick, has no known dedication. Corn and hops are the chief products of this scattered and sparsely-populated village.

Kingsley is on the Slea, a tributary of the Wey, and its eastern part lies between Woolmer and Alice Holt Forests. Its old church dates back 600 years, but the quaint little wooden bell-cote and the west end of the building on which it stands, were the only parts retained when restoration took place, in 1905, so that it could serve as a mortuary chapel. The new church was built in 1876, and occupies a commanding position: the communion plate dates from the latter half of the 16th century. Lode Farmhouse was a hunting lodge and later a residence used by King John, Henry III, Edward I, II and III, and Henry VIII when Prince of Wales: today it presents a pleasing prospect of a large farmhouse set back from the Oakhanger stream. Kingsley is always coupled in my mind with my uncle

Hugh, who often went there from Mapledurwell when his engineering skill was needed. He used to talk about Frank Dobson, the sculptor, who had a studio there during the Second World War.

Farringdon is off the Alton—Gosport road between Chawton (a source of the Wey) and East Tisted. Gilbert White was curate here from 1761 to 1785, and Jane Austen mentions Faringdon (as it was spelt in her day) in her letters. The 12th-century spired church has been restored and enlarged. In 1919 the rector died after 62 years' tenure of office: his immediate predecessor was appointed to the living in 1797, only four years after Gilbert White's death. In the churchyard are two ancient yew trees, renowned for their girth. The former schoolhouse, with herring-bone brickwork, has been converted into cottages.

On my way home I passed Jane Austen's house at Chawton, and the Robin Hood Butts, leaving the Basingstoke road at the point where the Odiham road branches off to the *Golden Pot.* Beyond a hurdled field, where sheep grazed, is South Warnborough in the valley, with a village pond, a pump, and a 'pub' with a spreading tree in front. From deeply-wooded country the spired bell-cote of the church is visible, and an avenue of chestnut trees leads to the churchyard. The north doorway is late Norman, and the rood loft and screen date from 1400, but what I remember best is a monument to an Elizabethan couple, Sir Thomas Whyte and his wife Agnes, and their 19 children shown behind them, all kneeling, under which an inscription reads 'God save the Quene': by reason of the Gothic text, this can be mistaken for 'God save the queue', which seems more appropriate!

Up a steep hill past thatched cottages and a chapel, a lane winds round to Hoddington Hill and Upton Grey. Bridle-paths near Bidden Farm and from the Greywell road to Five Lanes End are a short cut, and Mapledurwell lies in the valley beyond.

As a postscript, I must mention the hop-growing village of Holybourne, a mile or so from Alton, and also a tributary of the same name, which joins the Wey outside the parish. Like Alton, it was a place of call for pilgrims on the way to the shrine of St. Thomas a Becket at Canterbury. The most picturesque parts of the village are the pond and the Early English flint church, with a shingled wooden spire on its tower which, like the nave, is 12th-century. The chancel dates from a century later.

Mrs. Elizabeth Gaskell, novelist and author of a *Life of Charlotte Brontë*, lived at 'The Lawn', and died there in 1865, aged 55, but her body, together with that of her husband, lies in the graveyard of the beautiful old Unitarian chapel, opened in 1689, in Brook Street, Knutsford, the town she immortalised as *Cranford*.

29
Alton to Alresford

ALTON is a market town 11 miles from Basingstoke, and the centre of an agricultural and hop-growing district in the valley of the river Wey. It is an extensive parish, which in one direction spreads out several miles to include the *Golden Pot* inn, Beech and Alton Abbey, and almost reaches Thedden, all rich with forests and glades.

On the rare occasions when my grandfather drove us there in his trap, we went over the Down from Mapledurwell to Five Lanes End, and by grassy bridle-paths, just wide enough to permit the passage of farm carts, to Bidden Farm and Upton Grey. At the top of Hoddington Hill we branched off over a cart track near Humbly Grove where it entered a wood and came out on to the Odiham road between South Warnborough and the *Golden Pot*. There were two tree-lined avenues: one, opposite the *Pot*, descended by a rough road to Alton, coming out near the fine old parish church; the other, a most beautiful avenue of beeches, nearly two miles long, forked right at the *Golden Pot* cross-roads, but as spoliation on an unprecedented scale took place during the Second World War, four-fifths of its splendid trees were sacrificed to provide an airfield at Lasham.

I occasionally cycled over to Alton in succeeding years, but there was no bookshop in which I could make interesting acquisitions, though I recall a little shop belonging to a photographer with the Hampshire name of Aylward, whose views of villages round Alton I eagerly purchased: I also bought a small illustrated book about their history by Dr. William Curtis, a local antiquary. Several other medical

men and scientists who bore the same names have been
associated with Alton, chief among them the botanist
(1746-99), who was born in Lenten Street, which is at
right-angles to Amery Street, where Edmund Spenser, the
Elizabethan poet, lived: both houses bear commemorative
plaques, as also does an imposing building in the High Street
where in his young days, Cardinal Newman lived with his
parents.

I enjoyed looking inside the old parish church of St.
Lawrence, which has a Norman font, a heavy spired tower
120 feet high, and a large wooden door riddled with bullet
holes, souvenirs of the Civil War, and spared a thought
for its brave defender, Colonel Richard Boles, who died in
the pulpit, refusing to surrender. He is commemorated
by a brass, and was buried in Winchester cathedral.

I liked the greenness and homely look of the cricket
ground near the Robin Hood Butts, the tall buildings of the
brewery firm of Crowley, and the war memorial, in the
form of a cairn, in the hilly High Street. The buildings
and inns in this street are a mixture of differing styles, and
there is an interesting museum whose exhibits include a
15th-century parish bier from Long Sutton church.

In later years, I by-passed the town, preferring to visit
villages off the Gosport road, such as Chawton, Farringdon,
and East Tisted, a narrow lane from which led through
peaceful country to Stoner Hill and Petersfield. I had no
need to go all the way to Alton if I wished to see the forest
villages between it and Alresford. Shalden and Bradley
are small, out-of-the-way parishes which have much in
common: both lie hidden in deep wooded country equidistant from Lasham. Shalden is off the lane from the
Golden Pot to Lasham, whilst Bradley is between Lasham
and Preston Candover. Shalden consists of a common, a
farm, a church and some cottages; whilst Bradley had a
rectory, a church and a few houses. They—with Priors Dean
and Popham—must be among the least populated villages

in the county. Shalden church was built in 1863, retaining its predecessor's 15th-century font: Bradley church, rebuilt in 1877, incorporated more of the old edifice, including a piscina and some 13th-century lancet windows. Each has an open turret with a spire and a single bell. In shape and appearance, too, the buildings are somewhat alike. My visit to Bradley in 1922 was a sad occasion, for an aged incumbent, a lonely but brave and gentle figure, was on the point of leaving his beloved rectory.

This unspoilt countryside, 'far from the madding crowd', had a special appeal for me. If it were as readily accessible to me now as it was years ago, I should find pleasure in rediscovering that lovely wooded country, which also includes Beech, Bentworth, and Medstead.

Beech, resplendent with forest trees, is rightly named. It was the home of a very youthful Compton Mackenzie, who from 1896 to 1900 lived at 'Canadian Cottage' (since demolished). He was the founder and editor of *The Gramophone,* a monthly magazine devoted to the interests of lovers of recorded music ever since early 1923, to which I contributed occasional articles from 1930 to 1939. I treasure a copy of his book, *A Musical Chair* (a selection of his stimulating editorial talks), which bear an inscription 'To Robert W. F. Potter from Compton Mackenzie with best wishes to his flute and himself'. Reverting to his sojourn during his 'teens at Beech, the neighbourhood provided background material for some of his novels: this applies particularly to Alton Abbey, where a home devoted to the care and comfort of retired mariners was founded about the turn of the century. The small community of Anglican monks continues to look after these seamen. I have photographs of the abbey, the gatehouse and the beech glades, taken about 50 years ago, and I am glad to say that many of the splendid forest trees still survive.

Bentworth is a large, populous village four miles from Alton. The satirist and poet, George Wither (1588–1667), who, incidentally, wrote a poem in praise of Alresford pond, was born there and was christened in its 12th-century church. Noteworthy are the old arcades, arches and piers, the lancet windows, and a priest's doorway dating from 1250. The flint edifice, surrounded by trees, is spacious, having a nave and aisles, but the spired belfry and porch are modern.

Medstead is nearly 700 feet above sea level. The church, which is among trees, has a Norman arcade and a stone poor-box, and has been restored and enlarged. The tower and vestry were once depositories for smuggled goods. One usually associates contraband with coastal villages, but Medstead, Warnford, and other quiet inland places, served as secret storage depôts for cross-country illicit traffic.

Two other villages in pleasant country nearer Alresford are Ropley and Bishop's Sutton. Ropley is a large hilly parish close to the Pilgrim's Way, with a church, restored twice during the last century, which contains work from the 12th to the 15th centuries. Its registers go back to 1538, in which year they first came into general use: a chalice dates from 1592. The village of Bishop's Sutton, near which the river Alre rises, is about a mile and a half from Alresford. The interesting old church has a Norman nave, windows and two doorways, a piscina, and a little shingled bell-cote supported by heavy posts to the roof at the western end of the building. In the church is a memorial to Sister Rhoda (Ethel Rhoda McNeile) of the Community of St. Mary the Virgin, Wantage, who gave her seat in a lifeboat to a mother of a family of children when S.S. *Egypt* foundered in a fog in the Bay of Biscay in 1922.

30
Whitchurch to Andover

WHEN RIDING from Basingstoke to Andover, I usually
chose the road which goes through half a dozen villages
and follows the Test from Overton to Whitchurch, rather
than the open country route over Popham Beacon, which
is favoured by motorists because it does not pass through
any villages. For most of the way from Whitchurch to
Hurstbourne Priors, a high wall hugs one side of the road,
behind which the land rises steeply to the dense woods of
Hurstbourne Park. In Hurstbourne House there is a minstrels'
gallery. On the other side of the Andover road, fields and
copses slope down to water-meadows in the valley, where
roofs of buildings at Tufton are discernible a mile or so away.

Hurstbourne Priors—Cobbett's 'Downhusband', in contra-
distinction to 'Uphusband' (Hurstbourne Tarrant)—has
always appealed to me. Not only does that lovely stream,
the Bourne, flow through the village, but on summer evenings
cricket is played on the most beautiful of greens, almost
within the shadow of the church. I have seen many cricket
greens in Hampshire, the original home of the game, but
none more perfect than this. The church, its tower covered
with blood-red and shining green virginia creepers, completes
the picture. The west doorway and the arches over the north
chapel and elsewhere are fine examples of ornamental
Norman work, and nearby is the tomb of a knight who died
in 1574. There is a mass clock on the church wall, and
in the churchyard stands Hudson's favourite yew tree.

It was by the river Bourne that an Izaak Walton of our
time—Harry Plunket Greene (1865–1936), one of the most

famous of anglers—spent many of his happiest years. His book *Where the Bright Waters Meet*, a title which refers to the confluence of the Test and the Bourne, was first published in 1924, and relates how, over 20 years before, he walked into the village of his dreams. It was in the burial ground adjoining the churchyard, near the stream that was so dear to him, that he was laid to rest. Close by lies his son, David (1904–41), a grandson of the composer, Sir Hubert Parry. Plunket Greene was also a fine bass-baritone and a superb interpreter, who by his choice of songs helped to create a school of British song. Look through programmes of his concerts, whether in London, the provinces, or at the opening of the new hall at Hurstbourne Priors in 1909, and you will find songs by Hamilton Harty (incidentally, his accompanist at the village concert), Charles Stanford, and Arthur Somervell, all of whom were knighted for their services to music. His book, *Interpretation in Song,* has been the classic on the subject for 60 years. During the time when he lived at the 'Long House' (1902–13), he trained the church choir. Two stories—'Pilot' (his dog), and 'Iron-Blue' in his *Pilot and Other Stories* are about pleasant days spent in the village, which he revisited in the 1920s. His books are as good as his singing, especially the last, *From Blue Danube to Shannon,* which includes a fascinating chapter, 'What Schubert did for Song'. Such a superlative command of language must have interested many students in gems from amongst the composer's 603 songs.

The Bourne flows peacefully all the way from Hurstbourne Priors to St. Mary Bourne, for which we turn right at the crossroads near the *Portsmouth Arms* hotel. For years both villages have increasingly cultivated watercress, which, with the over-stocking of the river with trout, and the tarring of the roads, which polluted the stream, resulted in Plunket Greene leaving his beloved village.

Life in St. Mary Bourne followed an old pattern, its industries including hurdle-making and bee-keeping. Many of its cottages were thatched, and there were May-day celebrations, mummers, and even 'rough music', all of which customs and many more are recounted by Dr. Joseph Stevens (1818-99) in his *Parochial History of St. Mary Bourne*, and by Mrs. Kathleen Innes in *Life in a Hampshire Village* and *Village Story*. In 1962 a memorial plaque to Dr. Stevens—archaeologist, village historian, and doctor here from 1844 to 1879—was placed on the house in which he had lived. Inside the grey-towered church, close to the road, is the largest of the four black Tournai marble fonts in Hampshire— all with different carvings—also wall paintings and a lectern with chains. Dr. Stevens was buried here. The village square bears a quaint name, the Summerhaugh.

At the crossroads opposite the *Portsmouth Arms* is Hurstbourne Priors Hill, from the top of which one sees an old thatched farmhouse and barns so enclosed and sheltered by trees as to form a self-contained farmstead nestling in the dell deep down on the left. There is no village between here and Andover, only the hamlet of Andover Down, and a large turkey farm. Tall trees shade the road, making summer days cool, and the hedges are enriched with traveller's joy and wild roses. The new by-pass beyond Andover Down, which has been hewn out of the chalky downland on the east side of the town, makes a wide detour from the old straight road, leaving the *Queen Charlotte* inn high and dry on its now solitary track. Masses of poppies, oxeye daisies, and charlock cover the wide verges of the by-pass, which, after describing arcs and semi-circles, eventually reaches Andover. Our road joins the other main road from Basingstoke, which, after dropping down from Popham Beacon, passes Bullington Cross and Barton Stacey camp, and runs close to Bransbury Common, the former Longparish station, and Harewood Forest, in which is Dead Man's Plack.

As we approach the town centre and market square, the road narrows and becomes a veritable bottleneck for traffic, which has been Andover's major problem for a number of years. Through-traffic found it impracticable to avoid the town. Cars park crosswise in the centre of the wide section of the High Street, which is used as a market on certain days, vehicles on each side filtering through as best they can at a snail's pace.

Andover has its attractions—the stalls on market days, ancient inns such as the *Angel* and the *George*, the Town Mill, and the old bookshop and church at the narrow end of the High Street. I always enjoy a browse round the bookshop, full to the scuppers, including each side of the narrow staircase, and seldom do I come empty away. If ever it closes, I shall sadly miss it.

The parish church was built in 1842 on an eminence above the highest point of the High Street, and stands sentinel over the town. It has at least one historic relic, which is detached from the new building—a Norman archway. I find it pleasant on a summer day to sit near the war memorial in the churchyard, enjoying the peace of this quiet haven.

The town hall, built in 1825, may look a trifle drab at the best of times, and like a cold storage depôt at the worst, but is a familiar landmark.

Andover is a mixture of old and new, of the picturesque and the prosaic. It used to be noted for its woollen industry, and now has clean-looking modern printing works with well-kept grass frontages on the road to the aerodrome and Weyhill. It has always had two great attractions for me—first, it is the gateway to the Wiltshire downs and Salisbury Plain and to the Hampshire highlands in the north west, and second, it is the focal point of a smiling countryside rich in river scenery and in historic villages.

Andover, in common with other smaller towns in Hampshire—Alton, Romsey, and Petersfield—has long been the centre of a large agricultural district; but, like Basingstoke, is destined in a decade or two to become a London County Council overspill development area, six times the size it was in 1939.

Much of the hilly country round about has prehistoric evidence of hill-forts, barrows and tumuli. Some of their names are obvious evidence of this—Tidbury Ring (outside Bullington), Bury Hill (near Abbotts Ann and Upper Clatford), and Woolbury and Danebury Rings (near Stockbridge).

31
Highclere and Burghclere

A LOVE FOR OLD villages first moved me to journey all over Hampshire, which led to many personal discoveries over the years. Houses and even cottages can be common-place, but no two churches are ever alike. Their differing exteriors fascinated me, their interiors less so at that time, unless they were as distinctive and unforgettable as those of Dummer, Nately Scures, Upton Grey, and Minstead. During the half century in which I scoured the county on foot or on my bicycle, 1922 was the vintage year, for within 17 days I made 13 journeys on the machine, being young, energetic, and enthusiastic. The main roads from Basingstoke to Whitchurch, Andover, Amesbury, Reading, Newbury, Aldershot, Alton, Alresford, Farnham, Stock-bridge, Winchester, and Salisbury had become so familiar that I decided that the time had come to explore villages off the beaten track whose very names intrigued me when I spread out my road maps. In the realisation of my purpose, I added scores of snapshots and sketches to my ever-growing store. Those were the days and years when I really lived, when my enthusiasm was at white heat, when my interest never relaxed or grew cool; when the mind, like the aperture of a camera, captured the scene in detail and retained the image inviolate.

In 1922 my cycle run to Andover was uneventful until I reached the church at the top of the town. In those days I liked to ascertain how many bells the various Hampshire churches possessed, and I remember making my way to the ringing chamber, and from there to the belfry. I climbed up a ladder which led past the bells to a horizontal crossbeam high up in the tower, and experienced no difficulty in making my way astride the centre of the beam to the door leading out on to the roof, where I photographed the town below, with the river Anton winding its way through meadows on the outskirts to its source, and the Wiltshire downs in the distance. But when I came to make the descent, it was a different matter, for I was not climbing towards the light of the roof door, but with my back to it into the darkness, edging my way cautiously for the first few yards with no support on either side, to the descending ladder, and realising that my head for heights (or rather depths!) was not as good as it had been. What made matters worse was the sudden deafening noise of the bells when the clock struck noon. I was glad to be out in the open once again.

I then decided to explore the countryside round Tufton and Litchfield. The little Norman church of Tufton, in a meadow, has a chancel which goes back to Saxon days, and remnants of a wall painting of St. Christopher carrying the Christ-child on his shoulders. An uncommon feature is a grandfather clock in the nave. The exterior of the building, including the little bell-cote, was under scaffolding at the time. I took a snapshot of it, and cycled on to Litchfield, north of Whitchurch. The village lies in a valley, and it is here that the Hampshire highlands begin. The church, on a raised plot, has a Norman chancel, but was restored in the 1870s. A mile to the north are tumuli known as the Seven Barrows, and to the northwest are bare-topped Beacon Hill (858 feet), and wooded Sidown Hill, even higher, from which there are magnificent views, well attested in the vigorous and sturdy prose of Cobbett in his frequent accounts of Burghclere and district. Burghclere and Highclere have much in common, Highclere Park, 13 miles in circumference, occupying most of the two parishes. The park and castle are reputed to be among the finest in the country: two lakes cover 52 acres.

The railway stations of both villages are in Burghclere. The old church of Burghclere dates from 1100, but was rebuilt in 1861: there are two Norman doorways—the shapely, but plain, north, and the ornamental south. The new church, on a hill, dates from 1838; later a spire was added to the tower. Highclere's old church, inside the park and near the castle, was pulled down in 1870, and most of its mural tablets and carvings were transferred to the new broach-spired building erected in the village by the Earl of Caernarvon at the request of the parishioners, and was designed by Sir Gilbert Scott.

There are Iron Age hill-forts or barrow cemeteries. These are not confined to north Hampshire, but also occur near Petersfield (the Butser), the Meon valley (Old Winchester Hill), and north of the New Forest (Rockbourne and near Fordingbridge).

Curiosity prompted my first visit to the Sandham Memorial Chapel or All Souls' Oratory, near the *Carpenter's Arms* inn, and not far from Highclere station. It had been specially built to house the mural paintings of the late Sir Stanley Spencer (1891–1959), and in 1947 was taken over by the National Trust. Two of his foremost patrons, Mr. and Mrs. John Behrend, who lived at Burghclere for 36 years from 1919 onwards, became deeply interested early on in Spencer's peculiarly distinctive style of painting, which portrayed on walls and panels his memories of wartime days spent in an English military hospital and in Macedonia. His benefactors bore the cost of the erection of the building at Burghclere, and remunerated the artist for his work, which extended over several years. In 1927, the chapel was dedicated to the memory of Lieutenant H. W. Sandham of the Army Service Corps, who was killed in the First World War. Spencer's paintings were completed in 1932, and Burghclere is as inseparably associated with his name as is Cookham, a Berkshire village on the Thames, his artistic headquarters, where he spent most of his life.

32
Andover to Newbury and Kingsclere

THE ROAD FROM Andover to Newbury is a northerly one through Knight's Enham, King's Enham, Little London (not its namesake between Pamber and Silchester), Hurstbourne Tarrant, and Highclere. Though mullein and rosebay flourish near the Enham crossroads, the green at Enham village is as tidy as a lawn, and the beautiful thatched cottage on it is a paragon of its kind. The late Norman church of Knight's Enham, with a pretty bell-cote, stands secluded among the trees. Inside, a 12th-century font stands alongside its 19th-century successor.

The Enham Village Centre was established over 50 years ago as an industrial training centre for soldiers disabled during the First World War, and has been active ever since on behalf of ex-Service men. It is known as Enham Alamein, and in its workshops, furniture and baskets are made: market gardening also is carried on. These farmlands, woods and cottages were originally the property of the Dewar family, who settled at Knight's Enham over 200 years ago.

Fir trees become more plentiful as one nears Little London, but conspicuous in the woods and copses are oaks and silver birches, hazel bushes and bracken. From the top of steep Hurstbourne Hill—a gradient of one in eight—the slopes of Doles Wood descend to the valley in which lies Hurstbourne Tarrant. There are many thatched cottages in this large village, and people from far and wide bring their friends to admire the quality of the work on show at the Bladon Gallery, founded by Mrs. D. M. Bladon Hawton in 1949. In 1952 the Bladon Society of Arts and Crafts was

established. It originally occupied a chapel built in 1840,
but additional accommodation—cottages and a studio—
became necessary later. It is devoted to exhibitions of arts
and crafts—pictures, paintings, sculpture, pottery, glassware,
woodwork, weaving, textiles, and toys. A small admission
fee for non-members is charged, and most of the goods
are for sale, but the gallery is non-profit-making.

The 12th-century church of Hurstbourne Tarrant
resembles those of Yateley and King's Somborne as to length
and spaciousness, and the square-timbered towers and shingle
spires of all three are somewhat similar too. The ornamental
Transitional south doorway within the fine old porch heralds
the impressive interior which contains traces of old wall
paintings, and a memorial to Mrs. Anna Lea Merritt
(1844–1930), the American-born artist and author of
A Hamlet in Old Hampshire, who lived for a number of years
at 'The Limes', and died there. She painted the sign of the
George and Dragon. Joseph Blount, Cobbett's farmer friend
and host, lived at 'The Rookery' close by; Hudson also
stayed there. Some of the most readable portions of *Rural
Rides* are about 'Uphusband' and Burghclere not far away,
and recount how Cobbett frequently ranged over the entire
county on horseback, riding 40 miles a day in his 50s and
early 60s, from his farm at Botley, and visiting Hambledon,
Petersfield, Winchester, the New Forest, Southampton,
Selborne, Weyhill, and villages in the valleys of the Bourne,
Test and Itchen. He said that he never saw any inhabited
places more recluse than Woodcott and Binley, whose cottage
inn, *The Hurdler's Arms,* is a reminder that hurdles used
to be made at Hurstbourne Tarrant as well as at King's
Somborne, Longparish, and St. Mary Bourne. The river
Bourne or Swift rises here, but its bed is often dry for several
months of the year, between here and St. Mary Bourne.

The compelling attractions of this corner of Hampshire
are its highlands, its wooded countryside, and the remoteness
of its villages. The windswept hilltop parish of Tangley and

the Hampshire Gate—the boundary with Wiltshire—are
reached by a deviation from the Newbury road near
Hurstbourne Tarrant. The firs known as Tangley Clumps
are a well-known landmark. The church, rebuilt in 1875,
the spired tower having been added in 1898—is notable for
its 17th-century tub-shaped lead font (not unlike a milk
churn in shape), and for a fine yew tree in the churchyard.
It is the only Hampshire parish which has prehistoric sarsen
stones, apart from the Edward Thomas hillside memorial
near Petersfield; Shroner Wood between the *Lunways* inn
and King's Worthy; and a collection alongside the road at
Bramdean, assembled by a resident in 1861. It was at
Tangley that Cobbett spoke to an untravelled country-
woman whose furthest excursion in life was to Chute, just
over the Wiltshire border.

As I climbed the Hampshire highlands with occasionally,
as at Doiley Hill, a gradient of one in nine, I noticed, in
August 1965, several acres of beans, and in other fields
fires were burning in the charred stubble. I passed a long
white inn—now the 'Yew Tree' café—with a clipped yew in
front of it. Between here and *Red House* inn, the country
became more densely wooded. To the right of the Newbury
road, a lane led to Highclere church betwen fields in which
large ragwort flourished and great bindweed ran riot. The
oaks, firs, and silver beeches were so thick as to form a
forest. Further on, in a lane to the left of the main road,
was the *Derby* inn, and a signpost to East Woodhay, a large,
prosperous, residential village near the border, stated that
it was four miles distant. Crossing into Berkshire and before
reaching Newbury, I passed the church of St. George the
Martyr.

If you are returning to Basingstoke, a detour can be
made from the Newbury road after passing through the
border villages of Newtown and Headley—there is another
Headley, near Liphook. Instead of going straight on to
Kingsclere, turn right for Sydmonton, whose rebuilt church

tower looks elegant inside the park. The ancient features of the church are the Norman south doorway and the arch under the tower—near the font—which was originally the chancel arch. Fine views are obtainable from Ladle Hill (768 feet), which is best approached from Sydmonton. In the neighbouring village of Ecchinswell, the Enborne stream runs alongside quiet country lanes. The church, though not old, has interesting windows and an oak screen, as well as a friendly-looking spire and lychgate. From here it is but two miles through quiet by-lanes to Kingsclere, long famous for the Park House racing stables at Cannon Heath outside the town. Kingsclere church has a blocked-up Norman doorway, a font dating from 1200, and a Jacobean pulpit. On its heavy central tower is a curious weather-vane, shaped like a bed-bug: King John was so badly bitten by these creatures when he stayed a night in the village that he gave orders for such a sign to be placed on the tower, so that travellers would be warned of what they might expect!

33
Andover to Salisbury

THE DIRECT ROUTE to Salisbury is via what was the level crossing at Andover Town station, and forks left at the floral clock (where an old round house used to be) at the junction with the Weyhill road. The Salisbury road goes through the Anna valley, a side lane leading to Abbotts Ann, and another to Goodworth (or Lower) Clatford and to Upper Clatford on the other side of the main road.

Abbotts Ann is renowned for the chaplets or garlands carried at funerals of young persons: these have continued to be hung on the walls of the 18th-century church ever since 1716. The custom must have originated long prior to this, for in the early years of the present century, chaplets which had hung in the old church were found in cupboards taken from it when the present one was built. Some of the chaplets are disintegrating owing to old age, but it must be remembered that they were frail, some being made of cardboard arched like a crown and covered with paper rosettes, others resembling gloves made of paper. This touching custom—a symbol of blameless lives—used also to be observed at Selborne and Farringdon years ago. Washington Irving mentions it in his *Sketch Book,* written at a time when it must have been more prevalent than it is now.

The regularity of modern thatch on cottages at Abbotts Ann has much to commend it. Long may this handicraft continue to thrive and to add to the beauty of these enchanting villages.

The river Anton flows through Upper Clatford, and is joined by the Anna brook near the foot of Bury Hill, which is crowned with an ancient encampment. An avenue of pollard lime trees leads from the lychgate to the much-restored Norman church which is peacefully set between two farms, away from the village. It has an unusual Norman arcade between the nave and the chancel, resembling two wide chancel arches side by side, a piscina, dating from 1200, a pewter alms dish, and a pinnacled plain tower.

Goodworth Clatford church is also Norman, the massive pillars and the capital in the north arcade of the nave being noteworthy. There is a 12th-century font and an hour-glass stand. The perspective of the shingled steeple rising gracefully from the plain ashlar tower is captivating, viewed from the east end of the churchyard.

The 17 miles of main road from Andover to Salisbury are lined with beeches, oaks and hawthorn as far as Middle Wallop. This village is in the dip at the crossroads, where lanes branch off to Over Wallop and to Nether Wallop. The Wallop brook rises at Over Wallop. All three Wallop villages retain their old-world character, garden walls as well as cottages being thatched. Willow cricket bats used to be made at Nether Wallop, and had a national reputation. The Norman church is a mixture of 12th- and 16th-century work, but its plain tower is early 18th-century. It houses a 1436 brass of a prioress and several 15th-century wall paintings, including one of St. George and the Dragon: some were rediscovered as recently as 1931 behind whitewash! A pyramidal tomb in the churchyard commemorates an 18th-century 'doctor of physick'. Over Wallop church dates from the 12th and 13th centuries: it has a piscina and (like nearby Quarley and Kimpton) an Easter sepulchre. Its chancel and nave have been rebuilt, and the chancel screen and pulpit are of wrought iron.

Wallop aerodrome is just over the hill from Middle Wallop, alongside the main road. From there the downlands spread out on both sides with commanding views of the country towards Stockbridge, through which the Basingstoke road runs to Salisbury, joining the Andover road at Lobscombe corner on the Wiltshire side of the border, one of the highest points in the region.

From Lobscombe Corner to the *Pheasant* hotel, the Salisbury road is more hedged in. The *Pheasant* was formerly the *Winterslow Hut*, a coaching inn, which is associated with the essayist, William Hazlitt, who stayed there many times between 1819 and 1828. The sunny banks on which he liked to lie for hours at Winterslow and at Pitton (where Ralph Whitlock, the Wiltshire writer farms), are for the most part as they were in his day. There are a few scrawny hedges, with odd clumps of toadflax, ragwort, cow parsley, and poppies enlivening the swards, the downs of the vast Salisbury Plain rolling onwards and outwards, with an occasional wide carpet of yellow charlock between Winterbourne and Salisbury.

The visitor is gladdened by a sight of the matchless cathedral spire in the distance, and by the downhill run into the flat country which heralds the approach of the city. The valley falls sharply away from the main road on the high ridge. Names like Winterbourne Gunner and Stratford-sub-Castle on the signposts have a Wiltshire tang. A river runs under the road, and further on, a railway tunnel burrows into a hill before reaching Salisbury station which, like those of some other cathedral towns, stands on the outskirts of the city.

There is something for everybody in Salisbury—the cathedral (you cannot get away from 'the Spire' wherever you are) and the Close, so perfectly in harmony; the market, the fine half-timbered house of John A'Port (altogether apart from its contents!), Beach's bookshop, St. Thomas's and St. Edmund's churches, the ancient inns, the river Avon near City Mill (which each year becomes more beautiful and floral) and at Harnham Mill—both off Fisherton Street;

and roads with happy names like Blue Boar Row, Cherry Orchard Lane, Oatmeal Row, Penny-farthing Street, Shady Bower, Wain-a-long Road, and Endless Street, which, strange to relate, is named after a Mr. Endle.

34
Andover to the
Wiltshire Border

THREE MILES FROM Andover is Weyhill, where sheep fairs are held. From the Middle Ages until 80 or more years ago, all kinds of agricultural and village produce—cheese, hops and cloth, in addition to sheep and horses—were bought and sold. 'Wy and Winchestre faires' are mentioned in the 14th-century *Piers Plowman,* by William Langland. In 1753, 200,000 sheep were sold here in one day. The usual time for the hiring of farm labourers and shepherds was at Michaelmas, but it took place at Weyhill Fair between 10 and 13 October. Under the pseudonym of 'Weydon Priors', this village is the scene of the wife-selling incident in Thomas Hardy's *The Mayor of Casterbridge.* The long expanse of low pink walls makes the fairground easily identifiable to the passer-by. The church is modern, but the chancel arch dates from the 12th century, and the chancel itself from the 13th century.

A little further on is Thruxton. The tower of Thruxton's 13th-century church contains a brass to Sir John Lisle (1407), a wooden effigy to Lady Philpot and a list of rectors from 1243.

A few miles away, a lane near Park House, on the border with Wiltshire, leads to Shipton Bellinger, a village outside Tidworth Park in which Tidworth Tattoo was held. The camp, like its older neighbour, Bulford, outside Amesbury, is very tidy in its country surroundings. In the late 1920s and 1930s, we enjoyed the tattoos there, which included equestrian displays to the music of military bands, and horse-riding through glades in the thickly-wooded hills of

the park, lit up by searchlights as darkness fell on late
summer evenings. The performances, which were very
popular, lasted about three hours and ended with a magnificent display of fireworks. We thought the country setting
far preferable to that of the Aldershot Tattoo, which was
held in a more confined arena outside that town. Incidentally, South Tidworth is in Hampshire, whilst North
Tidworth is in Wiltshire.

Shipton Bellinger is in sheep-rearing country: its 14th-
century church was largely rebuilt 90 years ago. A hamlet on
the Wiltshire border bears the name of Hampshire Cross.

In the triangle formed by Andover, Ludgershall and
Nether Wallop are several secluded villages. A little north
of Thruxton is the small parish of Fyfield: Gilbert White
used to ride over on horseback from Selborne when visiting
his youngest brother Harry (1733-88), who was rector
here from 1782 until his death.

Adjoining Fyfield is Kimpton, in whose cruciform 13th-
century church is a brass (1522) of a knight, his two wives
and their large family, all kneeling. The tower, added in
1837, presents an effective contrast of light and shade
in its flint and brick structure. South of Thruxton is
Amport. Its church has a plain central tower, a fine east
window and an alabaster head of John the Baptist of
14th-century date.

North of Weyhill are Penton Mewsey, Foxcott and
Appleshaw. Weyhill (once part of the larger parish of
Penton Grafton and near where the river Anton rises),
has a hamlet with the quaint name of Ragged Appleshaw.
Penton Mewsey is prettily situated in farming country,
where the *White Hart* inn keeps company with the rebuilt
church, whose gable-end bell-turret can be seen among the
trees. Much of its 14th-century work—the font, aumbries,
piscina, consecration crosses and a mass clock—still
remains, and its bells date from 1555. Foxcott's most striking
characteristic is a solitary church tower with no vestige of

nave or chancel, which is now a mortuary chapel. The materials of the old edifice were used in building Charlton church: but neither here nor at Hatherden, is there anything of special interest, since both are relatively modern. Appleshaw lies off the Weyhill road to Ludgershall (pronounced Lugger-shawl), a leafy country lane with the railway running alongside most of the way. In 1896, Appleshaw was the scene of a spectacular find by a local clergyman antiquary (the Rev. R. H. Clutterbuck), who unearthed a collection of Romano-British pewter vessels and various kitchen utensils. The church has two fonts, and its low pinnacled tower with a steeple turret rising from the roof presents a striking façade.

The Andover road to the Wiltshire border climbs all the time. The views from the highest point range for miles in every direction, with Bulford to the right, the R.A.F.'s testing grounds on Boscombe Down on the left, and Amesbury in the valley straight ahead. A hedgeless lane almost doubles back on its tracks to remote Grately, once the residence of Saxon kings. It lies at the foot of Quarley Hill. Grately church contains not only old painted glass, including a medallion which came from Salisbury cathedral, but an iron bracket which served as a stand for an hourglass placed very appropriately near the pulpit in those days of wearisome sermons. In this neighbourhood is the Cholderton range of hills, but the village of that name is in Wiltshire.

The main attractions of this region are the magnificent views of vast stretches of Hampshire and Wiltshire, and particularly from that well-known landmark, Quarley Hill (562 feet), which is crowned by a clump of pines and beeches and by ancient entrenchments. Lofty hilltops fan out at intervals all the way along the border from Grately to Lobscombe and the Stockbridge hills.

The old church at Quarley, which has a 14th-century sepulchral slab and an even earlier font, is chiefly remembered for the three bells under a roofed frame slightly above ground level outside its walls, there having been no church tower since about 1882. It calls to mind the separate bell-tower of Chichester cathedral and the small external campanile in the Surrey churchyard of Tongham, near Aldershot, though they bear no resemblance to each other.

South of Weyhill is the village of Monxton (originally Monkston), with some charming colour-washed thatched cottages as pretty as any in Hampshire, and inside a tiny churchyard, a little oak-shingled spired church of stone and flint, in which are two brasses dated 1599 and 1660. A hamlet not far away bears the evocative name of Prospect.

35
The Meon Valley

THE YEAR 1922 stands out in my memory because of my earliest journeys through the valleys of two of Hampshire's prettiest rivers. The first was to the Meon valley, whose interesting villages—even including the ancient yew tree in West Tisted churchyard—are all mentioned in Domesday Book.

From East Tisted I deviated from the Gosport road to visit West Tisted, which is sparsely populated and little known compared with its residential neighbour and namesake. Its little church, except for the modern chancel and vestry is Early English, and noteworthy for memorials to the Tichborne family, a Norman arch and font, a 14th-century piscina, and a tiny wooden bell-cote which quietly proclaims its antiquity. Its registers, moreover, go back to 1538.

Further down the valley are three charming villages with thatched cottages, clustered together on the Meon river, with Beacon Hill, Old Winchester Hill (both over 600 feet high), and Corhampton Down in the vicinity. Old Winchester Hill (an Iron Age fort) is 12 miles from the ancient city. Meonstoke has a large ivy-covered church, with a modern double-tiered tower and a Norman font. The walled churchyard, the river, and the trees in the background combine to give it a most beautiful setting. Exton village, a small parish, adjoins Meonstoke. The church preserves its Early English appearance, and has a pre-Reformation bell, a piscina, and a Jacobean altar table. But by far the most interesting of the three is Corhampton, its Saxon church

built of rubble, being one of the oldest and best preserved
in the county. It is a joy to look upon, placed as it is on a
prehistoric mound encircled by a flint wall, and thus set
off to the best possible advantage. The little turret on the
roof contains two bells—one dated 1619—which were
formerly in the apertures in the gable-end below, the sloping
buttresses bulging out on either side enhancing the sense
of antiquity of this ancient church, especially when shadows
of large trees fall slantwise across it. Saxon architecture
is visible everywhere—the doorway, chancel arch, a stone
sanctuary seat, and a sundial. The font is Norman, the wall
paintings are 13th-century, and there is a venerable old yew
tree in the churchyard.

Warnford church is in Warnford Park, through which the
Meon flows: it also has Saxon origins, having been associated
with St. Wilfrid, a powerful missionary to the local Jutish
folk, the Meonwara. It is mainly 12th-century, but there
is a Saxon sundial on the wall of the tower, whose circular
belfry slats give it an owlish appearance.

Four miles south of Corhampton is the market town of
Bishop's Waltham. The ruins of the palace (which was the
home of the bishops of Winchester in the Middle Ages), the
abbot's pond, the flint and stone church with its staircase
turret rising several feet above the large embattled tower,
and the narrow, quaint streets are the outstanding features
of this small town, where William of Wykeham died
in 1404.

North-west of Bishop's Waltham is Upham. Oliver
Cromwell once stabled his horses in the church, as he did
at Old Basing. The poet, Edward Young (1681–1765), who
was born at the rectory, became a clergyman, but never
held a benefice in his native county. The death of his wife
brought forth his best-known work, *Night Thoughts on
Life, Death and Immortality*.

All of these valley villages are enchanting—particularly
the thatched cottages and bow-windowed village stores of

East Meon, and the river Meon (which rises a mile away, near the Butser) running alongside the High Street. The noble church—like Alfreton, in Sussex, a cathedral of the Downs—with a sturdy central tower and shingled spire, sits like a hen on her chickens, above the surrounding village, under the lofty expanse of Park Hill. It has one of the four 12th-century Tournai black marble fonts in the county, the others being at St. Mary Bourne, St. Michael's (the oldest church in Southampton), and Winchester cathedral. The walls of East Meon church are said to be four feet thick.

Some people regard West Meon as an even prettier river village. The curfew is still rung here at eight o'clock each evening. Its church, rebuilt last century, formidable and well-buttressed, stands four square to the winds. Thomas Lord (founder of the famous cricket ground), and also the parents of Richard Cobden, the political reformer, lie buried in the churchyard. The *Meon Hut* was an old coaching hostelry, whose name has as medieval a flavour as those of *The Deer's Hut* at Bramshott and *The Three-legged Cross* at Crux Easton.

The handsome towered church of Droxford has Norman nave walls and doorway, and homely, dormer windows in the long sloping roof, as seen across the meadow from the Meon, whose waters Izaak Walton fished when he stayed at Droxford rectory with his daughter, the wife of Prebendary Dr. William Hawkins. Here, as at Chilbolton and Barton Stacey, there are three piscinas. During the last war, the east window was badly damaged by bomb blast.

Soberton (pronounced Subbertun locally) is a mile from Droxford. Its church tower is said to have been built at the expense of a local dairywoman and butler: inside are several interesting features—nave and chancel arches, wall paintings, piscinas, and a squint. Nearly a century ago this large old church seated about 700 people.

I decided to return home by another way through unfamiliar deep country, passing Bighton church, whose heavy boarded bell-tower, large porch and buttressed chancel had an age-old look. Inside were arcades with Norman piers, a nave with two aisles, a 12th-century Purbeck marble font, a squint (or hagioscope), and two piscinas— altogether a combination of differing periods.

Making for Wield—with which village I had happy memories of pre-First World War days—I paused to photograph the ancient chapel and preceptory of Godfield, built in 1150, three or four miles from Alresford. It was a pathetic relic of the days when the Knights Hospitallers of St. John of Jerusalem used it, before the Black Death compelled them to move to North Baddesley, near Southampton, a little church which contains not only the tomb of a knight of their order, but a chained bible. The unglazed and otherwise derelict appearance of Godsfield chapel, made it seem desolate and forlorn. One end of the building (the priest's dwelling) was two-storeyed, whilst the other half, with three lancet windows in one wall, was the chapel itself. Remains of a chimney were visible, and the interior comprised a kitchen, fireplace, stone stairway, buttery, and a squint to the altar. Not long after my visit it became a youth hostel with a kitchen and bedroom at one end, the chapel being used as a lounge. Eight staddles, standing outside, looked like very large mushrooms.

Being within easy range of Wield, Lasham and Herriard, I was on home territory, and in an hour or two was happily relaxing in the low-ceilinged kitchen of our old cottage at Mapledurwell, talking to my uncle Charlie, who had just arrived from Sussex: he knew every inch of that county. One of his proudest possessions was a driving licence issued in 1906, when he drove his first Panhard car. He was as green-fingered as his father, and I envied him his gardening skill and enthusiasm. I have always wished that I had inherited those special gifts.

36
The Test Valley

FOLLOWING MY JOURNEY to the Meon valley, I explored villages in the valley of the silvery Test, in the vicinity of Stockbridge and Romsey. This river is roughly 40 miles long, whereas the Itchen is less than 30: both enter Southampton Water.

Whether one approaches Stockbridge by the switchback road over the many, hills from Sutton Scotney; from the direction of Andover through the Clatford villages, skirting the high, prehistoric encampments on Bury Hill and Danebury Hill, crowned by an extensive grove of splendid beeches; or by the more picturesque route through Wherwell, Chilbolton, Testcombe (originally Titcombe), where the railway and the river pass under a bridge; Leckford and Longstock, the views are exceptionally fine. The *Peat Spade* inn at Longstock is aptly named, for peat used to be dug in this village.

The thatched cottages, the Long bridge near Chilbolton common, and the 13th-century church with an ancient rood loft, three piscinas and a handsome, carved Elizabethan pulpit, its wooden panelling reaching down to the floor, leave one with a delightful memory of the village of Chilbolton. The Rev. Richard Durnford of Chilbolton kept a *Diary* (edited by H. Nicholl) of his angling activities on the Test from 1809 to 1819, but that of Colonel Peter Hawkins of Longparish extends from 1802 until his death in 1853.

Equally memorable in all respects is Leckford: the charm of its old-world cottages, the scenery of the Test and Anton rivers which meet here, Eel-pot bridge, and the church with

its age-old sanctuary and—most unusual—choir stalls with
arm rests and tip-up seats, brought from Venice and
presented to the church in 1925. Fishing at Leckford begins
below Testcombe bridge, and below Leckford are the waters
of the well-known Houghton Club, which has its headquarters in the *Grosvenor* hotel at Stockbridge. Danebury
used to be famous as a racecourse and training ground,
but after 1898, Stockbridge races ceased. Nowadays,
although Danebury Ring is a public open space belonging
to the County Council, there are difficulties in regard to
access to the innermost section, which is enclosed by a
wood.

My uncle Hugh, who accompanied me on later trips,
found the surrounding hills a tribulation, and was always
glad to reach the low-lying town, where sheep fairs were
held up to 1932. Stockbridge was not only angling country.
but loved by artists, too. What impressed us was the greenness and flatness of the well-watered valley in which the
quiet little town nestled, with the downs all round it; it
was as if we were viewing the promised land. Stockbridge
consists almost entirely of one long wide street, the so-called
High Street, with the low three-arched bridge spanning the
Test and some of its five tributaries hereabouts, and is the
most famous centre for dry-fly fishing. There are Tudor
houses and old inns, chief among them a Georgian hotel—
the *Grosvenor*—with a large porch on pillars projecting
towards the street, and a fine old-fashioned room above it.
Although the clock-tower of the town hall looks old, it only
dates from 1810: its weathervane, appropriately is a trout.
Perhaps the many halcyon days spent by anglers at Stockbridge have created an illusion of time lengthened out!
The spired parish church celebrated its centenary in 1966,
but the chancel of its predecessor still stands, and has long
been used as a mortuary chapel.

Three miles south of Stockbridge is King's Somborne
('Somborne Regis' in Domesday Book), large and prosperous,

with Park river, or the Somborne stream, which joins the Test at Horsebridge, running alongside the road past pleasing thatched cottages, many half-timbered, and one at least with a clipped yew in its front garden. At one time of day this was sheep-rearing country, when farmhouses sometimes served as woollen factories. The 13th-century flint church has an octagonal shingle spire above the wooden belfry, which also has a clock. Like Stockbridge, it has a fine Norman font of Purbeck marble. Behind the church is the site of John of Gaunt's palace.

I hastened on to Little Somborne. Field Marshal Earl Wavell's forebears have been associated with Hampshire for centuries. His father, Major-General A. G. Wavell (1843–1935) lived at Somborne House, Little Somborne, and it is said that a 13th-century collateral ancestor of his was Richard de Wauville, prior of Ellingham, where, at Moyles Court, Dame Alicia Lisle lived before she was executed for harbouring two fugitives after the battle of Sedgemoor. Marconi also lived for a time at Somborne House.

I found the unobtrusive church of Little Somborne surrounded by trees. Its diminutive wooden bell-cote and Saxon walls confirmed its ancient origin. I got the impression, more than in any church I have been in since, that this was a plain, simple edifice such as it might have been in the dawn of the English church, before the arrival on our shores of St. Augustine. The exterior particularly appealed to me, and the interior, especially the lancet windows, which shed light on the sanctuary and altar below, left an ineradicable memory. It was clear from all I saw within that it was in the most ancient traditions of worship and practice. An underground passage, said to be three-quarters of a mile long, ran from the church to Rookley House (formerly a monastery) in Upper Somborne (or Up Somborne), which village and modern church I also visited.

Braishfield is pronounced Brashfield, but Plaitford, not far away (which has a 13th-century church encircled by trees) is called Plateford. Braishfield church, built in 1855, did not detain me longer than it took to obtain a snapshot of the exterior, and so, by way of quiet lanes, I eventually reached lonely Upper Eldon, probably the smallest parish and certainly the smallest church I have ever seen in Hampshire. There are six consecration crosses on this 13th-century church.

From there I rode on to another solitary but lovely little church—Farley Chamberlayne—which has a small dormer window in the roof of the nave, behind the porch, and as satisfying an example of an old Hampshire weather-boarded bell-turret as any I know. It is about a mile from Farley Mount, a beacon hill (560 feet), commanding an extensive view. On the summit is a sharp pointed pyramidal monument commemorating the 25-foot leap of a horse into a chalk pit without mishap to animal or rider in 1833: it won the Hunters' Plate in a race on Worthy Down the following year under the name of 'Beware Chalk-Pit'. The rider on both occasions was the horse's owner, Paulet St. John. Beneath the monument the horse is buried.

Michelmersh is on high ground and well wooded, and its manor goes back to Saxon times. The church, too, may be Saxon in origin, and its oak tower is low and heavily boarded horizontally right down to the ground, ivy-covered and tile-roofed. There are several old features—monuments, glass, wall paintings, and an ancient cup-shaped font of 13th-century date—in the long, low building, despite considerable restoration, which took place last century.

In the region of Mottisfont are the Abbey (a massive house on the site of an ancient priory, whose arched vault is very satisfying aesthetically), white chalk cliffs, the river Test near the Cattle bridge, the leaning oak, and the foaming waters known as 'The Ginger Beer Stream'! The parish church, a flint building with a wooden belfry, has a wide Norman chancel arch, and the stained glass in the east window was originally in the now ruined Holy Ghost chapel, Basingstoke. There is a memorial to a member of the Meinertzhagen family from many years ago. Colonel Richard Meinertzhagen, author of *Diary of a Black Sheep* (published in 1964), is a well-known ornithologist, and receives honourable mention of his service in Palestine in the First World War in T. E. Lawrence's *Seven Pillars of Wisdom*. As I have a fondness for good diaries, I make mention of Meinertzhagen's autobiography, for he started keeping one at the early age of six.

Ashley church is of Norman and Saxon origins. The building is mainly 12th-century, but the small round arch leading to the altar belongs to an earlier period. Though the nave is partly sealed off from the disproportionately lengthy chancel by a wall, worshippers can see the well-lit altar through the chancel arch and the rounded openings on either side. A 16th-century canopied alms box was carved out of a solid oak pillar. Two bells hang in apertures in the west gable wall, and are as open to the weather as are those of Littleton church, nearer Winchester, which is also on raised ground above the road. The large expanse of roof and buttressing give Littleton church an unusual shape. Inside are 13th-century features including the font.

Crawley, midway between Winchester and Stockbridge, is a prosperous residential parish which, during the era of the Philippi family at Crawley Court, was transformed into a model village of renovated thatched cottages and timbered houses, with a superabundance of trees everywhere. The 15th-century church is darkly set amidst these, and has been restored during the last 80 years. On one of the five bells in the flint tower are inscribed the words: 'To the Church I will you call & to the grave sommonce you all'—an inscription which appears with slightly different spelling or variation on a few other Hampshire bells of 1746 date, such as those at Cheriton. For over a thousand years,

Crawley parish has been associated with the chapelry of
Hunton, six miles away. Hunton church is fenced off in the
middle of a meadow—as is its very near neighbour, Stoke
Charity—and has a small tower and a 14th-century piscina.
The village's perennial attraction is its pastoral and river
setting and picturesque water-wheel.

The high-lying village of Sparsholt is known chiefly for its
County Farm Institute and department of bee-keeping:
the Farm School at Old Basing moved here in 1913. The
Early English church has a wooden belfry and a peculiarly-
shaped roof, rather hotch-potch in appearance: inside are
wrought ironwork, Flemish wood carving, and a bassoon
(a relic of the band which provided the music for services
a century ago). The *Woodman* inn is National Trust property,
and, like the *Boot* at Vernham Dean, is thatched.

Next day I rode from Basingstoke to Romsey by main
roads which had grown commonplace, and was eager to
break new ground. I had not hitherto visited the southerly
villages bordering on Wiltshire, so decided to include Sherfield English, Lockerley, East and West Tytherley, and
East Dean in my itinerary, and to take my camera with
me. It was pleasant to realise that I should be in the vicinity
of Timsbury and East Wellow, with whose names I had
long been familiar. Sherfield English is four and a half miles
from Romsey, and if the latter's ancient abbey is uncommon
in shape, so also is the church of Sherfield English—twice
rebuilt (in 1858 and 1903)—with its flying supports, spire
on top of its tower, and ornate windows. In 1919, the
rector presented some old stocks, which were placed in
the churchyard. What was chiefly noticeable about these
villages was the density of woodland, yet unlike that of
the New Forest. By the time the border is reached, the
trees diminish and the view opens out. This early impression
was confirmed when I travelled by bus from Romsey to
Salisbury in the summer of 1965. The spired modern church
of Lockerley replaced a Norman edifice which itself

succeeded one on a Saxon foundation. Its pews are of Kauri-pine from New Zealand.

Both Tytherley churches are essentially modern, but two of the bells in West Tytherley are reputed to be ancient, whereas the peal of eight at East Tytherley date no further back than 1897. East Tytherley has not only a 13th-century chancel, nave and font, but a vestry window with the figure of St. Peter in stained glass of the same date. At West Tytherley, there was, in addition to the modern organ in its gallery, an old barrel organ, with a repertory of 30 tunes, in the nave below. The old Roman road from Winchester to Sarum passed through this beautiful village.

Mention of the Tytherleys, King's Somborne, Ashley, and Littleton, brings to my mind *Lift-Luck on Southern Roads* (first published in 1910), in which the author, the Rev. Tickner Edwardes (1865–1944) records impressions of a journey he made over much the same ground, but adds a touch of necromancy and romance to the narrative. He mentions Avington, Easton, Empshott, Farley Hill, Selborne, Tichborne, Winchester, and Woolmer Forest. He was vicar of Burpham, in Sussex, and wrote a number of other books—at least seven for apiarists, including *The Lure of the Honey-Bee, The Bee-Master of Warrilow* and *Bee-Keeping for All*; several nature books, among them *Neighbourhood, A Country Calendar* and *A Downland Year*; and some novels, the best-known of which was *Tansy*.

Timsbury village is in Test river country, and its manor has come into the news as a training ground in connection with world athletics. The 13th-century church has a little weather-boarded belfry, an old porch, a rood-screen, and a chained James I bible, which may be a first edition. East Dean, just inside the Hampshire boundary, left a deep impression on my memory. Alongside the road is the 700-year-old church, which resembles a chapel. It is timbered with oak from disused ships, as indeed are many cottages up and down the county, including ours at

Mapledurwell. Very beautiful were the cob-thatched cottages beyond the end of the road as seen from Dean station.

East Wellow is three miles from Romsey, and a mile away is Embley Park—a home of Florence Nightingale from 1825 to 1874. She visited it for the last time in 1891, and five years later it passed out of the hands of the family. In view of the proximity of Embley Park to Broadlands—on the Test just outside Romsey—where Lord Palmerston lived and fished, access to the then prime minister was easy. She died in 1910 at the age of 90, and chose to lie in the peaceful surroundings of her beloved Hampshire countryside, in East Wellow churchyard, in preference to Westminster Abbey. A tall family monument bears only her initials and the years of her birth and death, an inscription almost as simple as that on the obscure little headstone to Gilbert' White in Selborne churchyard. The church and its main door are of 13th-century date: its wooden bell-turret, not unlike that of Leckford, though smaller, is quaint and reminiscent of bygone days. There are wall paintings from the 13th to the 17th centuries, including one of the martyrdom of St. Thomas and another of St. Christopher, a handsome east window, a stoup and piscina, aumbries, bells, and sepulchral slabs.

West Wellow is in Wiltshire, and was therefore ouside my frontier in those days.

Turning homewards, I paused at Bossington (pronounced Bozzington)—a tiny village—and in order to obtain a snapshot of the little flint church, built in 1839, in the park of Bossington House, I left the road and walked towards it across a meadow. Not far away is Broughton, also in enchanting country. A dovecote in the churchyard adds beauty to the surroundings. The Norman flint church contains worn nave pillars, a charming piscina, and a 13th-century painted panel in its reredos. For a country church it is a large building, with a fine wide west door under the tower.

Two miles from Stockbridge is Houghton, which gives its name to the famous dry-fly fishing club which is as old as it is exclusive. It is a pretty village, especially the black poplars on the Houghton water below Boot Island. The 12th-century church and the churchyard are kept very tidy. The low, square wooden bell-cote is surmounted by a shingle broach spire added in 1890, and inside the church are piscinas, consecration crosses and squints.

As I left Stockbridge for home, via Sutton Scotney and Popham Beacon, and said goodbye to the newly-discovered churches in the Test valley, I realised how much that lovely river and its tributaries had contributed to my enjoyment of the glorious scenery through which I had passed. It was therefore with a sense of resignation that I faced the prospect of the switchback climb to Sutton Scotney, which my uncle called 'The Seven Sisters'—and detested! I remember our last ride together that way. No sooner had we climbed one hill than another loomed up, with the remaining five rising ever upwards above each other. We laughed about it afterwards whenever Stockbridge was mentioned, but he swore he would never cycle there again, and he never did! But for me, from that time right up to the present day, the river Test and the river Bourne have never ceased to exert their own special magic.

37
Petersfield to Portsmouth and Southampton

THOUGH I WENT to Portsmouth from time to time, having relatives there, I never knew the surrounding district as well as my father did, for he spent his early life in Cosham, and for years sang in Wymering church choir as man and boy. Living close to the forts on Portsdown Hill, he knew more about the Army—the various regiments, cap badges, march tunes and battle honours—than about Portsmouth's naval activities. It was unfortunate that in my childhood, his holidays did not often coincide with mine, and he was thus unable to introduce me to all the villages between Petersfield and Havant, and between Portsmouth and Southampton.

Portsmouth had its own special attractions—the harbour, the floating bridge, the dockyard and shipping, old and new. The naval reviews at Spithead brought in the country people on day outings in the first decade of this century, and for those who could stay longer, there was Southsea, with its beach and piers (Clarence and South Parade). It was as bracing as Bournemouth was relaxing, but both resorts were exceedingly popular.

The *Victory*, launched in 1765, was offshore until 1923, when she was transferred to H.M. Dockyard, and preserved in dry dock. In the harbour there were all manner of naval craft, from submarines to dreadnoughts—the pride of the Navy. There were not only large forts on the hills to the rear of the town overlooking the harbour, but small ones in the waters of Spithead which were to survive two world wars. Most Hampshire people were familiar with the fine pillared Guildhall, the garrison church, the two cathedrals and Charles

Dickens' birthplace, but few knew where Arthur Conan
Doyle practised medicine, in Elm Grove, Southsea. Isambard
K. Brunel, engineer and steamship designer, was born in
Britain Street, and George Meredith in the High Street.
'Pompey' was noted for people given to good works—John
Pounds (the crippled cobbler-schoolmaster of the ragged
children) and Agnes Weston (founder of the Royal Sailors'
Rest), to name but two.

Some knew Kingston and Portsea, for was not St. Mary's
an unrivalled training ground in social work for live wires
among budding curates whose vicars (including Dr. Garbett,
later Archbishop of York) were frequently on the short list
for bishoprics? Eastney, Fratton, Hilsea, Landport, and
Northsea had their minor attractions, and for the historically-
minded there was Portchester, whose castle encloses a
Norman church. Alverstoke (or Alverstock), two miles from
Gosport—the Navy's victualling station—has a Norman
church which was rebuilt in 1865. A local chapelry bears
the name of Anglesey. Ryde pier in the Isle of Wight was
just over four miles away. Lee-on-Solent and Hayling Island
(consisting of two country villages, North and South Hayling)
were fast becoming holiday resorts, and the shapes of the
tower and spire of these Hayling 13th-century churches,
and of Dollery's Farm, thatched and half-timbered,
were most attractive and satisfying to anyone with an
eye for a picture. Incidentally, St. Peter's, North Hayling,
is said to have the earliest known set of bells, all three
dating from 1350.

The route from Basingstoke and Alton to Portsmouth
by road went through woodland country as far as Petersfield, which has an open market in the square in front of the
Norman parish church, dating from 1100, and is silently
presided over by an equestrian statue of William III. The
large chancel arch and other Norman arches in the church,
and the tower, which is of 12th- and 15th-century dates,
are impressive.

The old bookshop was, of course, a compulsory halt, and there was the sunny, peaceful vista of 'The Spain' through ancient Sheep Street.

Between Petersfield and the Sussex border lay the parish of Buriton, heralded by a fine uphill sweep of country lane to the large village pond, the war memorial, and the Norman and Early English church crowning a ridge of the South Downs and sheltered by beech hangers. The manor house was the home of Edward Gibbon, author of *The Decline and Fall of the Roman Empire.*

The main road from Petersfield to Portsmouth carved its way through a mighty cleft of the Butser (889 feet), with a view straight ahead of the Isle of Wight: from its highest point on a clear, sunny day, Salisbury cathedral spire could sometimes be seen. Then came the welcome 'free wheel' into Horndean, and after that the descent through Cowplain, Waterloo (previously Waterlooville), Purbrook and Portsdown Hill to Cosham (pronounced Cossum), on the outskirts of Portsmouth. Wymering and Widley became part of Cosham before my time, but apart from my father's early associations with these places, there was little historically—apart from the late 12th-century north arcade of Wymering church and the early 13th-century arcade and chancel—or countrywise to draw me. Much restoration took place in Wymering church in 1860. Widley church, which has an apsidal chancel and an open gable-end bell turret, which are not unlike those of Nately Scures, was entirely rebuilt in 1849, and the only relic which was preserved from the old church is a small font with a slender bowl. Wymering lies back from the foreshore and the muddy channels extending from Portchester to Portsmouth.

My father sometimes talked of other places outside Portsmouth—Catherington, Chalton, Clanfield, Farlington, and Southwick—several of which are still surprisingly pretty. This tract of country revealed hitherto unknown and interesting hinterland villages of great downland beauty, large chalk dells and ancient churches—Chalton, for instance, with its windmill, chalk pit, thatched inn and 13th-century flint church; and Clanfield, whose rebuilt church retains the old font and pre-Reformation bells of its predecessor. It came as a revelation to me that there were Saxon churches at Boar-hunt, Idsworth and Warblington, which were well worthy of detailed examination. Boarhunt has a tub front and other Saxon features. Idsworth is a gem, standing lonely on a hill in a field which is part of Idsworth manor: it has box pews, wall paintings, a far-from-level stone floor, a stone altar, a Saxon doorway, which is sealed up, and a bell-cote which proclaims its pre-Conquest origin. The fine old timbered porch of Warblington church recalls that of Monk Sherborne: in the vestry is a pitch-pipe. A solitary tall turret is all that remains of the castle. In the churchyards of Bedhampton, Boarhunt, and Warblington are yew trees of great girth and age.

The Forest of Bere, mostly in Catherington parish, lies between Rowland's Castle and the picturesque village of Southwick, whose towered church of stone and flint has 13th-century characteristics and effigies of later date, as also has the Norman church of Catherington, restored in 1883: there are memorials to Admirals Sir Charles Napier and Lord Hood, who built Catherington House. A house in a park at Southwick was the headquarters of General Eisenhower before D-Day in 1944.

Rowland's Castle has a romantic name, also ancient Roman remains.

Havant, an old market town famous for the making of parchment for a thousand years, figures in Conan Doyle's *Micah Clarke,* whilst Emsworth, with its harbour, tidal mills, nautical industries and fishing activities, is especially famous for its oysters. Both are on the way from Portsmouth to the cathedral city of Chichester over the Sussex border.

On a sunny trip to Portsmouth and the Isle of Wight in 1958, we stopped in the broad market square of Wickham for morning coffee. The mellow buildings with bow windows, the quaint inns, and the general atmosphere of antiquity extended the same sort of welcome to the traveller that it used to do a century and more ago when coaches drew up for refreshments. William of Wykeham, chancellor of England and bishop under three kings, and forever associated with Winchester as the founder of its College, and of New College, Oxford, was born here in 1342. Wickham's cruciform church has a tower and broach spire, 14th-century sepulchral slabs, and monuments of later date—a combination of church and mausoleum.

Fareham, like other small Hampshire market towns and seaports, consists of a broad main street, and numbers tanning, flour milling and pottery-making among its occupations, as well as sailing and other shipping activities. An oaken man-of-war, the *Implacable,* a training ship for boys, was stationed in Fareham Creek, which forms the western portion of Portsmouth harbour. The parish church of SS. Peter and Paul bears traces of its Saxon origin. Sir John Goss, organist and composer, was born here, and the town also had associations with Thackeray in his *Roundabout Papers.*

Titchfield, an ancient town on the Meon, also has wide streets and a spired Norman church with Saxon origins, and is full of memorials, including the Wriothesley tomb containing the remains of the third Earl of Southampton, Shakespeare's patron, and a wall painting of the miraculous draught of fishes. There are other old buildings, such as Titchfield Abbey (Place House), with castle turrets still surviving, and Old Lodge, of 13th- and 15th-century dates respectively. The Rev. Pitt Cobbett, a former vicar of neighbouring Crofton, once brought out an edition of his kinsman's *Rural Rides.* The Meon reaches the Solent at Hillhead, near Lee-on-Solent.

Botley, a pleasant little town with quaint inns and shops and dignified old houses, was once a port, and is noted far and wide for its strawberries, and for the training ship

Mercury's association with Commander C. B. Fry, the famous cricketer. William Cobbett, who was very proud of his connection with Botley, once had a small farm here—Fairthorn Farm. The house has been pulled down, but a memorial stone, stating that this great Englishman, and champion of free journalism, lived near this spot from about 1805 to 1817, was placed here in 1957 by Hampshire members of the Institute of Journalists. The river Hamble, on which Botley stands, is only 10 miles long, and has two sources, at Durley and Bishop's Waltham. In the cruciform church of Durley is a Norman font, a stoup, a piscina, and, in a transept window, an old faded painting of a ship with a sailor climbing up the rigging.

Hambledon is famous for Broadhalfpenny Down and Windmill Hill, the nursery of English cricket, the *Bat and Ball* inn, and a memorial of granite commemorating the Hambledon Club. The village is justly proud of its ancient (Saxon, Norman, and Early English) church. On the Hamble estuary, also in strawberry country, is the beautiful village of Bursledon, which possesses an interesting, restored church with a Norman font. Netley Abbey ruins and Netley Castle, near Southampton Water, recall the Cistercians who settled here from the earlier foundation at Beaulieu. A mile away is the 13th-century church of Hound. Two miles from Netley is Hamble, or Hamble-le-Rice, an ancient village which once had a Norman priory, a part of which forms the present church, in which is a canopied double piscina. Rowner, a small parish mentioned in Domesday Book, is within a mile of the Solent, and on the river Alver. In a field stands its little 12th-century church which preserves an ancient piscina and sedilia, a Norman arch, monuments of hard chalk, and almost obliterated wall paintings.

Southampton stands on a peninsula between the estuaries of the Test and Itchen rivers. Much of Liverpool's passenger shipping, including its largest vessels, forsook the Mersey because of the double tides which the Solent and

Spithead provide. Between the wars it was a sight to see
mammoth liners like the *Mauretania, Berengaria, Aquitania,
Leviathan, Majestic,* and *Olympic*—and later the *Queen Mary*
and *Queen Elizabeth*—at the dockside, or from green fields
on either side of Southampton Water, though the mudbanks
on the outskirts of the town were unsightly.

Southampton had its historic side—the City walls, Bargate
(fortunately permanently preserved), West Gate, Tudor
House, and God's House, St. Michael's church, with its needle-
sharp spire, Canute's palace and King John's palace, the
ancient Wool House, and a memorial to the Pilgrim Fathers.
Not only did the *Mayflower* and *Speedwell* set sail from here,
but also the Crusaders in 1189.

The University of Southampton, when it was the University College, published periodically from 1928 an interesting
magazine, *Wessex,* but it ceased to appear after 1938.

For many years there was a good secondhand bookshop of
H. M. Gilbert & Son, at Above Bar, now at 2½ Portland
Street, which has always been well worth visiting. It is
associated with Gilbert's at Winchester.

Southampton was a great port in both world wars, especially for troopships. In 1956, I found that the transformation
which had taken place since pre-war days, and especially
because of the war-time bombing, was a revelation. The
new civic centre had been built, and also equally praise-
worthy was the layout of the town, particularly the grass
swards and open spaces on the outskirts, and the tree-lined
avenues leading out from the suburbs on the way to
Winchester. By 1966, the progress with the building of
Southampton—its new white buildings and shopping
precincts, wide streets, green verges and parks—was very
marked, and I was struck by the airport and its vicinity,
though Eastleigh is, as it has always been to the traveller
by rail, depressing. It now extends as far as Chandler's Ford,
which, with recent building and the prevalence of pines and
rhododendrons, has developed into a community somewhat

similar to Fleet. In this old-world village which received its name in coaching days, Chandler was the ancient miller, who occupied the then little mill in the valley, above the present railway station, and through the ford the stage-coaches passed on their slow, but often pleasant journeys. It was in this village that the Merrie Feast (of small black cherries) was held, and it is said that Richard Cromwell and his bride joined in its festivities on their honeymoon 300 years ago. Here also the family name of Purkess (descendants of the charcoal burner who conveyed William Rufus's body to Winchester) still occurs. The road through which they passed, although now diverted, is still known as the 'King's Lane', and the meadow they rested in as 'King's Mead'.

North Stoneham, between Southampton and Eastleigh, has a 15th-century church containing heraldic glass in its windows, and old monuments, including one to Admiral Lord Hawke, the hero of Quiberon Bay, who was buried here in 1781. On the tower is a one-handed clock. Canon Beadon was rector from 1810 to 1879, when he died at the age of one hundred and one! According to J. O. Johnston's *Life of Henry Parry Liddon,* Canon Beadon succeeded his own father, who had been rector here from 1740, and if it is so, then these two were incumbents successively for 139 years—surely a record! It was at a mill at South Stoneham (near Swaythling, a suburb of Southampton) that Henri de Portal learnt his trade as a paper manufacturer prior to becoming the tenant of Bere Mill, near Whitchurch. South Stoneham has no separate village of its own, and its relationship with Swaythling can best be described by the local jingle—'Stoneham has the steeple and no people, and Swaythling the people and no steeple'. Actually, St. Mary's church is towered, and its font, chancel arch and windows are all late Norman. Here is preserved a very old Bible—Coverdale (1572).

The urbanisation of the country on either side of the busy, modernised road to Winchester, has bereft the villages of some of their former beauty. At Twyford, on the Itchen, which last century was called 'the Queen of Hampshire villages', Alexander Pope is reputed to have attended school. The church, built by Sir Alfred Waterhouse, has a modern tower and spire 140 feet high, but the font and arcades on each side of the nave date from 1200. In the churchyard is a large yew clipped in pyramidal form. Colden Common is near Twyford, and its church, like that of Chilworth, is 19th-century, though the latter contains two of the oldest 12th-century bells in Hampshire, the original clappers of which are exhibited in a case. Between Twyford Down and St. Catherine's Hill is Death Pits, where victims of the Great Plague of 1665 were buried.

Otterbourne, too, is no longer as rural as it used to be. It is inseparably associated with its former vicar, John Keble (1792-1866), and with the writer, Charlotte M. Yonge (1823-1901), who was born here and buried at the foot of the Keble memorial cross outside the church, which was built of blue brick in 1839. The chancel of the old church, like those at Greatham and Stockbridge, is still in existence. The lychgate of the new church was provided out of a gift of £200 made to the authoress on her 70th birthday. She was devoted to the church and its maintenance, and the rood-screen was erected to her memory; she also built a chapel at Pitt Village which is not far away from Otterbourne.

38
Looking Forward

I CANNOT BRING MYSELF to head this brief closing chapter 'Conclusion' or even 'Epilogue'. I have tried to set down something of my feeling for Hampshire, which has been so closely woven into the texture of my life. Members of the families I knew so well in my childhood are still living in the old village or in nearby Up Nately, Newnham, and Nately Scures, and I know that their doors are always open to me, so that the place is still 'down home' as it used to be when I had relatives of the Prince family there.

I place on record my grateful thanks to Irene Goddard (née Brown) of Mapledurwell, whose family I have known so well for more than 60 years: through her kindness I spent three happy summer holidays with her family in the latter half of the 1960s, when I first set about the preparation of this book.

I have known the family of Mrs. Dora Young of Mapledurwell for an equally long period of time for, as mentioned in chapter 1, her brother 'Jack' (Charles) White was my best friend during my boyhood and youth: there was something so sincere and unchanging about each member of his family—the soldier father, the mother and their eight children —with never a rift over a lifetime.

The families of the older type of people in those days formed a well-knit community in a world of their own. Their dedication to their church had a great deal to do with the unchanging tenor of their lives, for where they were born and christened they performed their life work and were laid to rest.

Hampshire place-names, whether of parishes, farms, lanes, woods, or downs, have their own special fascination because they recapture ancient glories and so fittingly describe the landscape.

The countryside holds for me the same magical charm that it has always possessed, and I hope to spend many more happy hours travelling its roads and enjoying its villages, for to me it is not only the land of memories, but the country of dreams.

Index